The Dragon in China and Japan

THE DRAGON
IN CHINA AND JAPAN

PREFACE.

The student of Chinese and Japanese religion and folklore soon discovers the mighty influence of Indian thought upon the Far-Eastern mind. Buddhism introduced a great number of Indian, not especially Buddhist, conceptions and legends, clad in a Buddhist garb, into the eastern countries. In China Taoism was ready to gratefully take up these foreign elements which in many respects resembled its own ideas or were of the same nature. In this way the store of ancient Chinese legends was not only largely enriched, but they were also mixed up with the Indian fables. The same process took place in Japan, when Buddhism, after having conquered Korea, in the sixth century of our era reached Dai Nippon's shores. Before a hundred years had elapsed the Japanese mind got imbued with foreign ideas, partly Chinese, partly Indian. To the mixture of these two elements a third one, consisting of the original Japanese conceptions, was added, and a very intricate complex was formed. Whoever studies the Japanese legends has the difficult task of analysing this complex into its parts.

No mythical creature is more familiar to Far-Eastern art and literature than the dragon. It is interesting to observe how in Japan three different kinds of dragons, originating from India, China and Japan, are to be found side by side. To the superficial observer they all belong to one and the same class of rain bestowing, thunder and storm arousing gods of the water, but a careful examination teaches us that they are different from each other.

The Indian serpent-shaped *Nāga* was identified in China with the four-legged Chinese dragon, because both were divine inhabitants of seas and rivers, and givers of rain. It is no wonder that the Japanese in this blending of Chinese and Indian ideas recognized their own serpent or dragon-shaped gods of rivers and mountains, to whom they used to pray for rain in times of drought. Thus the ancient legends of three countries were combined, and features of the one were used to adorn the other. In order to throw light upon these facts we must examine the

Buddhist ideas concerning the Nāgas which came from India to
the East. Being not acquainted with the Sanscrit language, we
have to refer to the works of European scholars and to translations, in order to explain the western elements found in Chinese
and Japanese dragon legends. This being our only aim with
regard to the Nāgas, we will deal with them only by way of
introduction.

In the First Book we have systematically arranged the most
interesting quotations concerning the dragon in China, selected
from the enormous number of passages on this divine animal
found in Chinese literature from the remotest ages down to
modern times. In order to give the original conceptions we did
not quote the numerous poems on the dragon, because the latter,
although based upon those conceptions, enlarged them in their
own poetical way. The Second Book treats of the dragon in
Japan, considered in the light of the facts given by the Introduction and Book I.

I avail myself of this opportunity to express my hearty thanks
to Professor De Groot, whose kind assistance enabled me to
largely extend the Chinese part of this paper. Not only was his
very rich and interesting library at my disposal, but he himself
was an invaluable guide to me through the labyrinth of many
a difficult Chinese passage. Moreover, from the very beginning
his splendid works, especially the *Religious System of China*,
formed the basis of my studies in Chinese and Japanese religion
and folklore.

I also tender my best thanks to Professor Speyer, who with
great kindness gave me most valuable information concerning
the Nāgas, and to Miss E. Schmidt, who kindly put her knowledge and time at my disposal in undertaking the weary labour
of perusing the manuscript and correcting its language.

Leiden.   M. W. DE VISSER

CONTENTS.

INTRODUCTION.

THE NĀGA IN BUDDHISM, WITH REGARD TO HIS IDENTIFICATION WITH THE CHINESE DRAGON.

BOOK I.

THE DRAGON IN CHINA.

CHAPTER I

THE DRAGON IN THE CHINESE CLASSICS.

CHAPTER II.

DIVINATION AND GEOMANCY.

CHAPTER VI.

EMPERORS CONNECTED WITH DRAGONS.

CHAPTER VII.

TRANSFORMATIONS.

CHAPTER VIII.

THE INDIAN NĀGA IN CHINA

BOOK II.

THE DRAGON IN JAPAN.

CHAPTER I.

THE ORIGINAL JAPANESE DRAGON-GODS OF RIVERS, SEAS AND MOUNTAINS.

CHAPTER II.

THE CHINESE DRAGON AND THE DRAGON-HORSE AS OMENS IN JAPAN

CHAPTER III

CAUSING RAIN.

CHAPTER IV

THE INDIAN NĀGA IN JAPAN.

CHAPTER V.

CHINESE AND INDIAN DRAGONS IDENTIFIED OR CONNECTED WITH ANCIENT JAPANESE DEITIES.

CHAPTER VI

THE DRAGON-LANTERN.

CHAPTER VII.

THE CHINESE DRAGON'S EGGS IN JAPAN.

CHAPTER VIII

THE TATSUMAKI (龍卷), OR "DRAGON'S ROLL"

CHAPTER IX

JAPANESE, CHINESE AND INDIAN DRAGONS IN GEOGRAPHICAL, TEMPLE AND PRIEST NAMES

CHAPTER X

INTRODUCTION.

THE NĀGA IN BUDDHISM, WITH REGARD TO HIS IDENTIFICATION WITH THE CHINESE DRAGON.

§ 1. The Nāga according to European scholars.

In order to learn the Buddhist conceptions on the Nāga's nature, and the reasons why the Chinese identified this serpent with their four-legged dragon, we have to consult the works of some authorities on Buddhism: KERN, HARDY, GRÜNWEDEL and others. For the Nāga, known in the Far East, is clad in a *Buddhist* garb, and the legends about him which became popular in China and Japan were all imbued with Buddhism. KERN, in his *History of Indian Buddhism* [1], states that the Nāgas occupy the eighth rank in the system of the world, after the Buddhas, Pratyekabuddhas, Arhats, Devas, Brahmas, Gandharvas and Garudas, and before the Yakshas, Kumbhāndas (goblins), Asuras (demons), Rākshasas (giants), Pretas (ghosts, spectres) and the inhabitants of hell. "They are water spirits, represented as a rule in human shapes, with a crown of serpents on their heads". And in his *Manual of Indian Buddhism* [2] we read that they are "snake-like beings, resembling clouds". As to the enumeration of the beings, this is different in some other texts, as we learn from a note in the same *Manual* [3]. In the initial phrase of all the *Avadānas* Buddha is said to be worshipped by men, Devas, Nāgas, Yakshas, Asuras, Garudas, Kinnaras and Mahoragas [4]. These are, however, not exactly the "Eight classes" often mentioned in Chinese and Japanese Buddhist works. These are Devas, Nāgas, Yakshas, Gandharvas, Asuras, Garudas, Kinnaras and Mahoragas [5].

---

1 *Histoire du Bouddhisme dans l'Inde*, Annales du Musée Guimet, Bibl d'études, X et XI, Vol. I, p 310 (295)   2 P 59 seq   3 P. 60, note 1

4 LÉON FEER, *Avadāna-çataka*, Annales du Musée Guimet XVIII, p 2

5 The phrase "Devas, Nāgas and (the remaining of the) eight classes" (天龍八部) is very often found in the Chinese sūtras. EDKINS (*Chinese Buddhism*, p 217) says "Beings inferior to the Devas are called collectively the 'Eight classes" This is a mistake, for, as EITEL (*Sanscr-Chin. dict* s v Nāga, p 103) rightly explains, the

Hardy's *Manual of Buddhism* [1] gives the following details concerning the Nāgas. "The Nāgas reside in the loka (world) under the Trikuta-rocks that support Meru, and in the waters of the world of men. They have the shape of the spectacle-snake, with the extended hood (coluber nāga); but many actions are attributed to them that can only be done by one possessing the human form. They are demi-gods, and have many enjoyments; and they are usually represented as being favourable to Buddha and his adherents; but when their wrath is roused, their opposition is of a formidable character". With regard to Mount Meru Hardy says: "The summit is the abode of Sekra (Çakra), the regent or chief of the dewaloka called Tawutisa (Trayastrimçat), and around it are four mansions, 5000 yojanas in size, inhabited by *nāgas*, garundas, khumbaudas, and yakas" [2]. In describing the dewalokas he says· "The palace of *Virūpāksha* is on the *west*. His

---

Devas also belong to the Eight classes But according to Eitel, the ancient Chinese phrase speaks of "Nāgas, Devas and (others of) the eight classes (龍天八部) I never found them enumerated in this order in the Chinese sūtras, for the Devas were always placed before the Nāgas Moreover, in the jātakas and avadānas the Devas always precede the Nāgas in the often repeated order of beings In the "Sūtra on the original vow of the Bodhisattva Kshitigarbha" (Nanjo's Catalogue, nr 1003, translated from Sanscrit into Chinese at the end of the seventh century), p 2b, the terms 天龍鬼神, "Devas, Nāgas, Demons and Spirits", and 天龍八部, "Devas Nāgas, and (the remaining of) the Eight Classes", are met side by side I often found the phrase *Tenryū hachibu* in Japanese works This is, of course, the logical order, as the Devas are of higher rank in the system of the world than the Nāgas and therefore ought to be mentioned before the latter The fact that the Devas belong to the eight classes is stated in the *Ta-Ming san-tsang fah shu*, "Numbers (i e numerical terms and phrases) of the Law of the Tripitaka, collected under the Great Ming dynasty" (Nanjo, nr 1621), Ch 33, p 13 sq, s v 八部, where they are enumerated as Devas, Nāgas, Yakshas, Gandharvas, Asuras, Garudas, Kinnaras and Mahoragas.

There is, however, a second phrase, namely "Men, Devas and (the remaining of) the Eight Classes", 人天八部, which we find in the *Sūtrālamkāra çāstra* (Nanjo, nr 1182, Great Japanese Trip of Leiden, Ch X, p 4a and b), in two passages where the Buddhas Çākyamuni and Maitreya are said to honour Mahākācyapa "before men, Devas and (the remaining of) the eight classes" Huber (*Sūtrālamkāra*, nr 56, pp 278 seq) translates "Les huit classes des Devas", but the Devas are not divided into eight classes and the character 人 (men) belongs, of course, to the same sentence and not to the preceding one Men precede Devas when the different beings are enumerated, and the initial phrase of the Avadānas gives us their names Men, Devas, Nāgas, Yakshas, Asuras, Garudas, Kinnaras and Mahoragas (cf also Huber. l.l., pp 462 seq , Chavannes. *Cinq cents contes et apologues extraits du Tripitaka chinois* (1910), Vol III, p 61)

If the former phrase actually is found sometimes in ancient Chinese books in the wrong form given by Edkins, the Nāgas being placed before the Devas (I think I saw it once also in a Japanese work), this mistake must have risen from blending the former phrase with the latter, which mentions the Devas in the second place

attendants are the Nāgas, a kela-laksha in number, who have red garments, hold a sword and shield of coral, and are mounted on red horses"[1].

GRUNWEDEL[2]) states that the attributes of this Virūpāksha, one of the four lokapālas or Guardians of the World, also called the "Four Great Kings" (Caturmahārājas), are a caitya (a sanctuary) or a jewel in the form of a caitya in the right, and a *serpent* in the left hand.

Before Gautama's attainment of Buddhahood a Nāga king, Kāla by name, became aware of the approaching event by the sound the Bodhisattva's golden vessel produced when striking against the vessels of the three last Buddhas in Kāla's abode For they all had, like Siddhārtha, flung their golden bowls into the river[3].

As we shall see below, the Nāga king Mucilinda, who lived in the lake of this name, by his coils and hoods sheltered the Lord from wind and rain for seven days The Indian artists often represented the Buddha sitting under Mucilinda's extended hoods.

Not always, however, were the Nāga kings so full of reverence towards the Buddha; but in the end, of course, even the most obstinate one was converted. Nandopananda, e. g., tried to prevent the Lord's return from the Tushita heaven to the earth, but was conquered by Maudgalyāyana in the shape of a Garuda, and was then instructed by the Buddha himself[4]. When the Master had delivered a sūtra in one of the heavenly paradises, the Devas and Nāgas came forward and said: "We will henceforth protect correct doctrine"[5]. After Buddha's death the Nāga kings struggled with the kings of the Devas and eight kings of India to obtain a share in Buddha's relics[6], and got one third, and Ashōka gave Nanda a hair of Buddha's moustaches, while he threatened to destroy his kingdom if he refused. Nanda erected a pagoda of rock crystal for it on Mount Sumeru[7].

According to Northern Buddhism Nāgārjuna (± 150 A D.), the founder of the Mahāyāna doctrine, was instructed by Nāgas in the sea, who showed him unknown books and gave him his most important work, the Prajñā pāramitā, with which he returned

---

1 P 24

2 *Mythologie des Buddhismus in Tibet und der Mongolei*, p. 181

3 KERN, *Manual*, p 19, *Hist du Bouddhisme dans l'Inde*, Vol, I, p. 70 (64) (there he is called "roi du monde souterrain")

4 HARDY, II, pp 302 seq.

5 EDKINS, II, p 39   6 EDKINS, II, p 58

7 Ibidem, p. 59.

to India. For this reason his name, originally Arjuna, was changed into Nāgārjuna [1], and he is represented in art with seven Nāgas over his head [2].

The Mahāyāna school knows a long list of Nāga kings, among whom the eight so-called "Great Nāga kings" are the following · Nanda (called Nāgarāja, the "King of the Nāgas"), Upananda, Sāgara, Vāsuki, Takshaka, Balavān, Anavatapta and Utpala [3]. These eight are often mentioned in Chinese and Japanese legends as "the eight Dragon-kings", 八龍王, and were said to have been among Buddha's audience, with their retinues, while he delivered the instructions contained in the "Sūtra of the Lotus of the Good Law" (Saddharma Pundarīka sūtra, Hokkekyō, 法 華經) [4].

The Nāgas are divided into four castes, just like men, and form whole states. "They are", says GRUNWEDEL [5], "the Lords of the Earth more than any one else, and send, when having been insulted, drought, bad crops, diseases and pestilence among mankind".

With regard to the Nāgas in Indian art we have an excellent guide in GRÜNWEDEL's *Buddhistische Kunst in Indien.* After having stated that the Vedas not yet mention them [6], but that they belong to the Indian popular belief, extended afterwards by the official brahmanic religion, he further remarks that they often penetrated in human shape into the Master's neighbourhood and even tried to be taken up among his followers, as we see on a relief of Gandhāra (p. 102, Fig 47; the Nāga's true shape was detected in his sleep). For this reason one of the questions put, even to-day, to those who wish to be taken up into the Order is "Are you perhaps a Nāga?" There are three ways in which the Indian Buddhist art has represented the Nāgas. First: fully human, on the head an Uraeus-like snake, coming out of the

---

1 Translated into *Lung-shu*, 龍樹, or Dragon-tree, cf EDKINS, p 230, EITEL, l.l., p 103 We find the name Nāgārjuna in the *Kathāsaritsāgara*, Ch. XLI, TAWNEY's translation, Vol I, p 376 a minister, "who knew the use of all drugs and by making an elixir rendered himself and king Chirāyus (Long-lived) free from old-age, and long-lived"

2 GRUNWEDEL, l.l., pp. 30 seqq , p 46

3 GRUNWEDEL, l.l., pp 190 seq.

4 HARDY, l.l., p. 215.

5 L l , p 187.

6 Cf. L VON SCHROEDER, *Indiens Literatur und Cultur* (1887), p 377 "Im Rigveda sind dieselben (die Schlangengötter) ganz unbekannt, in Yajurveda aber finden wir be-

neck and often provided with several heads. This form has been taken up in Tibet, China and Japan [1]. Secondly: common serpents, and thirdly a combination of both, i e. snakes of which the upper part of the body looks human, snake's heads appearing above their human heads; the lower part of the body entirely snake-like [2] The first mentioned shape is to be seen in Fig. 5 (p. 29), a relief representing Nāgas worshipping a small stūpa on a throne, and in Fig. 103 (p 103), where a Garuda in the shape of an enormous eagle is flying upwards with a Nāgī (Nāga woman) in his claws, and biting the long snake which comes out of the woman's neck. A pillar figure of the stūpa of Bharhut represents Cakravāka, the Nāga king, standing on a rock in the water, with five snake's heads in his neck, while snakes are visible in holes of the rock [3]. Once, when Nāgas appeared before Buddha in order to listen to his words, he ordered Vajrapāṇi to protect them against the attacks of their enemies, the Garudas. An Indian relief shows us these Nāgas, the Nāga king Elāpatra and his consort, standing in the water, with snakes upon their heads, and worshipping Buddha, while in the background Vajrapāni is brandishing his sceptre against the expected Garudas. This Vajrapāni's main function is, according to GRÜNWEDEL, to give rain, and as a raingod he is the protector of the *rain giving snake-gods*, the Nāgas [4]

FOUCHER's very interesting paper on the Great Miracle of the Buddha at Çrāvasti [5] repeatedly mentions the Nāga kings Nanda and Upananda, represented at the base of the Buddha's lotus seat. At the request of King Prasenajit the Buddha wrought two miracles walking through the air in different attitudes he alternately emitted flames and waves from the upper or lower part of his body, and, secondly, he preached the Law after having multiplied himself innumerable times, up to the sky and in all directions. According to the *Divyāvadāna* the Buddha, after having completed the first miracle, conceived a wordly idea, which was immediately executed by the gods Brahma and Çakra placed themselves at the Buddha's right and left side, and the Nāga

---

1 Cf. p 114, Fig. 57, a Japanese picture, after Chinese model, representing Buddha's Nirvāna. Among the lamenting creatures, which surround the Master's body, also Nāga kings with snakes above their heads are to be seen

2 Cf GRUNWEDEL, *Myth des Buddhismus in Tibet und der Mongolei*, p. 89, Fig 73

3 GRÜNWEDEL, *Buddh in Tibet und der Mongolei*, p 15

4 L1, p 160.

5 FOUCHER, *Le grand miracle du Buddha a Çrāvasti*, Journal Asiatique, Série X, Tome XIII, pp 1—78

kings Nanda and Upananda (who were said so have bathed the
new-born Buddha and to have played a part in many episodes
of his life) created an enormous, magnificent lotus upon which
the Master sat down. Then the Buddha by means of his magic
power created a great number of Buddhas, seated on lotuses or
standing, walking, lying, over his head, up to the highest heavens,
and on all sides. This scene is recognized by FOUCHER on several
Indian monuments. Often the two Nāga kings are seen under or
on both sides of the lotus created by themselves. They are
represented supporting the lotus in a kneeling attitude, entirely
human but with five serpents over their heads [1], or with human
upper bodies and scaly serpent tails [2].

In the Jātakas the Nāgas are always described as enormous serpents; sometimes, however, they appear in later Indian (i. e Graeco-
Buddhist) art as real *dragons*, although with the upper part of
the body human. So we see them on a relief from Gandhāra [3],
worshipping Buddha's almsbowl, in the shape of big water-dragons,
scaled and winged, with two horse-legs, the upper part of the
body human Most remarkable is a picture [4] which represents
Garudas fighting with Nāgas before the preaching saint Subhūti.
The Nāgas are depicted there in all their three forms · common
snakes, guarding jewels; human beings with four snakes in their
necks, and winged sea-dragons, the upper part of the body
human, but with a horned, ox-like head, the lower part of the
body that of a coiling dragon. Here we find a link between the
snake of ancient India and the four-legged Chinese dragon.

§ 2 The Nāga according to some translated Buddhist texts.

After having referred to European scholars with respect to the
Nāga in Buddhism, we may compare their results with some
translated Indian texts. Being not acquainted with the Sanscrit
language, we thankfully make use of these translations in order
to illustrate the Buddhist dragon tales of China and Japan; for,
as I stated already in the Preface, this is the only aim of this
Introduction.

Professor COWELL's [5] translation of the *Jātaka*, the canonical

1 Pp. 19, 48 seq , fig 3, a sculpture of the rock-temples of Ajantā, cf pp 64 seq ,
fig. 11, pp 74 seq , fig 16, with two Nāgīs, pp. 58 seq , fig 8.
2 P. 56 seq , fig 7 (sculpture from Magadha)
3 GRUNWEDEL, *Buddh Kunst in Indien*, p. 20, fig 10
4 GRÜNWEDEL, *Buddh. in Tibet und der Mongolei*, p 189, fig. 160.

Pāli text, made up of those marvellous stories of the Buddha's former births, told by himself, contains seven tales which are vivid pictures of the great magic power of the Nāgas, especially of their kings, of the splendour of their palaces, and, on the other hand, of their helplessness against their deadly enemies, the Garudas [1]. The Nāgas are semi-divine serpents which very often assume human shapes and whose kings live with their retinues in the utmost luxury in their magnificent abodes at the bottom of the sea or in rivers or lakes. When leaving the Nāga world they are in constant danger of being grasped and killed by the gigantic semi-divine birds, the Garudas, which also change themselves into men [2]. Buddhism has, in its usual way, declared both Nāgas and Garudas, mighty figures of the Hindu world of gods and demons, to be the obedient servants of Buddhas, Bodhisattvas and saints, and to have an open ear for their teachings [3]. In the same way Northern Buddhism adopted the gods of the countries where it introduced itself and made them protectors of its doctrine instead of its antagonists.

Sometimes [4] we read that the Buddha, in a previous existence, succeeded in reconciling even such bitter enemies as a Nāga and a Garuda king. He himself was sometimes born as a mighty Nāga king. Thus he reigned as King Campeyya in his "jewelled pavillion" in the river Campā [5], as King Samkhapāla in the lake of this name [6], and as King Bhūridatta in the sacred river Yamunā [7]. In all these three cases he desired to be reborn in the world of men, and in order to attain this aim left his palace on fastdays and lay down on the top of an ant heap, observing the fast and offering his magnificent snake body to the passers-by.

---

1 Vol II, p. 10, Book II, nr 154, the Uraga-Jātaka; Vol III, p 174, Book VI, nr 386, the Kharaputta-Jātaka; Vol IV, p 281, Book XV, nr 506, the Campeyya-Jātaka, Vol. V, p 42, Book XVI, nr 518, the Pandara-Jātaka, Vol V, p 84, Book XVII, nr 524, the Samkhapāla-Jātaka, Vol VI, p. 80, Book XXII, nr 543, the Bhūridatta-Jātaka, and Vol. VI, p 126, Book XXII, nr 545, the Vidhurapandita-Jātaka

2 In Japan these birds have been identified with the Tengu comp my treatise on the Tengu, Transactions of the Asiatic Society of Japan, Vol XXXVI, Part. II, pp 25—98.

3 Cf. CHAVANNES, Contes et apologues, nr 343 (Vol II, p. 288), where a Garuda does not grasp a Nāga who has fled into the house of an ascetic on a small island in the sea; cf. Vol III, p. 82, where a wicked Nāga king is forced by an Arhat to go away, and Vol I, nr 151, p 423, where the Buddha converts a very evil Nāga, whom innumerable Arhats could not convert

4 Vol II, p. 10, nr 154

5 Vol IV, 281, Book XV, nr 506

6 Vol. V, p. 84, Book XVII, nr 524

7 Vol. VI, pp 80—113, Book XXII, nr 543.

Patiently he underwent the most terrible tortures, without using his enormous power against the puny rogues who caused him so much pain. As Saṁkhapāla he was freed by a passing merchant, whom he thereupon treated as a guest in his palace for a whole year, and who afterwards became an ascetic. In the two other cases, however, he fell into the hands of a snake-charmer, who by means of magical herbs, which he spit upon him, and by virtue of the "charm which commands all things of sense", as well as by squeezing and crushing, weakened the royal snake, and putting him in his basket carried him off to villages and towns, where he made him dance before the public. In both legends the Bodhisattva is just performing before the King of Benares, when he is released on account of the appearance of another Nāga, Sumanā, his queen, or Sudassana, his brother [1].

In the shape of a Garuda-king we find the Bodhisattva in another tale [2], where he finds out the secret way by which the Nāgas often succeed in conquering and killing the Garudas, namely by swallowing big stones and thus making themselves so heavy that their assailants, striving to lift them up, drop down dead in the midst of the stream of water, flowing out of the Nāga's widely opened mouths. Pandara, a Nāga king, was foolish enough to trust an ascetic, whom both he and the Garuda used to visit and honour, and told him at his repeated request the valuable secret of the Nāga tribe. The treacherous ascetic revealed it at once to the Bodhisattva, who now succeeded in capturing Pandara himself by seizing him by the tail and holding him upside down, so that he disgorged the stones he had swallowed and was an easy prey. Moved by Pandara's lamentations, however, he released him and they became friends, whereupon they went together to the perfidious ascetic The Nāga king caused this fellow's head to split into seven pieces and the man himself to be swallowed by the earth and to be reborn in the Avīci hell.

In the Kharaputta-jātaka [3] we read about a Nāga king who was nearly killed by boys, when seeking food on earth, but was saved out of their hands by Senaka, king of Benares. We do not read what made the mighty Nāga so powerless against those children; for there was apparently no question of fasting as in

---

1 A similar tale is to be found in CHAVANNES's *Contes et apologues extraits du Tripitaka chinois*, Vol. I, pp. 189 sqq , nr 50.

2 Vol. V, pp 42 seqq , Book XVI, nr 518

the above mentioned legends of the Bodhisattva. He went back
to the Nāga world and from there brought many jewels as a
present to the King, at the same time appointing one of his
numberless Nāga girls to be near the King and to protect him.
He gave him also a charm by means of which he would always
be able to find the girl, if he did not see her, and afterwards
presented him with another charm, giving knowledge of all
sounds, so that he understood the voices even of ants [1]. So we
find the Nāga king not only in the possession of numberless
jewels and beautiful girls, but also of mighty charms, bestowing
supernatural vision and hearing. The palaces of the Nāga kings
are always described as extremely splendid, abounding with gold
and silver and precious stones, and the Nāga women, when
appearing in human shape, were beautiful beyond description.
But the whole race was terribly quick-tempered, which made
them, considering their deadly poison and their great magic
power, very dangerous creatures [2]. Even the breath of their
nostrils was sufficient to kill a man, as we read in the above
mentioned Kharaputta-jātaka, where the Nāga king, angry because the girl whom he had appointed to protect King Senaka,
came back to the Nāga world, falsely complaining that the King
had struck her because she did not do his bidding, at once sent
four Nāga youths to destroy Senaka in his bedroom by the
breath of their nostrils.

Often we find stories of men staying as guests in some Nāga
king's palace and enjoying all its luxury, sometimes for seven
days [3], sometimes even for a whole year [4]. The most interesting
of all the Nāga tales is the Bhūridatta-jātaka [5]. We read there
about "the Nāga world beneath the ocean" [6], and about the Nāga
palace "beneath the Yamunā's sacred stream" [7], but at the same
time the Nāga maidens, frightened by the Ālambāyana spell, a
serpent spell obtained from a Garuda-king [8], "sank into the
earth", and the "jewel of luck" [9], which "grants all desires" [10],
when falling on the ground "went through it and was lost in

1 In nr 112 of CHAVANNES' *Contes et Apologues* (Vol II, p. 382) a Nāga king causes
a king to understand all animals.

2 Vol VI p 82, Book XXII, nr 543.

3 Vol. IV, p. 281, Book XV, nr 506.

4 Vol. V, p. 84, Book XVII, nr 524 In nrs 94 and 207 of CHAVANNES' *Contes et
Apologues* (Vol. I, p. 358, Vol II, p 87) an Arhat daily flies with his bed to the
palace of a Nāga king, where he receives food

5 Vol VI, pp 80—113, Book XXII, nr 543.

6 P. 80.   7 P 107.   8 Pp 93, 95

9 P 91.   10 P. 94

the Nāga world" [1]. So we see that whatever belongs to that world can disappear into the earth and needs not enter the water, because both are the Nāgas' domain [2]. The "jewel which grants all desires", which was guarded by the Nāga maidens but forgotten in their terror for the Garuda spell, is nothing but the "Nyo-i hōju", 如意寶珠, mentioned in the Chinese and Japanese legends The same story teaches us that children of men and Nāgi (Nāga women) are "of a watery nature", and cannot stand sunshine or wind, but are happiest when playing in the water [3].

So far the Jātakas of Cowell's edition. It is a strange fact that in all these tales no mention is made of the Nāga's nature of *god of clouds and rain*, although this is the main reason why the Chinese identified him with their dragon. In the legends, translated from the Chinese Tripitaka by Chavannes [4], however, so much stress is laid on the rain giving capacity of the Nāga, that we need not doubt as to its predominance in Northern Buddhism.

From the *Lalita vistara* [5] we learn that in the fifth week after reaching perfect Enlightenment the Buddha went to lake Mucilinda, and the Nāga king of the same name, who resided there, came out of the water and with his coils and hoods shielded the Lord from the rain for seven days, whereafter he assumed the shape of a youth and worshipped the Great Being. In the *Mahāvagga* [6] the name of the lake and the Nāga king is Mucalinda, and "in order to protect the Lord against the cold and the humidity, he seven times surrounded him with his coils and extended his hood over him". According to Hardy [7] "in the sixth week, he went to the lake Muchalinda, where he remained at

---

1 P 97.

2 Cf Hardy, *Manual of Buddhism*, p 183, where king Bimbisāra, hearing that a mysterious being (the Bodhisattva) was seen, is said to have ordered his courtiers to watch him when he should leave the town "If he be a demon, he will vanish, if he be a deva, he will ascend into the sky, if a *Nāga*, he will descend into the earth"

3 P 82

4 *Cinq cents contes et apologues extraits du Tripitaka chinois* (1910)

5 Ch XXII, Chavannes also refers to the *Yoga sūtra*, Sect III, 18, 19 and 49, cf Kern, *Manual of Indian Buddhism*, pp 21 seq , Oldenberg, *Buddha*, p 136 In painting and sculpture the Buddha is frequently sitting under the extended hood of the Nāga (Hardy, *Manual of Buddhism*, p 182, Grünwedel, *Mythologie des Buddhismus in Tibet und der Mongolei*, p 110, Fig 87 and 88)

6 I, 3, quoted by Kern, *Histoire du Bouddhisme dans l'Inde*, Annales du Musée Guimet X et XII Vol I p 86 (78)

the foot of a midella tree. At that time rain began to fall, which continued for seven days, without intermission, in all the four continents. The nāga Muchalinda having ascended to the surface of the lake, saw the darkness produced by the storm; and in order to shelter Budha from the rain and wind, and protect him from flies, mosquitoes, and other insects, he spread over him his extended hood, which served the purpose of a canopy".

It is highly interesting to compare with these passages the version of the same legend, found in the Chinese Tripitaka [1]. There he is said to have gone to Mucilinda's river (not lake) immediately after having reached Enlightenment. While he was sitting under a tree, his brilliant light penetrated into the Nāga's palace, just as in former times his three predecessors of this kalpa had spread their light, sitting on the same spot. The Nāga, delighted to see the new Buddha's light, arose from the water, and, surrounding the Lord with seven coils, covered him with his seven heads (not hoods). "*The Nāga, delighted, caused wind and rain for seven days and nights*" [2]. All that time the Lord sat motionless, protected by the royal snake, the first of all animals to be converted. This legend is to be found in the *Luh-tu tsih king*, [3] nr 143 of Nanjō's Catalogue, translated by Seng-hwui [4], who died A. D. 280 [5].

The same work contains many jātakas, in which the Nāgas are frequently mentioned, sometimes in company with Çakra, Brahma, the four devarājas and the gods of the earth [6]. One day, when the Bodhisattva and Ānanda were Nāgas in order to complete

---

1 CHAVANNES, l l, Vol I, Ch VI, p 275 sqq, ni 76 Tōkyō ed of the Tripitaka (1880—1885), VI, 5, pp. 82 sq, great Japan. ed, in Leiden and in the India Office, Ch. VI, pp 15 sqq

2 龍喜作風雨七日七夕. CHAVANNES translates "Pour s'amuser, le nāga déchaîna le vent et la pluie" I should prefer "The Nāga, delighted, caused wind and rain" He was delighted because he could shelter the Lord from the wind and rain caused by himself He did not think of amusing himself But the main point of the question is the fact that the Nāga in this version is said to have caused the wind and the rain himself, while the other versions only state that there was wind and rain

3 六度集經, "Collected sūtras on the six Pāramitās" CHAVANNES first thought that these sūtras had been collected by SENG-HWUI himself (Vol I, p. 1, note 1), but afterwards felt inclined to believe that it is a translation of one sanscrit text (Introd, p III)   4 僧會.

5 Nr 680 of NANJŌ's Catalogue, partly translated by BEAL under the title of "*Romantic legend of Sākya Buddha*", does not contain this legend

6 Cf CHAVANNES, l l, Vol I, Chap. V, pp. 160 sq, nrs 43 and 44, Trip VI, 5, p. 69; great Jap ed of Leiden, nr 143, Ch V, pp 5a, 6a.

the expiation of their former evil deeds, "expanding their majestic spirit, they made heaven and earth shake; *they raised the clouds and caused the rain to fall*" [1]. And when Devadatta was a terrible Nāga, "he expanded all his force; *lightning and thunder flashed and rattled*" [2].

The *Kiu tsah p'i-yu king* [3], "Old (version of the) Samyuktāva-dāna sūtra" (miscellaneous metaphors), translated in the third century A.D. by the same SENG-HWUI (NANJŌ's Catalogue, nr. 1359) in some of its apologues mentions the Nāgas as bringers of rain. Such a being by its rain made the dike, along which a çrāmanera carried his master's rice, so slippery that the man repeatedly tumbled down and dropped the rice into the mud. His master summoned the Nāga, who in the shape of an old man prostrated himself before the Arhat and invited him to dine in his palace all the days of his life The Arhat accepted this offer and daily flew with his bed to the Nāga's palace, after having entered abstract contemplation. But his pupil, anxious to know from where his master had got the splendid rice grains which he discovered in his almsbowl, hid himself under the bed and clinging to one of its feet arrived with the Arhat at the Nāga's abode. The latter, his wife and the whole crowd of beautiful women respectfully saluted the çramaṇa and the çrāmanera, but the latter was warned by his master not to forget, that he, the çrāmanera himself, was a must higher being than the Nāga, notwithstanding all the latter's treasures and beautiful women "The Nāga", said he, "has to endure three kinds of sufferings his delicious food turns into toads as soon as he takes it into his mouth, his beautiful women, as well as he himself, change into serpents when he tries to embrace them, on his back he has scales lying in a reverse direction, and when sand and pebbles enter between them, he suffers pains which pierce his heart. Therefore do not envy him". The pupil, however, did not answer, day and night he thought of the Nāga and forgot to eat. He fell ill, died and was reborn as the Nāga's son, still more terrible than his father, but after death became a man again [4].

---

1 奮其威神、震天動地、與雲降雨 Great Jap ed of Leiden, nr 143, Ch V, p 19*b*, CHAVANNES, Vol I, Ch V, p 181, nı 48, Trıp VI, 5, p 71

2 龍即奮勢、霆耀雷震. Great Jap ed of Leiden, nr 143, Ch VI, p. 27*a*, CHAVANNES, Vol I, Ch VI, p 254, nr 70, Trıp VI, 5, p. 78

3 舊雜譬喩經.

4 CHAVANNES, 11, Vol I, nr 94, pp 358 sqq (Trıp XIX, 7, p 19, gıeat Jap. ed. of

Another time the Buddha's disciples are compared to a great Nāga who liked to give rain to the earth, but, fearing that the latter might not be able to bear the weight of the water, decided to make the rain fall into the sea [1].

In the *Tsah p'i-yu king* [2], a work from the Korean Tripitaka, not to be found in NANJŌ's *Catalogue* (for nr 1368, which bears the same title, is a different work) we find the following Nāga tales. A Nāga ascended to the sky and caused abundant rains to fall: for the devas they brought the seven precious things, for mankind fertilizing water, and for the hungry demons a great fire which burned the whole of their bodies [3].

Another Nāga who by means of a single drop of water could give rain to one or two or three kingdoms, nay to the whole Jambudvīpa, placed it in the great sea that it might not dry up [4].

An exorcist of Nāgas went with his pitcher full of water to the pond of such a being and by his magic formulae surrounded the Nāga with fire As the water of the pitcher was the only refuge the serpent could find, it changed into a very small animal and entered the pitcher [5].

Here we see the Nāgas not only as rain gods, but also as beings wholly dependent on the presence of water and much afraid of fire, just like the dragons in many Chinese and Japanese legends.

With regard to the precious pearls in the possession of the Nāgas as gods of the waters, we may mention a tale to be found in the *Mo ho seng chi luh* [6] or "Discipline of the Mahā-sāmghikas" (NANJŌ, nr 1119), translated in 416 by BUDDHABHADRA and FAH-HIEN [7]. There we read about a Nāga who wore a necklace of pearls, which he liked so much that he preferred it to his friendship towards a hermit. The latter, daily tortured by the Nāga's coils, wound around his body, succeeded in getting rid

---

1 L l., Vol I, ni 138, p 410 (Trip XIX, 7, p 24)

2 雜譬喩經, cf CHAVANNES, 11, Vol II, p 1, note 1 Both this work and the *Chung king chwen tsah p'i-yu king*, 眾經撰雜譬喩經 (NANJŌ, nr 1366) are said to be compiled by the bhiksu TAO LIOH, 道畧, but are probably two different editions of his work, KUMĀRAJIVA seems to have translated TAO LIOH's work in 401 A D.

3 CHAVANNES, 11, Vol II, nr 167, p. 23 (Trip. XIX, 7 p 3)

4 L.l., Vol II, nr 193, p. 63 (Trip XIX, 7, p 8)

5 L l., Vol. II, nr 179, p 42 (Trip. XIX, 7, p. 5)

6 摩訶僧祇律, Mahāsāmghika vinaya

7 NANJŌ, *Catal*, App. II, nrs 42 and 45.

of him only by asking him for the precious necklace [1]. Also the Chinese dragons were said to have pearls at their throats.

The *Avadāna-çataka*, a hundred legends translated from the Sanskrit by LÉON FEER [2] contain a few passages concerning the Nāgas. The most important one is the 91th legend [3], where Suparni, the king of birds, is said to have seized from the ocean a little Nāga, which after having been devoured was reborn as Subhūti and by following the Buddha's teachings reached Arhatship. He remembered to have had five hundred rebirths among the Nāgas on account of a long row of wicked thoughts in previous existences. Now he used his supernatural power to convert both Nāgas and Garudas by protecting the former against five hundred Garudas and the latter against a gigantic Nāga, which he caused to appear. In this way the law of love was taught them, and they followed his teachings.

In another legend [4] a Brahman is said to have been reborn as a Nāga because he had broken his fast; seven times a day a rain of burning sand came down upon him till he succeeded in keeping a special fast. Then, after having died with abstinence of food, he was reborn in the Trāyastrimçat heaven.

In a third passage [5] Virūpāksha, one of the four guardians of the world, who reigns on the West side of Mount Meru, is said to be surrounded by Nāgas (his subjects, who live in the West).

Finally, the Nāgas are mentioned among the divine beings who came to worship the Buddha: Çakra, the king of the gods, Viçvakarma and the four great kings surrounded by Devas, Nāgas, Yakshas, Gandharvas and Kumbhāndas [6]; another time they are enumerated as follows Devas, Nāgas, Yakshas, Asuras, Garudas, Kinnaras and Mahoragas [7].

In Açvaghosa's *Sūtrālamkāra* [8], translated into French from KUMĀRAJĪVA's chinese version by EDOUARD HUBER, the Nāgas are often mentioned. "When the great Nāga causes the rain to fall, the ocean alone can receive the latter; in the same way the

---

1 CHAVANNES, 11, Vol II, ni 955, p. 319 (Trip. XV, 8, p 44)

2 *Annales du Musée Guimet*, Tome XVIII (1891)

3 Pp 366 sq. 4 Nr 59, pp 227 sqq 5 Nr 19, p. 83.

6 Ni 12, pp 57 sq 7 Nr 17, p 77.

8 Kumārajīva translated this collection of tales about A D 410, the original sanskrit text is lost, except some fragments, which, according to HUBER, show that Kumārajīva not always understood the text HUBER's translation is based upon the TŌKYŌ edition of the Tripitaka (XIX, 4) It is nr 1182 of NANJŌ's Catalogue, entitled 大莊嚴

Samgha (alone) can receive the great rain of the Law"[1]. When a merchant, Kotīkarna by nâme, visited a town of pretas, these hungry demons uttered a long complaint, which contains the following verse "When on the mountains and valleys the Heavenly Dragons (the Nāgas) cause the sweet dew to descend, this changes into bubbling fire and spouts upon our bodies"[2]. "Elāpatra the Nāgarāja, having violated the commandments by maltreating the leaves of a tree, after death fell among the Nāgas, and none of the Buddhas has predicted the time when he shall be able to leave them"[3].

"The tears (of those who, on hearing the Law of the twelve Nidānas, are moved by pity and weep with compassion) can entirely destroy the Nāga Vāsuki who exhales a violent poison"[4].

"The Rāksasas and the Piçācas, the evil Nāgas and even the robbers dare not oppose the words of the Buddha"[5].

An evil Nāga guarded a big tree which stood in a large pond, and killed all those who took a branch or a leaf from it. When the bhiksus came to hew down the tree in order to build a stūpa, the people and a brahman warned them not to do so on account of the danger, but the bhiksus answered: "With regard to the poisonous Nāga, you, brahman, glorify yourself. But we rely upon the Nāga of men (the Buddha), and, placing our trust in Him, glorify ourselves ... . Among all the poisonous Nāgas, for this Nāga king you show yourself full of respectful thoughts. The Buddha is sweet and calm, He is the King of all beings, it is Him whom we revere, the Perfect one, the Bhagavat. Who would be able to subdue the poisonous Nāga, if not the Buddha's disciples?" Then they cut down the tree, and, to the astonishment of the brahman, no *clouds*, no *thunder*, no miraculous signs bore witness to the Nāga's wrath, as had formerly been the case even when one leaf of his tree was taken by a human hand[6]. The brahman, after having uttered his amazement and anger,

---

1 Ch I, m 3, p 30, great Jap Tripitaka of Leiden, nr 1182, Ch I, p 19

譬如大龍雨
唯海能堪受、
衆僧亦如是
能受大法雨。

2 Ch. IV, nr 10, p. 100, great Jap Trip. of Leiden, m 1182, Ch IV, p 3a
3 Ch III, nr 11, p 64, great Jap Trip of Leiden, Ch. III, p 2a
4 Ch VIII, nr 45, p. 215, great Jap Trip of Leiden, Ch. VIII, p. 2a.
5 Ch IX, nr 52, p. 255; great Jap. Trip. of Leiden, Ch. IX, p. 6a.
6 Ch. XV, nr 80, p. 447, great Jap. Trip. of Leiden, nr 1182, Ch XV, p. 21a

because he thought that they had used magic incantations, fell
asleep, and in a dream was addressed as follows by the Nāga:
"Be not angry; what they did was done to show me their vene-
ration. They have neither despised nor wounded me, for my
body supports the stūpa, moreover, the tree has become a
beam of the stūpa, and I can protect it; the stūpa of the Daça-
bala, of the Exalted one, should I ever have been able to protect
it (if not in this way)?... There was still another reason, why
I had not sufficient power (to resist the Buddha). I am going
to tell you this reason, listen attentively: Takṣaka, the Nāga
king, came here in person and took possession of this tree;
could I protect it? Elāpatra, the Nāga king, himself came to
this spot with Vaiçramana· was my power sufficient to resist
those Devas and Nāgas, full of majesty?" When the Brahman
awoke, he became a monk

This remarkable story shows us the Nāga as an inhabitant of
a pond, but at the same time as a tree demon, in which function
we often found the serpent in Chinese and Japanese tales, but
never in Indian Nāga legends As a rain and thunder god he is
said to produce clouds and thunder when he is angry. Takṣaka
and Elāpatra are mentioned here as the mightiest of the Nāga
kings, and Vaiçramana, the guardian of the North, king of the
Yakshas, is probably confounded with Virūpāksha, the guardian
of the West, king of the Nāgas. The whole legend is a typical
specimen of the way in which Buddhism subdued the other cults.

After having learned the Nāga's nature from these Buddhist
writings which made him known in China and Japan, we may
venture one step into another direction, in turning to the *Kathāsaritsāgara* or "Ocean of the streams of story". This "largest and
most interesting collection" of tales was composed by the Kashmi-
rian court poet SOMADĒVA, "one of the most illustrious Indian
poets" [1], in the eleventh century of our era [2], but the original
collection, its source, entitled the *Brhatkathā*, is must older, and,
according to Prof. SPEYER [3], "must have been arranged in that
period of Indian history, when *Buddhism* exercised its sway over
the Hindoo mind side by side with Çaivism and so many other
manifold varieties of sectarian and local creeds, rites and theoso-
phies" "The main story and a large number of the episodes are

---

1 Cf SPEYER, *Studies about the Kathāsaritsāgara*, Verhandelingen der Koninklijke
Akademie van Wetenschappen te Amsterdam, Afd. Letterkunde, Nieuwe Reeks, Deel
VIII, n° 5 (1908), p 2.

Çaiva tales, as was to be expected from the supposed first narrator being no other than the Supreme God Çiva himself"[1]. Next to legends of the *Buddhists* even mythological narrations from the Vedic age are to be found in this work, smaller collections being incorporated into it[2]. Among the great number of interesting legends, contained in the *Kathāsaritsāgara*, tianslated by TAWNEY (1880—1884), there are several in which the Nāgas play a more or less important part.

The first thing which strikes us is the total absence of passages devoted to their capacity of *giving rain*. Combining this with the same observation made above with regard to the *jātakas* of COWELL's edition, we feel inclined to believe that this part of the Nāgas' nature has been particularly developed by the Northern Buddhists. The original conceptions regarding these semidivine serpents, living in the water or *under the earth*, seem to have attributed to them the power of raising *clouds* and *thunder*, and of appearing as clouds themselves, but not as rain giving beings. It is, of course, a very obvious conclusion that cloud gods produce rain, but it seems that this idea, which made them the benefactors of mankind, first rose in the minds of the adherents of the Mahāyāna school. According to the original ideas, on the contrary, they seem to have only given vent to their *anger* in terrifying mankind by means of dense clouds, thunder and earthquakes. Highly interesting in this respect is the following story, to be found in the *Kathāsaritsāgara*[3].

In the Vindhya forest in the northern quarter there was a solitary açoka tree, and under it, in a lake, stood the great palace of a mighty Nāga king, Pārāvatāksha by name, who obtained a matchless sword from the war of the gods and the Asuras In order to get this sword an ascetic, assisted by a prince and his followers, threw enchanted mustard-seed upon the water, thus clearing it from the dust which concealed it, and began to offer an oblation with snake-subduing spells. "And he conquered by the power of his spells the impediments, such as *earthquakes, clouds*, and so on. Then there came out from that açoka tree a heavenly nymph, as it were, murmuring spells with the tinkling of her jewelled ornaments, and approaching the ascetic she pierced his soul with a sidelong glance of love And then the ascetic lost his self-command and forgot his spells; and the shapely fair one, embracing him, flung from his hand the vessel of oblation.

---

1 Ibidem   2 Ibidem.
3 Ch LXX, Vol II, p 149 sq.

Veih. Kon Aknd v Wetensch (Afd. Letterk) N R Dl XIII, N° 2   2

And then the snake Pārāvatāksha had gained his opportunity, and he came out from that palace *like the dense cloud of the day of doom* Then the heavenly nymph vanished, and the ascetic beholding the snake terrible with *flaming eyes, roaring horribly* [1], died of a broken heart When he was destroyed, the snake lay aside his awful form, and cursed Mrigānkadatta (the prince) and his followers, for helping the ascetic, in the following words: 'Since you did what was quite unnecessary after all coming here with this man, you shall for a certain time be separated from one another'. Then the snake disappeared, and all of them at the same time had their eyes dimmed with darkness, and were deprived of the power of hearing sounds. And they immediately went in different directions, separated from one another by the power of the curse, though they kept looking for one another and calling to one another".

Nāgas injuring the crops are mentioned in another passage, where Svayamprabhā, queen of the Asuras residing in Pātāla land, "makes herself surety (to king Merudhvaja) that the Nāgas shall not injure the crops" [2]. The seven Pātālas are the netherworld [3], the "home of the serpent race below the earth" [4], but also the Asuras, "who escaped from the slaughter in the great fight long ago between the gods and asuras", had fled to Pātāla [5] and lived there. As to the Nāgas having their abode in Pātāla land, we may refer to the following passages of the *Kathāsaritsāgara*. "On the extreme shore he set up a pillar of victory, looking like the king of the serpents emerging from the world below to crave immunity for Pātāla" [6]. "Do you not remember how he went to Pātāla and there married the daughter of a Nāga, whose name was Surūpā" [7] When Kadrū and Vinatā, two wives of Kaçyapa, had a dispute as to the colour of the Sun's horses, they made an agreement that the one that was wrong should become a slave to the other. Kadrū, the mother of the snakes, induced her sons to defile the horses of the Sun by spitting venom over them; thus they looked black instead of white, and Vinatā, the mother of Garuda, king of birds, was conquered by this trick and made Kadrū's slave When Garuda came to release her, the snakes asked the nectar from the sea of milk, which the gods had begun to churn, as a substitute,

---

1 This is probably thunder and lightning
2 Ch CXIX, Vol II, p 551
4 Vol I p 185 note 3

3 Vol II, p 549, note 1
5 Ch CXVIII Vol II p 530

and Garuda went to the sea of milk and displayed his great
power in order to obtain the nectar. "Then the god Vishnu,
pleased with his might, deigned to say to him 'I am pleased
with you, choose a boon'. Then Garuda, angry because his mother
was made a slave, asked a boon from Vishnu — 'May the snakes
become my food'". Vishnu consented, and Garuda, after having
obtained the nectar, promised Indra to enable him to take it
away before the snakes should have consumed it. He put the
nectar on a bed of Kuça grass and invited the snakes to take
it there after having released his mother. They did so, and
Garuda departed with Vinatā, but when the snakes were about
to take the nectar, Indra swooped down and carried off the vessel.
"Then the snakes in despair licked that bed of Darbha grass,
thinking that there might be a drop of spilt nectar on it, but
the effect was that their tongues were split, and they became
double-tongued for nothing. What but ridicule can ever be the
portion of the over-greedy? Then the snakes did not obtain the
nectar of immortality, and their enemy Garuda, on the strength
of Vishnu's boon, began to swoop down and devour them. And
this he did again and again. And while he was thus attacking
them, the snakes *in Pātāla* were dead with fear, the females
miscarried, and the whole serpent race was well-nigh destroyed
And Vāsuki the king of the snakes, seeing him there every day,
considered that the serpent world was ruined at one blow· then,
after reflecting, he preferred a petition to that Garuda of
irresistible might, and made this agreement with him — 'I will
send you every day one snake to eat, O king of birds, on the
hill that rises out of the sand of the sea. But you must not act
so foolishly as to enter Pātāla, for by the destruction of the
serpent world your own object will be baffled' When Vāsuki said
this to him, Garuda consented, and began to eat every day in
this place one snake sent by him· and in this way innumerable
serpents have met their death here". Thus spoke a snake, whose
turn it was to be devoured by Garuda, to Jīmūtavāhana, "the
compassionate incarnation of a Bodhisattva" [1], son of Jīmūtaketu,
the king of the Vidyādharas on Mount Himavat. And Jīmūtavāhana, "that treasure-house of compassion, considered that he
had gained an opportunity of offering himself up to save the
snake's life. He ascended the stone of execution and was carried
off by Garuda who began to devour him on the peak of the
mountain". At that moment a rain of flowers fell from Heaven,

1 Vol I, p 174.

and Garuda stopped eating, but was requested by Jīmūtavāhana himself to go on Then the snake on whose behalf he sacrificed his life, arrived and cried from far, "Stop, stop, Garuda, he is not a snake, I am the snake meant for you". Garuda was much grieved and was about to enter the fire to purify himself from guilt, but following Jīmūtavāhana's advice determined never again to eat snakes, and to make revive those which he had killed. The goddess Gaurī by raining nectar on Jīmūtavāhana made him safe and sound, and Garuda brought the nectar of immortality from heaven and sprinkled it along the whole shore of the sea. "That made all the snakes there (whose bones were lying there) rise up alive, and then that forest, crowded with the numerous tribe of snakes, *appeared like Pātāla* come to behold Jīmūtavāhana, having lost its previous dread of Garuda" [1].

Pātāla-land, the seven under-worlds, one of which was called Rasātala [2] (sometimes equivalent to Pātāla) [3], was inhabited by Nāgas, Asuras, Daityas and Dānavas (two classes of demons opposed to the gods and identified with the Asuras). There were temples of the gods (Çiva [4], Durgā [5], the Fire-god [6]), worshipped by the demons. As to its entrances, these are described as mountain caverns [7] or "openings in the water" [8]; or wonderful flagstaffs rising out of the sea with banners on them showed the way thither [9]. Sometimes human kings were allowed to visit this Fairy land Chandraprabha e. g., after having offered to Çiva and Rudra, with his queen and his ministers, with Siddhārta at their head, entered an opening in the water pointed out by Maya, and after travelling a long distance, arrived there [10]. And king Chandasinha with Sattvaçīla plunged into the sea and following the sinking flagstaff reached a splendid city [11]. Also king Yaçahketu, after diving into the sea, suddenly beheld a magnificent city, with palaces of precious stones and gardens and tanks and wishing-trees that granted every desire, and beautiful maidens [12]. This agrees with the description of the Nāga palaces which we found in the Jātakas.

A temple of Vāsuki, the king of the snakes, is mentioned in the

---

1 Ch XXII, Vol I, pp 182 sqq , cf Ch XC, Vol II, pp. 312 sqq

2 Vol I, p 417, II, 544   3 II, 185, note 4

4 II, 198, in the form of Hātakeçvara We read on p 109 of the *Sang hyang Kamahāyānikan*, an interesting old-Javanese text translated by J Kats, that Içvara, Brahmā and Vishnu by order of Vairocana filled heaven with gods, the earth with men, and the netherworld (Pātāla) with Nāgas   5 II, 267   6 II, 547

7 I, 446 "There are on this earth many openings leading to the lower regions", II 197   8 I 447   9 II 269   10 I 417   11 II 060

same work [1] There was a festive procession in his honour, and great crowds worshipped him His idol stood in the shrine, which was full of long wreaths of flowers like serpents, "and which therefore resembled the abyss of Pātāla". To the South of the temple there was a large lake sacred to Vāsuki, "studded with red lotusses, resembling the concentrated gleams of the brilliance of the jewels on snakes' crests; and encircled with blue lotusses, which seemed like clouds of smoke from the fire of snake poison: overhung with trees, that seemed to be worshipping with their flowers blown down by the wind".

Other passages relate about Nāgas assuming human shapes [2], either to escape Garuda (who in this work is always mentioned as one being), or to embrace a Nāgī In the former case Garuda himself persecuted the Nāga in human form, in the latter the snake-god, discovering that he was deceived by his wife during his sleep, "discharged fire from his mouth, and reduced them both (her lover and herself) to ashes".

§ 3. The Nāga as a giver of rain.

We have seen above that the Nāga's capacity of raising clouds and thunder when his anger was aroused was cleverly converted by the Mahāyāna school into the highly beneficient power of giving rain to the thirsty earth. In this way these fearful serpents by the influence of Buddha's Law had become blessers of mankind It is clear that in this garb they were readily identified with the Chinese dragons, which were also blessing, rain giving gods of the water.

The four classes into which the Mahāyānists divided the Nāgas were:

1 *Heavenly Nāgas* (天龍), who guard the Heavenly Palace and carry it so that it does not fall.

2. *Divine Nāgas* (神龍), who benefit mankind by causing the *clouds to rise and the rain to fall.*

3. *Earthly Nāgas* (地龍), who drain off rivers (remove the obstructions) and open sluices (outlets).

---

1 Ch LXXIV, Vol. II, p 225 Vāsuki is also mentioned Vol. I, p. 32, where Kīrtisena, his brother's son, is said to have married Crutārthā, the daughter of a Brahman His daughter Ratnaprabha is mentioned Vol I, p 544 He cursed a Nāga king who had fled from battle, Vol II, p 171 The serpent Vāsuki served as a rope with which to whirl round mount Mandara, when the sea was churned and produced Çrī or Lakshmī, Vol II, p 568, note 1

2 Ch LXI, Vol II, p 54, Ch. LXIV, Vol. II, p. 98.

4. *Nāgas who are lying hidden* (伏藏龍), guarding the treasuries of the "Kings of the Wheel" (輪王, Cakravartī-rājas) and blessing mankind [1].

The *Taiheiki* [2], a Japanese work, relates an Indian tale in which a Dragon (i e. Nāga) king is said to have caused rain. A *sien* (仙, the Chinese equivalent for a wonder-working ascetic), annoyed by this, caught all big and small dragons of the inner and outer seas, and shut them up in a rock. Owing to their absence not a drop of rain fell for a long time, and the crops were spoiled by the heavy drought. Then the king, moved with compassion for his people, asked his advisers how this ascetic's power could be broken and the dragons let loose. The answer was, that a beautiful woman could seduce him and thus put a stop to his magic capacity. So the King despatched the greatest beauty of his harem to the cottage of the ascetic, who immediately fell in love with her and, losing his supernatural power, became an common man and died. The dragons, no longer under his influence, flew away to the sky, and caused the winds to blow and the rain to fall.

A passage from Jin-Chʻau's *Buddhist Kosmos* [3], dealing with the Nāga kings, and translated by Beal in his *Catena of Buddhist scriptures from the Chinese* [4], mentions four sūtras, one of which, the *Mahāmegha sūtra*, shall be treated below in § 4. As to the *Lau-Tán*(?) sūtra, the title of which is not explained by Beal, so that we know neither the Chinese characters nor the Sanscrit equivalent, this sūtra is said there to contain the following passage: "To the North of Mount Sumeru, under the waters of the Great Sea, is the Palace of Sāgara Nāgarāja, in length and breadth

----

1 Cf the Japanese Buddhist dictionary *Bukkyō iroha jiten*, 佛教ヤ３は字典, written in 1901 (sec ed 1904) by Miura Kensûke, 三浦兼助, Vol II, p 56 s v 龍, the Chinese work *Tsʻien kʻioh ku lei shu*, 潜確居類書, written in the Ming dynasty by Chʻen Jen-sih, 陳仁錫 The same Chinese work enumerates as follows the three sorrows (患) of the Indian dragons

   1 Hot winds and hot sand, which burn their skin, flesh and bones
   2 Sudden violent winds, which blow away the palaces of the dragons and make them lose their treasures, clothes, etc , so that they can no longer hide their shapes
   3 Golden-winged bird-kings (Garuda kings) who enter the dragons' palaces and devour their children.

2 太平記, written about 1382, Ch XXXVII, p. 6

3 *Fah-kai-on-lih-to* (法界, *Fah-kai* is *Dharmadhātu*).

80000 yōjanas; it is surrounded by precious walls, a beautiful railing, garden and parks, adorned with every species of decoration". This Sāgara, one of the eight Great Nāga kings mentioned above, apparently obtained the principal rank among the rain bestowing Nāgas of the sea, worshipped by the Northern Buddhists.

From the *Saddharma smrtyupasthāna sūtra*[1], which BEAL, without giving the Chinese title, wrongly calls *Saddharma Prākasa sāsana sūtra*, but which I found in NANJŌ's Catalogue sub nr 679, BEAL quotes the following passage: "Down in the depths of the Great Sea 1000 yōjanas is a city named Hi-loh, its length and breadth 3000 yōjanas; it is occupied by Nāgarājas. There are two sorts of Nāgarājas 1. Those who practise the Law of Buddha; 2. Those who do not do so. The first protect the world, the second are opposed to it. Where the good Nāgas dwell it never rains hot sand, but the wicked Nāgas are subject to this plague, and their palaces and followers are all burned up. Whenever men obey the Law, and cherish their parents, and support and feed the Shamans, then the good Nāgarājas are able to acquire increased power, so that they can cause a small fertilizing rain to fall, by which the five sorts of grain are perfected in colour, scent, and taste.... If, on the contrary, men are disobedient to the Law, do not reverence their parents, do not cherish the Brahmans and Shamans, then the power of the wicked dragons increases, and just the opposite effects follow, every possible calamity happens to the fruits of the earth and to the lives of men".

Finally, the *Buddhāvatamsaka mahāvaipulya sūtra*[2] contains a large number of interesting passages with regard to the Nāgas as gods of clouds and rain. BEAL translates as follows: "In the midst of the Palace of the Nāga-rāja *Sāgara* there are four precious gems, from which are produced all the gems of the Ocean Here also is the Palace of Jambuketu, the Nāga-rāja's eldest son, also the palace of *Vāsuki* Nāga-rāja, and eighty myriads of other Dragons, each having his separate palace".

"There are five sorts of Dragons 1. Serpent-dragons; 2. Lizard-dragons; 3. Fish-dragons; 4. Elephant-dragons; Toad-dragons".

1 正法念處經 (NANJŌ, nr 679)

2 NANJŌ, nrs 87 and 88 大方廣佛華嚴經, litt *Mahāvaipulya Buddhāvatamsaka sūtra*, nr 87 is translated by BUDDHABHADRA (覺賢, who worked A. D. 398—421, cf. NANJŌ, Appendix II, nr 42, p 399) and others, nr 88 is a later and fuller translation by ÇIKSHĀNANDA, A.D. 695—699.

"*Sāgara* Nāga-rāja, assuming the appearance of Maheshvara, exerting his great strength, mightily assists all sentient creatures. His influence extends from the four continents up to the Para-nirmita Vaçavartin Heaven. He spreads out the *clouds* diversified with every colour, excites the varied brightness of the *lightning*, causes the changing peals of *thunder*, raises propitious *breezes*, distils *fertilizing showers*. But though this Nāga-rāja is well affected towards men, the good principles which prevail in the world are the real source of propitious rain falling. Again it is said that *Anavatapta* Nāga-rāja raises the widespreading vapoury clouds which cover Jambudvīpa and distil soft and nourishing rain, causing the various herbs and grains to spring up and flourish, and the fountains and rivers to swell with refreshing streams".

Beside in this passage translated by BEAL the same sūtra often mentions Sāgara and the other Nāga-kings as givers of rain. In the Chinese translation of the end of the seventh century A. D. (NANJŌ, nr 88) we read e. g. "Further, there are innumerable Great Nāga-kings, called Virūpāksha, Sāgara, etc. etc. ..., who by raising the clouds and diffusing the rain put an end to the vexations caused to all living beings by burning heat"[1].

"When the Great Sea-Nāga-king (Sāgara) sends down the rain, He (the Enlightened One) can separately count the drops, and in one thought make out (their number)"[2].

Comparisons especially, mostly in stanzas, of the rain-giving Nāga kings to Buddha and his Law, are very numerous[3]

"The Supreme Nāga king Sāgara, when raising the clouds covers the whole earth and distributes the rain over all places, and in his heart there is but one thought — so do also the Buddhas, the Kings of the Law. great clouds of compassion spread everywhere, and, on behalf of all those who practise religious austerities, rain down on each and on all without distinction"[4]

"Like Anavatapta Nāgarāja sends down the rain everywhere on Jambudvīpa and thus can cause all the plants and trees to shoot up and grow, and it (the rain) does not come forth from his body but from his heart — in the same way also the

---

[1] 復有無量諸大龍王所謂毗樓博叉王、娑竭羅龍王 ⋯ 興雲布雨令諸眾生熱惱消滅。Ch I, p 18a, b   [2] Ch XV, p. 18b
[3] Cf Ch XV, p. 21b, XVII, 19a, XXXVIII, 22b, XLII, 6b, 15b, LI, 11b, LII, 1b, LII, 3b, LXXX, 22a.
[4] Ch II, p. 48

beautiful words of the Buddhas everywhere rain upon the Universe (Dharmadhātu)" [1].

Thus this sūtra is a striking evidence of the great blessing power attributed by Northern Buddhism to the Nāga kings as givers of rain.

§ 4 Sūtras recited in rain ceremonies

The most important of the sūtras, recited by the Northern Buddhists for causing rain in times of drought, is the *Mahāmegha sūtra*, "The Sūtra of the Great Cloud". NANJŌ's *Catalogue of the Buddhist Tripitaka* contains four Chinese translations of this text nrs 186—188, and 970. The titles of the translations are a little different from one another [2], but the original work is the same JNĀNAGUPTA translated it first between A. D. 557 and 581 (nr 187), and a second time between A. D. 589 and 618 (nr 186). In A. D. 585 another translation was made by NARENDRAYAÇAS (nr 188). Nr 970, which has the same Chinese title as nr 188, is a later translation. The Sanskrit text still exists, and an extract of it is given by BENDALL, in the Journal of the Royal Asiatic Society [3], this agrees with nr 186, while BEAL, in his *Catena of Buddhist Scriptures from the Chinese*, gives an abstract of nr 188. According to DE GROOT [4] the sūtra was translated by AMOGHAVAJRA, the second patriarch of the Yoga school in China, disciple of VAJRABODHI (the first patriarch of the same school, who in 719 arrived in China). This is apparently nr 970 of NANJŌ's Catalogue, designated as "a later translation".

From BENDALL's extract we learn that the contents of the *Mahāmegha sūtra* are as follows. "On one occasion the Venerable One dwelt in the palace of the Snake-Kings Nanda and Upananda, in the summer pavilion of the circle of mighty clouds filled with

---

1 Ch LI, p. 11b.

2 Nr 186 佛說大方等大雲請雨經, "Mahāvaipulya Great Cloud sūtra, for asking rain"

Nr 187 大雲請雨經, "Great Cloud sūtra for asking rain"

Nr 188 大雲輪請雨經, "Great Cloud-wheel sūtra for asking rain" On p. 11b of the Chinese text we find the name of the Tathāgata "Great Cloud-wheel" BENDALL (p 303) translates "great cloud-circle", but 輪 is *wheel*

Nr 970: same title as nr 188.

3 New Series, Vol XII (1880), pp. 286 sqq

4 *Le Code du Mahāyāna en Chine*, Verhandelingen der Koninklijke Akademie van Wetenschappen, Afd Letterkunde, Deel I, n° 2 (1893), Ch VIII, pp 148 sqq.

precious gems and jewels, accompanied by a mighty assemblage of bhikshus, and by a mighty assemblage of bodhisattvas, and a mighty host of kings, to wit, Nanda the Snake King, and Upananda (here follows a list of 185 snakes) [1], attended, I say, by 84 hundreds of thousands of millions of krores of snakes assembled and seated together". All the Nāgas saluted the Lord, bending their clasped hands towards him, whereupon they stood on one side and made supplications. "Let us worship, let us reverence, esteem, honour the samudras (infinite numbers) of Bodhisattvas... *riding upon the sea-clouds*, immeasurable and innumerable, with samudras of *cloud-bodies*". Then the "Great Supreme King of Snakes" asks. "How, O Venerable One, may all the troubles of all the snakes subside; (and how) may they (thus) gladdened and blessed, send forth rain-torrents here, seasonably for Jambudvīpa; make all grasses, bushes, herbs, forest-trees to grow; produce all corn, give rise to all juices, whereby the men of Jambudvīpa may become blessed?" The Master answers, that all the troubles of the Nāgas may subside and they may be reborn in the Brahma-world by exercising charity. Further, they must put into action the Sarvasukhandadā dhāranī, and repeat the names of the Tathāgatas, "whose families and races are sprung from the one hair-tip of Vairocana, speedy producers of happiness [consisting of] a circle of clouds" Here follows a large number of names of Tathāgatas, among which in the Chinese text [2] such are found as. "Tathāgata who stores up the great clouds" [3], "Tathāgata the displaying of whose nature sends forth the clouds" [4], "Tathāgata who holds in his hands (and directs) the clouds and the rain" [5], "Great raiser of the clouds" [6], "Great disperser of wind and

---

1 Among these Nāga-kings the Chinese text gives names as Moon-cloud, Sea-cloud, Great Cloud-receptacle (store-house), Nāga-king who sends down the rain, Nāga-king of Clouds and Rain, Great Rain, King of Clouds, etc (月雲、海雲、大雲藏、降雨龍王、雲雨龍王、大雨、雲王) On p 2a of nr 188 we find the Nāga-king Kumbhīra (Crocodile) (金毗羅龍王), i e, as BEAL (*Catena*, p 423) rightly remarks, the well-known god *Kompira* of Japan When at the Restauration the Shintōists reclaimed all their temples from the Buddhists, they wrongly declared Kompira to be an obscure Shintō deity, called Kotohira, and thus took possession of all the shrines of this Nāga-king, the protector of sailors and of those who travel on sea.

2 P 11 sq

3 藏大雲如來.

4 性現出雲如來.   5 持雲雨如來.

clouds" [1], "Great cloud wheel" [2] etc. "By the utterance of these
names of Tathāgatas, O snake-king, all woes of all snakes are
set at rest, and [though] fraught with ills they create here in
Jambudvīpa showers in season and for a season, and make all
grass, shrubs, herbs, forest-trees, and corn to grow". At the
request of the Nāga king the Buddha utters a Dhāranī called
Mahākarunodbhava, "which causes rain in time of drought and
checks excessive rain", and invokes the Nāgas: "O mighty snakes,
bring rain here by the appointment of the truth of all Devas,
hail! By the appointment of the truth of Brahma, rain here in
Jambudvīpa, hail!"

Then follow prescriptions for the Great Cloud-circle (or *wheel*)
rite. "He who desires a mighty rain must perform this rite in
an open space, overspread by a blue canopy, shaded by a blue banner, on a clear spot of earth, (being) a prophet of the Law,
seated on a blue seat, fasting according to the ashtānga, with
well-washed limbs, clad in pure raiment, anointed with fragrant
odour, wearing the three white stripes, he must recite it for a
day and night continuously facing the east; he must place four
full vessels, filled with pure blue water, after prayers to the
Tathāgatas also, according to his power, an oblation, and flowers
and odours, then the prophet of the Law, after having painted
towards the four quarters with liquid cow-dung on a reed, in
the eastern quarter three hastas high must depict the snake-king
called Triçīrshaka (Three-crested), with cow-dung, in the southern
quarter him called Pancaçīrshaka (Five-crested) five hastas high,
in the western, seven hastas high, Saptaçīrshaka (Seven-crested);
in the northern, Navaçīrshaka (Nine-crested), nine hastas high... .
Afterwards, at a season of drought, he shall recite this chapter,
'The Great-cloud-circle', for one day or for two, until it needs
shall rain seven nights".

Then by numerous invocations the snake kings are summoned.
On p. 309 we read that this "Whirlwind" chapter, also called
"The Heart of all Serpents" must be recited by the prophet of the
Law, after three snake kings with their retinues having been
painted with cow-dung for thrice seven days uninterruptedly ·
a triple-crested one in the East, a seven-crested one in the West,

---

1 大散風雲如來.

2 大雲輪如來 Cf the name of the sūtra itself "Great Cloud wheel sūtra
for asking rain", translated by NANJŌ into, "Sūtra on asking rain of the Great
Cloudwheel".

and a nine-crested one in the North. "A blue canopy and blue dress, blue banner (are to be used) and all the offering is to be made blue". "The cloud-monarchs too must be depicted, emitting a shower, and rubbing against one another, at the end masses of rain-birds and lightning are to be painted", and offerings of parched rice, fish, flesh and honey-food without curds must be made. After all these preparatory measures the prophet of the Law, pure and clad in pure raiment, must recite this "Whirlwind" chapter, "the Heart of Snakes".

BEAL [1] gives a short abstract of this sūtra (nr 188), as he found it in the Chinese Tripitaka. Of the great Nāga kings enumerated in the beginning the third one is *Sāgara* [2], the principal sea god of Chinese Buddhists, who often called him simply "The Sea-dragon-king". By this name he is also indicated in the titles of the two sūtras nrs 456 and 457 of NANJŌ's Catalogue [3]. The fourth Nāga king, *Anavatapta* [4], was well-known in Japan, as we will see below [5]. To him nr 437 of NANJŌ's Catalogue is devoted (translated A. D. 308) [6]. In the fifth place the Nāga king *Manasvin* [7] is mentioned. Then follows *Varuna* [8], the Nāga king, different from the deity of this name, called in China the Deva of the Water [9], which name reminds us of the famous *Suitengū* [10] of Tōkyō. Professor SPEYER had the kindness to point out to me that in the *Mahāvastu* [11], where the Buddha blesses Bhallika and Trapuṣa, among the protectors of the West Virūpāksha, the Nāgas and Varuna are mentioned. As to Virūpāksha, one of the four guardians of the world, he is the sovereign of all the Nāgas. Varuna, the Brahmanic god of heaven, is at the same time the regent

---

1 *A catena of Buddhist scriptures from the Chinese* (1871), p. 419 sqq

2 The first and second are *Nanda* and *Upananda Sāgara* is written 娑伽羅, cf. EITEL, *Sanskrit-Chinese dictionary*, s v. (there wrongly 婆 instead of 娑)

3 Nr 456 佛說海龍王經, "Buddhabhāshita Sāgara Nāgarāja sūtra"

Nr 457 佛爲海龍王說法印經, "Sūtra on the Seal of the Law, spoken by Buddha for the sake of the Nāga-king Sāgara"

4 阿那婆達多.

5 Book II, Ch III, § 4

6 Anavatapta nāgarāja paripṛkkhā sūtra The Chinese title is quite different.

7 摩那斯 Cf EITEL, 11 s v. Mānasa, where Manasvin is wrongly said to be the tutelary deity of lake Mānasarovara (in Tibet identified with lake Anavatapta, cf. KAWAGUCHI, *Three years in Tibet*, Ch XXVI, pp. 139 sqq).

8 婆婁那.   9 水天.   10 水天宮.

of the sea, and, as one of the eight Lokapālas, guardian of the West [1]. It is remarkable that there were apparently two beings of the same name, both deities of the water and of the West, Varuna the deva and Varuna the Nāga king.

After *Takshaka* [2], *Dhrtarāshtra* [3] and *Vāsuki* [4], of whom the first and the third both belong to the eight great Nāga kings of Northern Buddhism [5], *Mucilinda* [6], also called *Mahāmucilinda*, who, as we have seen above, protected Çākyamuni during the seven days of meditation, and *Elāpatra* [7], who consulted the Buddha about rebirth in a higher sphere, are enumerated, followed by 176 others.

The same Nāga kings, except Mucilinda and Elāpatra, are mentioned in the so-called *Anumantrana*, an invocation of the Nāgas found in the Bower MS. from Mingai, about which R. MORRIS [8] writes the following· "As regards to the contents of the MS., fol. 3 apparently contains a charm which is intended to force the Nāgas or snake-deities to send rain The mutilated line 1 enumerates, it would seem, various plants which are to be used as ingredients for an oblation. Line 2 gives the Mantra for the oblation.. ... The end of line 2 and the following lines to the end of the page contain the so-called *Anumantrana*, a further invocation of the snake-deities, intended to propitiate them by a declaration of the worshipper's friendly relations with various individual Nāgas. This snake-charm, which appears to be *Buddhistic*, was probably composed in Southern India. For it mentions 'the district on the banks of the Golā', i. e the Godāvarī..... The language of this piece is the incorrect Sanskrit, mixed with Prākrit forms, which is common in the Buddhist works of *the early centuries of our era*, as well as in the Buddhist and Jaina inscriptions of the same period".

MORRIS compares the list of names found in the Anumantraṇa,

---

1 Cf EITEL, l l., s v

2 德大迦

3 提頭剌吒 , BEAL calls him *Ditarāksha*, but MORRIS writes *Dhritarāshtra* (Dhṛtaraṣṭra)

4 婆修吉.

5 See above p 4, cf pp 20, 21, 23

6 目真隣陀.

7 伊羅跋那 (Elāpatna)

8 Journal of the Pāli Text Society, 1891—3, pp 63 seqq , Notes and queries by the Rev. R MORRIS, nr 44 Cf. the Wiener Zeitschrift für die Kunde des Morgenlandes, Vol. V, nr 2

each time preceded by the words "l keep friendship with", with those mentioned in the Great Cloud-wheel Rain-asking sūtra in BEAL's Catena, those found in the *Saddharma Pundarika sūtra* and those of Southern Buddhism. Nanda and Upananda, Anavatapta, Takshaka, Dhrtarāshtra and Virūpāksha are mentioned in all these lists, Sāgara (wrongly called Samhāraka in the Mingai MS.) in the three former, as well as Vāsuki, while Varuna and Manasvin are not found in the Lotus and in Southern Buddhism. Further, the MS. gives several other names, as Naīrāvana, Krshna, Gautamaka, Mani, Dandapāda etc. Dhrtarāshtra and Virūpāksha are the regents of the East and the West, and also Nāga kings; as to Naīrāvana, this is, according to MORRIS, perhaps Vaiçravana, the regent of the North. Kishna and Gautamaka are mentioned in the Divyāvadāna as two Nāga kings.

Prof. DE GROOT [1] gives a very interesting description of the whole rain ceremony, as it is performed in Chinese Buddhist monasteries in times of drought, by order of the authorities or of influential laymen. Au altar is erected, mostly in the court-yard before the great temple of the Triratna, but sometimes at the foot of the mountain on which the monastery is situated; there a Kwan-yin temple is often appointed for these ceremonies and for the prayers for rain, sent up by the mandarins and the people. Once or twice DE GROOT saw a shrine dedicated to Sāgara Nāgarāja, the special sea-god of the Chinese Buddhists, it was opened only in time of drought.

The altar corresponds with the prescriptions of the sūtra, mentioned above [2]. On the gates of the four sides dragons are painted, two on each, with their heads turned to the inside. The cow dung of the Hindus is replaced in China by a yellow reddish clay, which is used for adorning the platform inside the enclosure. The estrade upon this platform is covered with *blue* silk, as well as the tables for the sūtras, utensils, offerings, and the chairs of the performing monks, of whom the leader looks to the East, the others to the North and South.

According to DE GROOT, the colour blue is chosen in China because this is the colour of the East, from where the rain must come; this quarter is represented by the Azure Dragon, the highest in rank among all the dragons. We have seen, however, that

---

1 *Code du Mahāyāna en Chine*, Ch VIII, pp 148 sqq.

2 Cf. also nr 177 of the Supplement of the Tripitaka (third volume of bundle 3), p 380 b 大雲經祈雨壇法, 'Doctrine concerning the altar for praying for

the original sūtra already prescribed to use the blue colour and to face the East. Moreover, the Azure Dragon has nothing to do with Buddhism. The Chinese Buddhists only copy an ancient Indian rite. Indra, the raingod, is the patron of the East, and Indra-colour is *nīla*, dark blue or rather blue-black, the regular epitheton of the rain clouds [1]. If the priest had not to face the East but the West, this would agree with the fact that the Nāgas were said to live in the Western quarter and that in India the West corresponds with the blue colour. Facing the East, however, seems to point to an old rain ceremony in which Indra was invoked to raise the blue-black clouds.

On the eastern, southern, western and northern tables tablets are placed on which the principal dragons of these quarters, whose Indian names are mentioned above, are painted, with three, five, seven and nine heads instead of the crests or hoods of the Nāgas. Often other tablets representing attendants of these great dragons stand at their sides. All the dragons have waves at their feet and clouds above their heads Finally, twenty eight black poles with long blue flags, each with a burning oil lamp between four flower vases filled with fresh flowers, represent the twenty eight constellations. We find these twenty eight blue banners mentioned on p 21a of the Chinese text of the sūtra (NANJŌ, nı 186), BENDALL's translation of the Sanscrit text, however, speaks only of one blue banner [2] DE GROOT explains the fact that all the poles are black by the connection of this colour with the North, with Yin and the water [3]. This may be right, as the sūtra itself does not mention the colour of the poles, so that the Chinese in this respect could follow their own ideas

In the morning of the first day of the ceremonies the leading priest with the abbot and the highest authorities of the monastery offer incense in the great temple of the Tiiratna, and, while the dhāranīs of Kwan-yin are recited, the temple and the rain altar are purified by sprinkling pure water upon them (as amita). Now the Buddhas and Bodhisattvas, dragon-kings and saints may descend upon the altar without contaminating themselves. The leading monk and the abbot rise from their seats and offer incense; at the same time the choir thrice sings a lamentation about the

---

1 Professor SPEYER had the kindness of pointing this out to me One of the many passages where a blue-black colour is mentioned is *Mahābhārata*, Book III, 16, 13

2 Pp 303, 309

3 *Black* horses were the principal offerings to the rain gods of Japan, see below, Book II, Ch. III, § 2

drought and a prayer for rain, followed by an invocation of the Triratna. Then some moments of profound silence allow the officiating monk to sink into dhyāna and to see by his mental eyes the Buddhas, Bodhisattvas, dragon-kings and saints descending and listening to the prayers. On awakening he orders to recite seven times the dhāranī of the "Light-king of the Great Wheel" (i e the sun), in order to correct the mistakes which might be made in the ritual. Thereupon the monks invoke by name all the 187 Nāga kings mentioned in the sūtra and thrice recite the first kind of dhāranīs, given by the Buddha to these kings according to the same holy text. These magic formulae are accompanied by the sound of vajra bells, and followed by a terrible noise of drums and cymbals in order to make them more powerful. Then follows the invocation of all the 54 rain-giving Tathāgatas, enumerated in the sūtra, each monk having a small incense-burner in his hand, which they also used in invoking the Nāga kings. After a second dhyāna of the leading monk having rendered efficacious the second kind of dhāranī, given by the Buddha and recited by the monks in the same way as the former, the ceremony is closed by expressing the hope that the rain may soon come, sent by the Triratna and the dragon kings. A little later, in the course of the forenoon, the offerings, placed on the altar, are solemnly presented to the dragons, and songs and prayers are sent up to them, as well as to the Triratna and all the devas'. Often a paper figure of one of the Taoistic "Celestial Generals", with a written request for rain in his hand, is burned, that he may take it to Heaven.

In the afternoon the leading monk with the abbot and as many other monks as they want take their seats upon the altar and recite the Great-Cloud-Wheel sūtra. All these ceremonies are daily repeated till it rains sufficiently. If the drought lasts too long, Kwan-yin's dhāranīs and prayers for rain are continued night and day, small groups of monks relieving one another in all the buildings of the monastery. The main point of the ceremony is the purity of the altar and of the priests themselves; for the drought, like all calamities caused by some crime of men, can only be stopped by pure ceremonies performed by pure priests. Especially because they never eat animal food, the monks are religiously cleaner and therefore much more able to make rain than laymen.

As to the ceremonies for stopping too abundant rains, called "praying for good weather" ', these are described by DE GROOT

in the same chapter. The same sūtra may be used, because it
has the power of ruling the rain, but these ceremonies are seldom
performed on such an extensive scale. As a rule a yellow paper
tablet with an invocation of the Buddhas and Bodhisattvas who
reside above the rays of the sun and are mentioned in the
"Sūtra of the vajra brilliant flames (the beams of the sun), which
puts a stop to wind and rain"[1], is erected in the hall of the
Triratna and offerings are made to them Then Kwan-yin is
invoked and this Bodhisattva's dhāranīs are recited, or those of
the "Medicine-Master, Tathāgata of the *lu-li* (one of the sapta-
ratna, probably the bluish precious stone called vaidūrya) light"[2],
i. e. the sunlight, and the latter's name is invoked a thousand
times. DE GROOT explains this Medicine-Master to be the oriental
Sun, who cures Nature and drives away all illnesses caused by
the demons of Darkness His cult, the counterpart of that of
Amitābha, the occidental Sun, is based upon a sūtra, which we
find mentioned in NANJŌ's Catalogue sub nr 171[3]. This Tathāgata
is the well-known *Yakushi Nyorai* of Japan. It is quite clear
that he is considered to be most powerful in causing the rains
to stop and refreshing the earth by his rays Thereupon Çākyamuni, the Buddhas who are above the brilliant flames, and all
the Nāgas are supplicated to grant good weather, and besides
the two former the Medicine-Master and Kwan-yin are each
invoked thrice in kneeling attitude. Finally, the Buddha, Dharma
and Sangha are, as always, praised as the refuge of all. The
same ceremonies are repeated by other monks till the rain stops,
and then a larger number of them for the last time celebrates
the rites as a sign of gratitude and satisfaction.

In Japan, which in summer time has much more to suffer from

---

[1] 金剛光燄止風雨經

[2] 藥師瑠璃光如來·

[3] 藥師瑠璃光如來本願功德經, *Bheshajyaguru vaidūrya-
prabhāsa Tathāgata pūrvapranidhāna guna sūtra*, "Sūtra on the merits and virtue of
the original vow of the Medicine-Master, the Tathāgata Vaidūrya light, translated by
HUEN TSANG, A D 650 Cf nrs 170, 172, 173 According to NANJŌ, nrs 170, 171 and
172 are later translations of the twelfth Sūtra of nr 167, the main title of this work is
佛説大灌頂神咒經, *Buddhabhāshita mahābhishekarddhidhāranī sūtra*,
"Sūtra on the divine dhāranī of the Great washing of the top of the head (baptism),
spoken by Buddha". This is apparently the *Kanjō-kyō*, 灌頂經, "Sūtra on the
washing of the top of the head", recited in the fifth month of A D 880 in the Sacred
Spring Park at Kyōto, for stopping the abundant rains (*Sandai jitsuroku*, Ch XXXVII,
p. 541)

continuous and heavy rains than China, ceremonies for stopping
rain are frequently mentioned in the annals, as we shall see
below [1]. But also rain prayers were very frequent, and the Buddhist priests eagerly took advantage of the opportunity to surpass
the Shintoists and extend their sphere of influence. Thus the
Great-Cloud-Wheel sūtra (NANJŌ, nr 188), mentioned above, was
recited by fifteen Buddhist priests in the Sacred Spring park
(*Shinsen-en*) at Kyōto, in the sixth month of the year 875 of our
era [2]. At the same time sixty other priests in the Taikyokuden,
one of the buildings of the Imperial Palace, recited parts of the
Mahāprajñāpāramitā sūtra [3], which is very often mentioned in the
Japanese annals as having been partly read in rain ceremonies [4]).
Sometimes also the *Vajra-prajñāpāramitā sūtra* [5] was used. In the
fifth month of A.D. 880 the *Kanjō-kyō* [6], "Sūtra on washing the
top of the head (baptism)", was recited in the Sacred Spring park
for stopping the abundant rains.

Also in China other sūtras are used in rain ceremonies, e. g.
the *Vajra-prajñāpāramitā sūtra*, the *Buddhabhāshita Sāgara Nāga-
rāja sūtra* [7], "Sūtra on the Sea-dragon-king (i. e. Sāgara), spoken
by Buddha", etc. This is logical, for, as DE GROOT [8] remarks,
according to the 39th commandment of the Mahāyāna code all
punishments for crimes committed — and drought is such a
punishment — are to be taken away by reciting the sūtras and
vinayas of the Mahāyāna.

---

1 Book II, Ch. III

2 Cf below, Book II, Ch III, § 3, *Sandai jitsuroku*, Ch. XXVII, p 414

3 大般若經, *Mahāprajñā sūtra*, NANJŌ's *Catalogue*, nr 1, gives the full
title 大般若波羅蜜多經, and states that it was translated in A D
659 by the famous pilgrim HÜEN TSANG

4 Cf *Sandai jitsuroku*, Ch XX, p 335 (sixth month, 871), Ch XXIII, p. 372, (fifth
month, 873), Ch XXV, p 386 (second month, 874), Ch XXXII, p 466 (seventh month,
877), Ch. XXXVII, p 543 (sixth month, 880)

5 金剛般若經, *Sandai jitsuroku*, Ch XXIII, p 372, NANJŌ, nrs 10—12

6 灌頂經, see above, p 33, note 3, *Sandai jitsuroku*, Ch XXXVII, p 541;
NANJŌ, nr 167

7 佛說海龍王經, NANJŌ, nr 456, translated A D 265—316. Cf nr 457.
佛為海龍王說法印經, "Sūtra on the Seal of the Law spoken by
Buddha for the sake of Sāgara Nāgarāja" These sūtras were spoken in Sāgara's palace
at the bottom of the sea

8 L 1, p 156, cf p. 72

BOOK I.

THE DRAGON IN CHINA.

CHAPTER I.

THE DRAGON IN THE CHINESE CLASSICS.

§ 1. Yih king

The oldest Chinese work which mentions the dragon is the *Yih King* [1]. We read there the following explanation of the lowest line of the first of the diagrams, which corresponds with Heaven. "*First, nine · a dragon hidden in the water is useless*" [2]. According to the commentators the meaning of this sentence is that the lowest line of this diagram, representing the dragon lying in the deep, is a sign that it is not the time for active doing Therefore LEGGE [3] translates: "In the first (or lowest) line, undivided (we see its subject as) the dragon lying hid (in the deep). It is not the time for active doing". This translation is more explicative than true, for the text simply gives the words "First, nine · a dragon hidden in the water is useless". As to the word *nine*, this is explained by the commentary entitled "*Traditions of Ch'eng*" [4] to mean the "fullness of Yang", because it is three times three, i. e. a multiplication of the undividable number which represents Yang. As the undivided strokes of the diagrams are symbols of Yang and the divided ones of Yin, the meaning of the two first words of the sentence is, as LEGGE translates, that the lowest line is undivided. The characters 勿用, however, do not mean: "it is not the time for active doing", but simply. "*useless*" [5]. The dragon, symbolized by the lines of the diagram of Heaven, because he is the Yang creature κατ' ἐξοχήν, is represented by the

---

[1] Book 御纂周易折中, Ch I, 上經, 乾.
[2] 初九. 潛龍勿用.   [3] Section I, p 57   [4] 程傳.
[5] Prof. DE GROOT kindly pointed out to me the simple and clear meaning of this and the following sentences

lowest line as still lying in the depth of the waters. In this condition the heavenly giver of fertilizing rains is still useless to mankind. This must be the original meaning of these words, but the diviners concluded from this uselessness of the hidden dragon that one had to abstain from active doing.

The second line of the same diagram is explained by the *Yih king* as follows. *"Nine, second; a dragon is seen in the rice fields, advantage, a great man will be seen"* [1]. LEGGE translates. "It will be advantageous to meet with the great man". Although this translation follows the commentators, the meaning is clearer if we divide the sentence as we have done above. The appearance of a dragon in the rice fields gives advantage, i. e. the fertilizing rain gives good crops The original meaning of the character 利, which consists of *rice* and a *knife*, is apparently *harvest*, which was, of course, identical to advantage. Further, "a great man will be seen". Here we see the dragon representing great (especially holy) men, who are as full of Yang as the dragon himself. Even in those olden times his appearance apparently was considered to be an omen of the birth of great and holy men, especially of Emperors, the holiest men on earth.

In the third line the dragon is not mentioned, but in the fourth we read that he is *"perhaps leaping in the pool"* (but not yet rising above the surface). *"There will be no evil* (咎)" [2]. The word *evil* seems to be more logical in a divinatory sentence than "mistake".

The fifth line is described as *"A flying dragon in the sky; advantage, a great man will be seen"* [3]. It is, of course, of the utmost benefit to mankind, if the rain-bringing dragon is soaring in the sky. At the same time it is an omen of the appearance of a great man.

Finally, the topmost line is explained as *"The dragon exceeding the proper limits* (i. e. flying too high). *There will be regret"* [4]. The simplest explanation of these words is that, if a dragon flies too high, he is too far from the earth to return and the rain does not reach it, a reason of regret to himself and to mankind. At the same time the great man, symbolized by the dragon, repents all exaggeration on his part.

---

[1] 九二。見龍在田。利。見大人。

[2] 九四。或躍在淵。无咎。

[3] 九五。飛龍在天。利。見大人。

The *Yih king* goes on as follows: "*The number nine is used* (in this diagram). *If a herd of dragons is seen divesting themselves of their heads, this means good fortune*" [1]).

The lowest line of the second diagram, which represents Earth (坤, *Kw'un*), is explained as "*Dragons fighting in the open field, their blood is dark* (not *purple*, as Legge translated) *and yellow*" [2]. Apparently a thunderstorm, with dark and yellow clouds flying through the sky, is described in this way. For in a passage of Appendix V of the *Yih king* [3], ascribed to Confucius, we read: "*K'ien* (Heaven) is a horse, *Kw'un* (Earth) is a cow, *Chen (Thunder) is a dragon*" [4] And, again, in the same Appendix [5]. "*Chen* is thunder, is a dragon, is dark and yellow" [6]. The same diagram represents also *Spring* and the *Eastern quarter*, which are identified with the *Azure Dragon* [7].

In Ch. 11 (p. 2) of the *Yih king* the words "*A dragon lying in the deep is useless*" are illustrated by "*Yang is below*" [8], which means. "The Sun is under the horizon, i. e. the dragon lying in the deep is as useless as the sun under the horizon

In the same chapter (same page) we read: "*A dragon is seen in the rice fields; blessing power* (德) *is spread everywhere*" [9]). This is a clear explanation of the word *advantage* in the above passage on the fifth line of the first diagram.

As to the "*Dragons fighting in the open field*", in this chapter these words are followed by. "*Their way (tao) is exhausted*" [10], i. e. their blessing actions are completed to the last. As rain is the blessing conferred upon mankind by the dragons, this sentence may easily be explained by the fact that in a thunderstorm, when the dragons fight in the sky, the rain comes down in torrents.

---

[1] 用九。見羣龍无首。吉。

[2] 上六。龍戰于野。其血玄黄。

[3] *Shwoh-kwa chu'en*, 說卦傳 (Ch 17), p 12 Legge, Appendix V, p 429, Chapter VIII, 12

[4] 乾爲馬。坤爲牛。震爲龍。

[5] Ch 17, Legge, p 430, Ch. XI, 17.

[6] 震爲雷。爲龍。爲玄黄。

[7] Cf De Groot, *Rel Syst*, Vol I, p 317; III, p 964, 987.

[8] 潛龍勿用。陽在下也。

[9] 見龍在田。德施普也。

[10] 龍戰于野。其道窮也。

An Appendix of the *Yih king* [1] says: "*The hibernating of dragons and snakes is done in order to preserve their bodies*" [2]. Here we see dragons and snakes being closely connected and regarded as belonging to the same kind of animals. Also in later times the same fact is to be observed.

On considering the above passages of the *Yih king* we arrive at the conclusion that the ideas on the dragon prevailing in China at the present day are just the same as those of the remotest times. It is a water animal, akin to the snake, which uses to sleep in pools during winter and arises in spring. It is the god of thunder, who brings good crops when he appears in the rice fields (as rain) or in the sky (as dark and yellow clouds), in other words, when he makes the rain fertilize the ground. But when he flies too high and cannot return, the thirsty earth must wait in vain for his blessings, and sorrow prevails. As this beneficient being is full of Yang, it symbolizes those among men who are fullest of Light, namely great men, and its appearance is considered to be an omen of their coming, i. e. of their birth. In the first place the greatest and fullest of Yang among them all, the Emperor, is, of course, symbolized by the dragon. He is, indeed, the representative of Imperial power, as we shall see later on.

When black and yellow clouds covered the sky, and thunder and lightning raged, the ancient Chinese said, like those of to-day. "The dragons are fighting; look at their blood spreading over the sky". And at the same time the heavenly dragons caused the rain to pour down upon the grateful earth.

Even when the dragons were only leaping in their pools, no calamity was to be feared, and when a herd of them, even headless, was seen in the sky, this was a felicitous sign. Winter, when they hibernate and sleep in pools, is the dry season in China. But in spring, in the third of the twenty four seasons into which the year was divided even in olden times, the "Resurrection of the hibernating animals" [3] takes place, and it begins to rain a little. In the "beginning of summer" [4], however, i. e. in the first of the six summer seasons, "the winds arrive

---

[1] 繫辭下傳 (Ch XV), p 11.

[2] 龍蛇之蟄以存身也。

[3] 驚蟄, "Resurrection of hibernating animals", is the name of this season, cf DE GROOT, II, Vol III, p. 968

and the dragons ascend to the sky" [1], for this is the time when the abundant rains come down, a blessing to mankind.

§ 2. Shu king.

In the *Shu king* [2] we read the following words of the Emperor Shun to Yu "I wish to see the emblematic figures of the ancients: the sun, the moon, the stars, the mountain, the *dragon*, and the variegated animals (pheasants) which are depicted (on the upper sacrificial garment of the Emperor)". So we see that even in the early times of Shun's predecessors, i e. in the days of Hwang Ti (who is said to have reigned in the 27th century B. C.) and Yao, the dragon belonged to the six symbolic figures painted on the upper garment of the Emperor. This was, no doubt, due to its blessing power as rain-giving god of thunder and clouds.

§ 3 Li ki

The *Li ki* [3] says: "What is called the four *ling* (靈)? The unicorn, the phoenix, the tortoise and the dragon, they are called the four *ling* As the dragon is considered to be a domestic animal, fishes and sturgeons do not flee away" [4]. COUVREUR translates *ling* by. "animaux qui donnent des présages", but it has a stronger meaning, as we may learn from DE GROOT's *Religious System* [5]. Therefore I should prefer to translate it by "*spiritual beings*" The effective operation of the *tsing* (精) or vital spirit of these four creatures is, indeed, enormously strong, and therefore they may be justly called "the four *spiritual* animals par excellence". It is no wonder that their appearance was considered to

---

1 *Yih wei*, 易緯、通卦驗, quoted in the famous encyclopaedia entitled *K'in ting ku kin t'u shu tsih ch'ing*, 欽定古今圖書集成 (published in 1725, cf. DE GROOT, 11 Vol I, Introd p XXI), which we henceforth shall quote as T.S, Sect 禽蟲, Ch 127, 龍部彙考, p 5b· 立夏風至而龍升天.

2 予欲觀古人之象、日、月、星辰、山、龍、華蟲、作會. Sect. 益稷, *Yih Tsih*, LEGGE, Sacred Books of the East, Vol III, Part II, Book IV, § 1, p 58

3 Ch VII, *Li un*, 禮軍, art 3, nr 10 COUVREUR, *Li ki*, Vol I, p 524

4 何謂四靈。麟鳳龜龍、謂之四靈、故龍以爲畜、故魚鮪不淰。 5 Vol. IV, p 12

be an omen, but this was only the consequence of their *"spirituality"*.

In art 4 of the same Chapter of the *Li ki* [1], where the halcyon days of the holy emperors of antiquity are described, we read "The male and female phoenixes, and the male and female unicorns were all in the marshes beyond the city walls; the tortoise and the dragon were in the ponds of the Imperial Palace" [2], i. e the four *ling* were all in the neighbourhood, spreading their blessings over the Palace and the country.

Further, in another passage of the *Li ki*, also devoted to the ancient sovereigns [3], the following words are to be found: "They (the monarchs of old) chose (litt. followed, accommodated themselves to) felicitous places in order to make sacrifices to the Emperor of Heaven in the suburbs. The sacrifices ascended and reached Heaven. Then phoenixes descended, and tortoises and dragons arrived" [4].

Finally; in the first, second and third months of spring [5], "the Emperor ascends his carriage adorned with bells, drawn by azure dragons [6] and carrying a blue banner (旂, *k'i*, adorned with dragons joined [7])". The azure dragon is, as we stated above, the symbol of Spring, the season when "thunder resounds, lightning begins to flash, and the hibernating animals all move, open their doors (i. e. come out of their chrysalides) and begin to come out" [8].

§ 4. Cheu li

We have seen the dragon mentioned in the *Shu king* among the twelve symbolic ornaments of the ancient sacrificial robe of

---

1 COUVREUR, p 586, nr 16

2 鳳皇麒麟、皆在郊椒、龜龍在宮沼。

3 Ch VIII, *Li k'i*, 禮器, art 2, nr 12, COUVREUR, Vol. I, p 563

4 因吉土以饗帝於郊、升中於天。而鳳凰降、龜龍假。

5 *Li ki*, Ch XXI, *Yueh ling*, 月令, "Monthly Precepts", COUVREUR, I, Ch IV, pp 332 (first month), 340 (second month), 347 (third month) 天子…. 乘鸞路、駕蒼龍、載青旂

6 Horses higher than eight ch'ih, i e 1 60 meter, were called dragons (COUVREUR, I, p 333)

7 *Cheu li* 周禮, Section *Ch'un kwan*, 春官, "Spring officials", s v. 司常, *Szĕ shang*, Ch. XXVII, p 24, gives the names of the nine banners ruled by the *Szĕ shang*, "Banner rulers". "Dragons joined form the *k'i*, 旂, (the second banner)", 交龍爲旂

the Emperor. Further, the *Cheu li* has taught us (above p. 40, note 7) that the banner called *k'i*, 旂, was adorned with *dragons joined* (i.e. twisted about each other). The same work [1] states the following: "In general as *tsieh* [2] (official tablets) of the envoys of the Empire, in mountainous countries *tiger* tablets are used, in plain countries tablets *painted* with *human* figures, and in watery countries *dragon* tablets. The tablets are all made of metal" [3]. It is clear why the ornaments of these official tablets were divided in this way. For, as the commentator CHING K'ANG-CH'ING remarks on this passage, "in the mountains are many tigers, in the plains many men, and in the waters many dragons" [4] Thus the dragon symbolized the water.

A third passage of the *Cheu li* [5], which treats of the Winter officials, says that, in painting and embroidering, "Water is represented by means of dragons" [6]. CHAO P'UH'S [7] commentary explains these words as follows. "The dragon is a divine being in the water. If one represents water without representing dragons, there is nothing to show the divinity of its phenomena" [8] As to CHING K'ANG-CH'ING, he simply states: "The dragon is a water creature; it is (depicted or embroidered) on clothes" [9].

§ 5. I li

A dragon banner is mentioned in the *I li* [10], where Imperial hunting parties are described. We read there: "In the frontier

---

1 Section *Ti kwan*, 地官, s v *chang tsieh*, 掌節, Ch XIV, p 39

2 節.

3 凡邦國之使節。山國用虎節。土國用人節。澤國用龍節。皆金也。

4 土平地也。山多虎。平地多人。澤多龍。

5 Section *Tung kwan*, 冬官, Ch XLII, 老工記、畫繢 (painting and embroidering) 之事、雜五色, p 5b   6 水以龍.

7 趙溥, a commentator of the Sung dynasty Although only his family name is mentioned, and there was another commentator of the same family name, namely CHAO KW'ANG, 趙匡, of the T'ang dynasty, probably we have here to do with the former

8 龍水中神物。畫水不畫龍則無以見變化之神。

9 龍水物。在衣。

10 儀禮, Sect 鄉射禮記, Ch X, p 48a 於竟。則虎中。龍旝。

regions: when a tiger is hit: dragon banner". This is, at least, probably the meaning of the very short text. CHING K'ANG-CH'ING explains it as follows: "'In the frontier regions' (竟 is used here for 境) means shooting with the rulers of neighbouring countries. They paint a dragon on the banner [1]; moreover it is a variegated pattern. 'Full silk' forms the banner" [2]. In hunting parties with foreign rulers probably a signal was given with this dragon banner when a tiger (the dragon's deadly enemy) was shot.

The ancient texts referred to in this chapter are short, but sufficient to give us the main conceptions of old China with regard to the dragon. He was in those early days, just like now, the god of water, thunder, clouds and rain, the harbinger of blessings, and the symbol of holy men. As the Emperors are the holy beings on earth, the idea of the dragon being the symbol of Imperial power is based upon this ancient conception.

For the sake of clearness the further texts will be treated in separate chapters according to the kind of information they give. In each chapter, however, chronological order will be observed.

---

1 旃, *chen*, according to WELLS WILLIAMS, Dict. s. v. p. 44 "a silken banner of a reddish color, plain and triangular"

2 於竟。謂與鄰國君射也。畫龍於旃。尚文章也。通帛爲旃 (通帛, *t'ung poh*, was, according to CHING K'ANG-CH'ING, in the same work, Ch XXVII, p 24b, "deep red, in accordance with the main colour of the Cheu dynasty") .

CHAPTER II.

DIVINATION.

§ 1. Lucky omens

The birth of great sages and Emperors was preceded by the appearance of dragons and phoenixes. In the night of Confucius' birth (B. C. 551) two azure dragons descended from the sky and came to his mother's house. She saw them in her dream and gave birth to the great sage [1]. The biography of the Emperor Wu [2], the famous man of the Han dynasty (B. C. 140--87), contains the following passage in regard to his birth· "The Emperor Hiao Wu of the Han dynasty was the son of the Emperor King. Before he was born the Emperor King dreamt that a red hog descended from the clouds and straightly, entered the Ch'ing fang koh (Exalted Fragance Corridor). The Emperor King awoke and sat down under the corridor Actually there was a red dragon. It was like fog and in coming darkened the doors and windows. When the Imperial harem went to look (what was happening), there was above the corridor a cinnabar coloured vapour which increased enormously and, rose. After the vapour had dispersed they saw a red dragon coiling and revolving between the rafters. The Emperor King called a diviner, the Old Yao by name, and asked him about the matter. The old man said 'This is a lucky omen. This corridor certainly will produce a man who shall rule the world. He shall expel the barbarians and thus bring with him lucky omens. Therefore he shall be the most glorious ruler of the Liu family. But it (may mean) also a great prodigy'. The Emperor King ordered the Imperial Consort Wang to move to the Exalted Fragrance Corridor, wishing thereby to act in accordance with Old Yao's words. Thereupon he changed the

---

1 *Shih i ki*, 拾遺記, written by WANG KIA, 王嘉, probably in the 4th century, Ch. III, 周靈王, p 4b

2 *Wu Ti nei chw‘en*, 'Inner traditions on the Emperor Wu", 武帝內傳, ascribed to the famous historiographer PAN KU, 班固, who died A D 92, p 1a.

name of the corridor into *I lan tien*, 'Hall of the Florishing Orchid' [1]. After more than ten days the Emperor King dreamt that a divine woman held up the sun in both her hands and gave it to the Consort Wang. She swallowed it, and after fourteen months gave birth to the Emperor Wu. The Emperor King said· 'I dreamt that a red vapour changed into a red dragon. The diviners considered this to be a lucky omen; (therefore) he (the new-born son) must be called Lucky (*kih*)'".

One of the ten lucky signs which were seen in the course of one day under the reign of Yao, one of the five holy Emperors of ancient times, was a dragon which appeared in the pond of his palace [2].

The appearance of *yellow* or *azure* dragons, often mentioned in the annals [3], was nearly always considered to be a very good omen. Only if they came untimely or on wrong places they were harbingers of evil, as we shall see below. They were mostly seen in the night, spreading a brilliant light all over the neighbourhood. Such a nightly apparition illuminated the palace of Kung Sun-shuh [4] under the reign of the Emperor Kwang Wu (25—57 A.D.). The former considered it such a good omen, that in 25 A.D. he proclaimed himself Emperor of Shu (White Emperor) and changed the name of the era into Lung-Hing [5], "Dragon's rise" [6]. A black, horned dragon was seen one night by Lu Kwang [7], who lived in the fourth century A. D. Its glittering eyes illuminated the whole vicinity, so that the huge monster was visible till it was enveloped by clouds which gathered from all sides. The next morning traces of its scales were to be seen over a distance of five miles, but soon were wiped out by the heavy

---

1 The orchid being the symbol of harmony, because the *Shi king* compares the dwelling together in harmony of brothers with the smell of orchids, the new name of the corridor was still more felicitous than the former

2 *Shuh i ki*, 述異記, written by JEN FANG, 任昉, in the earlier part of the 6th century 堯爲仁君。一日十瑞、宮中芻化爲禾、鳳凰止於庭、神龍見于宮沼。Ch 上, p 4b

3 Cf T S, Ch 128, 龍部、紀事一, p 7b, 8a, 9, Ch 129, 紀事二, pp 1 sq

4 公孫述.　　　5 龍興.

6 *Tung kwan han ki*, 東觀漢紀, Ch. XXIII, written in 107 A D by LIU CHEN, 劉珍, and continued in 172 A D by TS'AI YUNG, 蔡邕

7 呂光 cf GILES *Chin. Biogr. Dict* s v pp 555 sq In 396 he took the style

rains. Then one of Lu Kwang's attendants said to him: "A dragon is a divine animal and an omen of a man's rise to the position of a ruler So you will attain this rank". On hearing this, Lu Kwang was very much rejoiced; and actually he became a ruler after some time [1]. The dragons being such important omens, it is no wonder that Imperial proclamations often were issued on account of their appearance [2].

Finaly, we may quote a divinatory work [3] which says: "When the beginning rise of an Emperor or King is about to take place, a dragon appears in the Yellow River or in the Loh. All examine his head: if the head is black, men are correct, if white, the Earth is correct; if red, Heaven is correct" [4].

§ 2. Bad omens.

A. Fighting dragons.

From olden times high floods, tempests and thunderstorms have been ascribed by the Chinese to dragons fighting in rivers or in the air. Although, according to the *Yih king* [5], "the *tao* of dragons, fighting in the open field, is exhausted", i. e their blessing power makes the rain pour down in torrents, on the other hand such severe thunderstorms often cause much damage and calamities. Therefore, however welcome a dragon fight in the air might be in times of drought, in ordinary circumstances the threatening armies in the sky were looked at with great fright. Moreover, the people believed the damage produced by dragon fights in rivers or in the air to be not limited to the actual calamities of the present, but to extend itself to the near future, in other words, they were considered to be very bad

---

1 *Pao P'oh-tsze*, 枹朴子, written by KOH HUNG, 葛洪, in the fourth century, 外篇, Ch. IV (廣譬)

2 The Emperor - Wen of the Han dynasty e g did so in B C 165, *Books of the Early Han Dynasty*, 文帝本記, Ch IV, comp the Emperor Suen's proclamation in the summer of B C. 52 (ibidem, 宣帝本記, Ch VIII, p. 14a

3 The *Yih k'ien tsoh tu*, 易乾鑿度, quoted in the T. S., Sect 禽蟲, Ch. 130, 龍部, 雜錄, p 2b

4 帝王始興將起河洛龍見．皆察其首．黑者人正、白者地正、赤者天正。

5 See above, p 37.

omens, foreboding inundations, disorder, war, nay even the
dynasty's fall. As gods of water, clouds and rain they caused
high floods by their fights, and as representatives of the Imperial
power their victory or defeat meant rebellion, war, and even the
fall of the reigning House.

According to the *Tso chw'en* [1] a high flood was ascribed to
dragons fighting in a pool in the nineteenth year of the reign
of Chao, Duke of Lu (523 B. C.) "There were great floods in
Ch'ing; and [some] dragons fought in the pool of Wei, outside
the She gate. The people asked leave to sacrifice to them; but
Tsze-ch'an refused it, saying. "When we fight, the dragons do
not look at us. Why should we look at them, when they are
fighting? If we offer a deprecatory sacrifice to them, they will
leave their abodes. If we do not seek the dragons, they also will
not seek us". Then the matter was given up.

The *Yih lin* [2] says. "If six dragons have angry fight with one
another under an embankment, and the azure or yellow dragons
do not conquer, the travellers will meet hardships and trouble" [3].
As we have seen above, the azure and yellow dragons especially
were harbingers of felicity; so their defeat was a sign of coming
trouble, probably caused by inundations.

In regard to impending war and ruin we may quote the following passages from the Histories.

In the *Books of the Sui dynasty* [4] we read: "In the Liang dynasty
(A. D 502—557), in the second year of the T'ien kien era (503),
there were dragons fighting in a pool in Northern Liang province.
They squirted fog over a distance of some miles As to the evils
of dragons and snakes the *Hung fan wu hing chw'en* [5] says · 'These
are trouble and damage of dragons and beasts. That which belongs to Heaven is symbol of the Ruler. If the Heavenly breath
is injured, and the Tao of the Ruler is wounded, also the dragons
are injured. Their fights are symbols of weapons and shields'.

---

1 LEGGE, *Chinese Classics*, Vol V, Part II, pp. 674 sq (Book X, year XIX).

2 易林, a work on divination, quoted by the T S, Ch. 130, 龍部雜錄, p 3a

3 六龍共怒戰於陂下、蒼黃不勝、旅人艱苦。

4 隋書, Ch XXIII, m 18, 五行志、下, p 17a.

5 洪範五行傳, cf DE GROOT, Vol V, p 491, note 1 "A work based on
a section of the *Shu king* entitled *Hung fan* or The Great Plan It seems to have
been held in great esteem in the sixth century as an expositor of prognostics. It was
then composed of eleven chapters, with a commentary by Liu Hiang so that it must

King Fang [1] says in his *Yih fei heu* [2] ("Flying observations on divination"): 'When the hearts of the multitude are not quiet, dragon fights are the bad omens thereof' [3]. At that time the Emperor for the first time ascended the throne, and there was a riot of Ch'en Poh-chi and Liu Li-lien. Danger and fear prevailed in the empire".

The same annals [4] contain the following passage: "In the sixth month of the fifth year of the P'u t'ung era (524 A D) dragons fought in the pond of the King of K'uh o (?). They went westward as far as Kien ling ch'ing. In the places they passed all the trees were broken. The divination was the same as in the second year of the T'ien kien era (503 A D.), namely that their passing Kien ling and the trees being broken indicated that there would be calamity of war for the dynasty, and that it was a sign that the Imperial tombs would be destroyed. At that time the Emperor considered the holding of discussions to be his only task, and did not think of ploughing. His fighting generals were careless, his soldiers idle, and the Tao of the Ruler was injured. Therefore there was the corresponding fact of the dragons' evil. The Emperor did not at all become conscious (of the danger). In the first year of the T'ai Ts'ing era (547 A D.) there was again a dragon fight in the waters of Li cheu The waves seethed and bubbled up, and clouds and fog assembled from all sides. White dragons were seen running to the South, followed by black dragons. That year Heu King came with troops to submit, and the Emperor accepted his submission without taking precautions. The people of the realm were all frightened, and suddenly rebellion arose. The Emperor in consequence thereof had a sad death". He died in 549, and eight years later the Liang dynasty came to an end

In A. D. 579 a black dragon was killed by a red one. Moreover, in the same year there was a fight of a white dragon with a black one, the result of which was that the white one ascended

---

1 京房, a famous diviner of the first century of our era, author of the *Yih chu'en*, 易傳 (cf De Groot, Rel. Syst , Vol IV, p. 204) and of the *Yih yao*, 易妖 (cf below, Bad omens, D.)

2 易飛候.

3 龍獸之難害者也。天之類君之象、天氣害、君道傷、則龍亦害．鬭者兵革之象也．京房易飛候日、衆心不安．厥妖龍鬭．

4 Same chapter, section and page.

to the sky and the black one fell on the earth and died [1]. As black was the colour of the Later (i e. Northern) Cheu dynasty, these dragon fights were forebodings of its approaching fall, which actually took place two years later.

As to inundations announced beforehand by dragon fights, we may refer to the *History of the Sung dynasty* [2], where we read that in the fifth year of the K'ien Tao era (A D. 1169) such a battle in the air was seen amidst a heavy thunderstorm "Two dragons fled and pearls like carriage wheels fell down on the ground, where they were found by herdsboys. In the following years inundations afflicted the country".

Sometimes dragon fights are mentioned not as omens, but only as causing heavy storms which destroyed a large number of houses and government buildings and killed hundreds of people, carrying them into the air together with their domestic animals, trees and tiles, over a length of more than ten miles. Such a storm raged in the fourth month of the ninth year of the Hwang t'ung era (1149) above the Yü lin river in Li cheu [3].

Devastation caused by lightning was believed to be the result of sacred fire, sent by Heaven to stop dragon fights. "In the fifth month of the year yih-wei (probably 1295) on a place near the lake at I hing, all of a sudden there were two dragons which twisting around each other and fighting both fell into the lake. Their length had no sharp limits In a short space of time a heavy wind came riding on the water, which reached a height of more than a chang (ten ch'ih or feet). Then there fell from the sky more than ten fire balls, having the size of houses of ten divisions. The two dragons immediately ascended (to the sky), for Heaven, afraid that they might cause calamity, sent out sacred fire to drive them away. Supposed that Heaven had been a little remiss for a moment, then within a hundred miles everything would have turned into gigantic torrents. When I recently passed by boat the Peachgarden of Teh Ts'ing, those

---

1 *Wang Shao chw'en*, 王劭傳, "Biography of Wang Shao", *Books of the Sui dynasty*, Ch LXIX, 列傳, nr 34, p 2a

2 Sect 五行志 (Ch 61—67) 乾道五年七月乙亥武窜 縣龍鬭于復塘村、大雷雨二龍奔逃、珠墜大車輪、 牧童得之。自是連歲有水災。

3 *Kin shi*, 金史, History of the Kin Dynasty (A. D. 1206—1368), Ch XXIII,

paddy fields were all scorched and black, some tens of acres in all. Then we moored the boat to the bank and asked those villagers (for the reason). They said · 'Yesterday noon there was a big dragon which fell from the sky. Immediately he was burned by terrestial fire and flew away. For that what the dragons fear is fire'" [1].

B *Dead dragons.*

When dragons, wounded in a battle, tumbled down and died, this was believed to be a very bad omen. The *Books of the Han dynasty* [2] relate the following· "On the day jen-tszĕ of the sixth month of the seventh year of the Yen-hi era (A. D 164), under the Emperor Hwan, there was a dragon which died on Mount Yé Wang in Ho néi (one of the districts of that time). Its length was about some tens of chang. Siang K'iai was of the following opinion. Taking into consideration that the dragon is a felicitous. symbol of an Emperor or King, and that the *Yih lun ta jen* says: "In the T'ien-feng era (A.D 14—19) there was a dead dragon in the Hwang-shan palace. The Han troops killed Mang (i. e the Emperor Wang Mang, killed in A. D. 22), and Shi Tsu (i e. Kwang Wu, the first Emperor of the Eastern Han dynasty) rose again (ascended the throne, in A. D. 25)", this omen must be a sign of change (of the dynasty)'. In the 25th year of the Kien-ngan era (A. D. 220) the Emperor Wen of the Wéi dynasty replaced the House of Han" [3].

---

1 *Kwei sin tsah shih,* 癸辛雜識 (cf DE GROOT, *Rel Syst* Vol II, p 399· "a collection of miscellanies written by CHEU MIH, 周密, in the earlier part of the fourteenth century), quoted T S , Sect 禽蟲, Ch 130, 龍部紀事三, p 8b 乙未歲五月宜興近湖之地忽有二龍交闘俱 隊于湖。其長無際。頃刻大風駕水、高丈餘而至、 即有火塊、大如十間屋者十餘、自天而墜。二龍 隨即而升、蓋天恐其爲禍驅神火逐之、使少緩 須臾則百里之內皆爲巨壑矣。余向者舟經德清 之棑園、其稻田皆焦黑、凡數十畝。遂艤舟、問其 里人云、昨午有人龍自天而墜下、墜即爲地火所 燒而飛去、蓋龍之所畏者火也。

2 *Shuh Han shu,* Ch XVII, Sect 五行, ni 5, 龍蛇孽, p 2a

3 桓帝延熹七年六月壬子河內野王山上有龍

In the fifth year of the Kien-teh era (A. D. 576), under the
Later Cheu dynasty, a black dragon fell from the sky and died.
The dragon is the symbol of the Ruler, black was the colour
of the dynasty, and falling and dying is a most unlucky omen [1]
So it was a foreboding of the Emperor's death, which happened
two years later (A. D. 578), and of the dynasty's fall (A. D. 581),
which was announced also by the dragon fights mentioned above.

C. *Dragons appearing at wrong times.*

When dragons appeared at wrong times, they were forebodings
of evil instead of omens of felicity. The time is wrong for a
dragon to appear, when the Son of Heaven himself does not
walk in the Tao, thus throwing into disorder both the Tao of
Heaven and men. So did the Emperor Kʻung Kiah of the ancient
Hia dynasty, twenty centuries before Christ Szĕ-ma Tsʻien [2] says
the following about this monarch. "The Emperor Kʻung Kiah
having ascended the Throne, loved the matters of the kwéi and
the shen and was disorderly (in his behaviour, i.e. he disturbed
the Tao). As the virtue of the House of the Hia rulers was
declining, the feudal lords rebelled against it. Heaven sent down
two dragons, a female and a male. Kʻung Kiah could not feed
them; he had not yet found the Dragon-rearer Family [3]. Tʻang
of Tao (i.e. the House of the Emperor Yao) having declined,
one of his descendants was Liu Léi, who from the Dragon-rearer
family learned to tame dragons, in order to serve Kʻung Kiah.
Kʻung Kiah bestowed upon him the family name of Yu-lung [4]

死、長可數十丈。襄楷以爲、夫龍者爲帝王、瑞易
論大人、天鳳中黃山宮有死龍、漢兵誅莽而世祖
復興、此易代之徵也。至建安二十五年魏文帝
代漢。

1 *Books of the Sui dynasty*, Sect. 五行志: 後周建德五年黑
龍墜於亳州而死。龍君之象、黑周所尙色、墜而
死不祥之甚。

2 *Historical Records*, Ch II, 夏本紀, Jap ed. with commentaries and notes,
史記評林（八尾版）, Vol. II, Ch II, p 21b. Cf Chavannes' translation,
Vol I, p 168.

3 *Hwan-lung shi*, 豢龍氏

(Dragon-ruler), and he received the succession of Shı Wéi. The first of the dragons, the female, dıed, (whereupon) he took it and gave ıt the Emperor to eat. As Hıs Majesty ordered to seek (the dragon), Lıu Léi got afraıd and fled Kᶜung Kıah dıed, and hıs son, the Emperor Kao, ascended the Throne" [1].

A different form of the same legend, according to whıch Kᶜung Kıah was presented by the Emperor of Heaven with two teams of dragons, whıch were reared by Lıu Léi tıll one of them dıed and was given as food to Hıs Majesty, is to be found ın a passage of the *Tso chwᶜen*, whıch we wıll partly quote ın Chapter IV § 8, ın regard to the Dragon-rearer famıly havıng been invested wıth this name by the Emperor Shun. As to our present subject, however, ı. e the evıl omen of dragons appearıng at a tıme when the Tao is vıolated, we may refer to another passage of the *Historical Records*, where the fall of the Hıa dynasty, ıs apparently brought into connectıon wıth the appearance of two dragons. We read there the followıng. "In the thırd year (of hıs reign) (B. C. 779), King Yıu fell deeply ın love wıth Pao Szĕ [2]. Pao Szĕ gave bırth to a son, Poh Fuh, and Kıng Yıu wıshed to degrade the Crownprınce. The mother of the Crownprınce was the daughter of the Marquıs of Chen and was queen. Afterwards, when Kıng Yiu had got Pao Szĕ and loved her, he wıshed to degrade Queen Chen and at the same time send away the Crown-prince I Kıu, (ın order to) make Pao Szĕ queen and Poh Fuh Crown-prınce The great astrologer of Cheu, Poh Yang [3], after havıng read the hıstorical records, saıd. "(The House of) Cheu is lost".

Now follows the explanatıon why the astrologer had such pessımıstıc vıews. CHAVANNES [4] poınts out that the followıng ıs borrowed from the *Kwoh yu* [5], one of the many works used by

---

[1] 帝孔甲立、好方鬼神事、淫亂。夏后氏德衰、諸侯畔之。天降龍二、有雌雄。孫甲不能食、未得豢龍氏。陶唐既衰、其後有劉累、學擾龍于豢龍氏、以事孔甲。孔甲賜之姓曰御龍氏、受豕韋之後。龍一雌死、以食夏后。夏后使求、懼而遷去。孔甲崩、于帝皐立。

[2] 褒姒.　　　[3] 伯陽.

[4] *Les Mémoıres Hıstorıques de Se-ma Tsᶜıen*, Vol I, p. 281, cf Introductıon, Chap III, pp CXLVII, sqq.

[5] 國語, "Dıscourses concernıng the States", often called the "Exterıor Com-mentary" on the *Chᶜun tsᶜıu*, and ascrıbed to the author of the *Tso chwᶜen*

Szĕ-ma Tsʻien. "In olden times, when the rulers of the Hia dynasty were declining (in virtue and power), there were two divine dragons which stopped at the palace of the Emperor and said·'We are two rulers of Pao'. The Emperor tried to find out by divination whether he should kill them, send them away or keep them, but to none of these questions he received a favourable answer. When he cast lots, however, as to the question whether he should request (the dragons) to give him their foam to store it away, the answer was favourable. Then a piece of cloth was spread and a written communication was offered to them. The dragons disappeared and their foam remained, it was put in a case and stored away. When the Hia dynasty was lost, this case was transmitted to (the House of) Yin; when (the House of) Yin was lost, it was transmitted again to (the House of) Cheu. During these three dynasties no one dared open it; but at the end of the reign of King Li it was opened and looked into. The foam flew through the palace and could not be removed. King Li ordered his wives to undress and to raise cries in unison (naked) against the foam. The foam changed into a black lizard[1] and in this form entered the rear departments of the palace (the female departments). A young concubine of the seraglio, who had reached the age when one loses his milk-teeth (seven years), met it. When she had reached the age when young girls put a hair-pin in her hair (i. e. the age of fifteen, when they get marriageable), she was pregnant. Without having a husband she gave birth to a child, which she abandoned with fright. At the time of King Süen (King Li's son) a little girl sung, saying: 'A bow of wild mulberry wood and a quiver of reed are sure to destroy the dynasty of Cheu'. King Suen heard this, and as there were a married couple who sold these utensils, he ordered them to be seized and put to death. They escaped and being on the road saw lying there the child which the young concubine of the seraglio had just abandoned. They heard it crying in the night, pitied it and took it up. The man and his wife then fled to (the land of) Pao. The people of Pao, having committed some crime, asked for (permission to) present to the King the girl whom the young concubine had abandoned, in order to atone therewith for their misdeed. (Thus) the girl came from Pao, and this became Pao Szĕ. In the third year of King Yiu's reign the King went to the seraglio, saw Pao Szĕ and fell

1 玄黿, *huen yuen* Chavannes (p. 282, note 5) remarks that *yüen*, which means

53

in love with her. She gave birth to a son, Poh Fuh. Finally the King degraded Queen Chen and the Crownprince, and made Pao Szĕ queen and Poh Fuh crownprince. The Great Astrologer Poh Yang said: 'The misfortune is complete; there is no help for it'". Then we read that the Emperor, who by all manner of devices tried to make the woman laugh, did not succeed until by a false sign of an enemy's attack he caused the lords to come up in great haste. This made Pao Szĕ burst into laughter, but it was the cause of the King's death and the ruin of the dynasty, for when the enemy actually came, the lords, whom the King had deluded several times by false alarms, did not come to the rescue. Thus the King was killed, Pao Szĕ was taken prisoner, and the treasures of the House of Cheu were all taken by force. Japanese legends tell us that Pao Szĕ was reborn in the twelfth century as *Tamamo no mae*, the Emperor Konoe or Toba's concubine, who changed into a fox [1].

It is clear that in the above passages the dragons were harbingers of evil, because the Emperors did not walk in the Tao.

In A. D. 553 a dragon was seen ascending near the Imperial Palace, and the next year a huge black serpent rose from the Palace moat to the sky, spreading a dazzling light and followed by a small snake. Calamity was predicted on account of these apparitions, and the Emperor tried to avert the evil by offerings of money [2], magic, Buddhist prayers and philanthropy; but it was all in vain, for at the end of the same year he was killed [3]

The *History of the Liao dynasty* [4] says: "[In the first year of the T'ien-hien era (A D. 926)] the Emperor (T'ai-Tsu, 907—926) stopped at Fu-yŭ-fu and did not take any precautions That evening a big star fell before his tent, and on the day sin-szĕ, when he captured the castle of Tau-tszĕ, the Emperor saw a yellow dragon coiling and winding, about one mile in length. The brightness of its light blinded the eye; it entered the Imperial

---

1 Cf my treatise on "*The Fox and the Badger in Japanese Folklore*", Transactions of the Asiatic Society of Japan, Vol XXXVI, Part 3, pp 51 sqq

2 The dragons are fond of money, comp the Japanese work *Seiyŭki*, 西遊記 (written by TACHIBANA NANKEI, 橘南谿, in 1795—1797), *Zoku Teikoku Bunko*, Vol XX, Ch II, p 259. This has perhaps something to do with their liking for the vital spirit of copper (cf below, Book II, Ch III, § 3)

3 *History of the South* (*Nanshi*, 南史, written by YEN SHEU, 延壽, who lived in the first half of the seventh century A D), Ch VIII (梁記, 下).

4 *Liao shi*, 遼史, (906—1168), Sect 大祖本紀, 下, T'ai-Tsu pen ki, "Fundamental history of (the Emperor) T'ai-Tsu", Ch II, p 6a

lodging house. There was a purple, black vapour which hid the sky, remained the whole day, and then dispersed. That very day the Emperor died" [1].

Sometimes a dragon's appearance was a sign of impending calamity in the form of inundations. Such was the case in A. D. 967, according to the *Books of the Sung dynasty* [2]. We read there the following· "In the summer of the fifth year of the K'ien-teh era (967) it rained in the capital, and a black dragon appeared. Its tail was on the border of the clouds, and it flew from North-west to Southeast. The diviners explained it to be (an omen of) big floods. The next year in twenty four prefectures the water destroyed the ricefields and the houses" [3].

D. *Dragons appearing in wrong places.*

If a dragon, symbol of Imperial power, is born in a commoner's house or comes out of his well, this is a very bad omen for the dynasty, the Emperor personally, or one of his feudal lords, for it means degradation from the highest dignity to a common state, and death of the ruler or of one of his representatives.

The *Books of the Tsin dynasty* [4] contain the following passage. "Under the reign of Sun Hao of the Wu dynasty (the fourth and last Emperor of that dynasty, A. D. 242—283), in the T'ien-ts'eh era (A D 275—276), a dragon was hatched in (the house of) a family in Ch'ang-sha, and ate the chickens KING FANG [5] says in his *Yih yao* [6]· 'If a dragon is hatched in a man's house, a

---

1 次扶餘府上不豫。是夕大星隕於幄前。辛巳平旦了城、上見黃龍繚繞、可長一里、光耀奪目、入於行宮。有紫黑氣蔽天、踰日乃散.是日上崩。

2 宋書, *Sung-shu* (A D 960—1279), Sect 五行志.

3 乾德五年夏京師雨、有黑龍見、尾于雲際、自西北趨東南。占主大水。明年州府二十四水壞田廬。

4 晉書 (A D 265—420), Ch XXIX, nr 19, Sect. 五行志，下, p 24a (龍蛇之孽)

5 京房, the famous diviner of the first century before our era, mentioned above, p. 47, note 1

6 易妖

king will become a commoner'. Afterwards Hao submitted to
Chin (the Chin dynasty)[1].

In the same section of this work[2] we read the following.
"Under the Emperor Ming of the Wei dynasty (A D. 227—239),
in the first year of the Ts'ing-lung era (233), on the day kiah-
shen of the first month, a blue dragon appeared in a well at
Mo-p'o (a place) in the suburbs If only a lucky omen rises
at a wrong time, it becomes an evil. How much more is this
the case, when it (the dragon) is in straits in a well! This is
not a felicitous omen![3] It was wrong that Wei on account of
it changed the name of the era. Yu Pao says 'From the end of
the reign of the Emperor Ming under the Wei dynasty the
appearances of blue and yellow dragons were signs corresponding
with the fall and rise of its rulers. As to the fate of the land
of Wei, blue is the colour of wood and yet it does not conquer
metal; it was a sign of yellow getting the throne and blue losing
it. The frequent appearance of blue dragons means that the
virtue of the sovereign and the fate of the dynasty are in inner
conflict with each other[4]. Therefore Kao Kwei Hiang Kung[5]
(Ts'ao Mao, A. D. 241—260, who in 254 became the fourth
Emperor of the Wei dynasty) was utterly defeated in war.''

"According to Liu Hiang's[6] explanation the dragon, the symbol
of dignity, when being imprisoned in a well means calamity
consisting in a feudal lord being about to be secretly seized.
In the Wei dynasty there was no dragon which was not in a
well. It was an omen of the oppressive measures of those men
who occupied the highest ranks[7]. The poem on the 'Dragon lying
in the deep', written by Kao Kwei Hiang Kung, has this meaning".

The *Books of the Early Han dynasty*[8] relate the following. "In

---

[1] 吳孫皓天册中龍乳於長沙人家、噉雞雛。京房
易妖日、龍乳人家王者爲庶人。其後皓降晉。

[2] 晉書, Ch XXIX, nr 19, 五行志, 上, p 23b (龍蛇之孼).

[3] 只瑞與非時則爲妖孼、况困于井、非嘉祥矣。

[4] 青龍多見者君德國運內相尅伐也。

[5] 高貴鄉公.

[6] 劉向 (B C 80—9), a famous author and minister, cf GILES, *Biogr Dict*, p
501, nr 1300.

[7] 按劉向說龍貴象而困井中諸侯將有幽執之
禍也。魏世龍莫不在井、此居上者逼制之應。

[8] Ch XXVII, Sect 五行志, m 7

the second year of the reign of the Emperor Hwei (B.C. 193), in the morning of the hwei-yiu day of the first month, there were two dragons which appeared in a well at Li-wen-ling (a village), east of the palace of Lan-ling They were seen till the evening of the yih-hai day, then they went away. Liu Hiang is of the following opinion 'If a dragon, a symbol of dignity, is in straits in the well of a commoner, this means calamity consisting in a feudal lord being about to be secretly seized'[1]. Afterwards the Empress-Dowager Lü secretly killed Ch'u, the king of San Chao[2], and also Lu was finally murdered. KING-FANG says in his *Yih chw'en*[3]: 'When those who have virtue meet injuries (i. e. are put to death), the bad omens of this are that dragons appear in wells'. Further, he says: 'In cases of execution or violent cruelty black dragons come out of wells'"[4]

The "*Biography of Chang Wen-piao of Ch'u*"[5] gives the following tale. "When Wen-piao was going to plot his rebellion and, still being engaged in preparing it, had not yet settled (his plans), one of his followers dreamt at night that a dragon was coiling above Wen-piao's chin. Wen-piao was very much rejoiced and said. 'This is Heaven's appointment' (to the Throne, i. e. it is a sign that I shall ascend the Throne). Then he settled his plans, raised troops, and was defeated Men of knowledge said: 'As the dragon is a divine being and yet came out of his chin, this was an omen that calamity should be at work and that his shen (soul) should go away'".[6] Here again the dragon appeared in a wrong place.

§ 3. Dragon horses.

The *Li ki*[7] says: "The Ho (river) sent forth the horse with

1 劉向以爲龍貴象而困於庶人井中象諸侯將有幽執之禍。

2 Cf GILES, 11 p 553, nr 1442, s v *Lu Hou* "To make the throne secure, she poisoned the Prince of Chao, another son of the late Emperor by a concubine"

3 易傳

4 京房易傳曰、有德遭害厥妖龍見井中。又曰、行刑暴惡黑龍從井出。

5 楚張文表傳, quoted T S Ch 129, 龍部紀事二, p 14a.

6 識者以龍神物而出於頷、是禍將作神去焉之兆也。

7 LEGGE, Sacred Books of the East, Vol XXVII, Book VII (Li yun), Sect IV, nr 16, p 392 COUVREUR, *Li ki*, Vol I, p 536 河出馬圖.

the map (on his back)" This was the "River Map" from which Fuh-Hı fashıoned the eıght *kwa* (八卦), the dıagrams used in dıvınatıon The *Shu king* [1] mentıons thıs map among the precıous objects pıeserved at the Court ın B. C. 1079. LEGGE [2] treats of ıt in his Introductıon to the *Yi king* wıth regard to the well-known passage of an Appendıx of thıs Classıc [3], ıunnıng as follows: "The Ho gave forth the scheme or map, and the Lo gave forth the wrıtıng, (both of) whıch the sages copıed" Accoıdıng to one of the commentators on the *Yıh king* "the water of the Ho sent forth a *dragon horse*; on ıts back there was curly hair, like a map of starry dots The water of the Lo sent forth a dıvıne tortoıse; on ıts back there were rıven veıns, like wrıtıng of character pıctuıes" [4] Thıs conceptıon, apparently based upon the above passage of the *Lı kı*, became common ın later tımes, and the *San tsʻaı fʻu hwuı* [5] gıves a pıcture of thıs dragon horse As to the appendix of the *Yıh king* [6], quoted by SZĔ-MA CHENG ın the *"Annals of the three sovereigns"* [7], neıther the rıver nor the horse aıe mentıoned, but ıt ıs sımply stated that Fuh-Hı was the fırst to trace the eıght dıagrams.

In the *Shui yıng tʻu* [8] the followıng descrıptıon of a dragon horse ıs gıven: "It ıs a benevolent horse, the vıtal spıut of rıver water. Its heıght ıs eıght chʻıh five tsʻun, ıts neck is long, and its body ıs covered wıth scales. It has wıngs at ıts shanks, and its haır hangs down ıts sıdes Its cry consısts of nıne tones, and ıt walks on the water wıthout sınkıng. It appears at the tıme of famous sovereıgns". Thıs remınds us of the descrıptıon gıven

---

1 LEGGE, Sacred Books of the East, Vol. III, *Shu kıng*, Part V, Book XXII, p. 239.

2 Sacred Books of the East, Vol XVI, Introductıon, pp 14 sqq

3 Appendıx III, Sect I, Ch 11, § 73, LEGGE, 11, p 374, Ch V, 繫辭上傳, 卷三, p 14b 河出圖、洛出書、聖人則之。

4 河水中出龍馬、背有旋毛、如星點之圖。洛水中出神龜、背有坼文、如字畫之書。

5 三才圖會, wrıtten by WANG KͥꞶ, 王圻, at the tıme of the Mıng dynasty

6 繫辭, Ch. XV, p. 4, LEGGE's tıanslatıon, p 382

7 *San-hwang pen-kı*, 三皇本紀 (補史記), by 司馬貞, p. 1b, CHAVANNES' translatıon, Vol I, p 6

8 瑞應圖, wrıtten before the Chʻen dynasty (A.D 557—589) by SUN JEU-CHI, 孫柔之, and quoted ın the *Tʻıen chung kı*, 天中記 (wrıtten undeı the Mıng dynasty by CHʻEN YAO-WEN, 陳耀文), Ch LV

by Kʻung Ngan-kwoh [1] in his commentary on the *Shu king* [2], which runs as follows· "A dragon horse is the vital spirit of Heaven and Earth. As a being its shape consists of a horse's body, yet it has dragon scales. Therefore it is called 'dragon horse'. Its height is eight chʻih five tsʻun A true dragon horse has wings at its sides and walks upon the water without sinking. If a holy man is on the throne it comes out of the midst of the Ming river, carrying a map on its back" [3].

The *Tʻung kien tsʻien pien wai ki* [4], which refers to this passage, says: "At the time of Tʻai Hao (i. e. Fuh-Hi) there was a lucky omen consisting of a dragon horse which carried a map on its back and came out of the Ho river Therefore in giving titles to the officials he began to arrange them by means of the dragon, and called them 'Dragon-officers'" [5]. As to these titles we read in the *Annals of the Three sovereigns* [6]· "He (Fuh-Hi) had the lucky omen of a dragon; by means of the dragon he arranged the officials and called them 'Dragon-officers'". The *Tso-chwʻen* [7] gives the same matter in an extensive passage regarding the titles of the officials of the first Emperors.

The *Tʻai-pʻing yu-lan* [8] describes a dragon horse which appeared

---

1 孔安國, a famous scholar in the reign of the Han emperor Wu (B C 140—85), who in B C 97 transcribed the ancient tablets discovered in the wall of the house of the Confucian family, and made a commentary on the whole. Cf Legge's Introduction to his translation of the *Shu king*, Sacred books of the East, Vol III, p 8.

2 Sect 雇命, quoted in the T S, Sect 禽蟲, Ch 128, 龍部紀事一, p 1b

3 龍馬者天地之精。其爲形也馬身而龍鱗、故謂之龍馬。高八尺五寸、類骼有翼、蹈水不沒。聖人在位、負圖出于孟河之中焉。

4 通鑑前編外紀, "Extra writings" belonging to the "Preceding part" of the *Tszě-chi tʻung kien kang-muh*, 資治通鑑綱目, "A chronological survey of the Mirror of History, composed to assist Government", an imperial edition of 1707, based upon the *Tszě chi tʻung kien* written by *Szě-ma Kwang*, 司馬光, between 1065 and 1084 It consists of three parts 前編, from Yao's time to B C. 402, the main work (B C 402—A D 960), and the Supplement (A D 960—1367)

5 因而名官始以龍紀、號曰龍師·

6 P. 2a, Chavannes, Vol I, p 7 有龍瑞。以龍紀官、號曰龍師。

7 Book X, year XVII (17th year of Duke Chao), Legge, *Chinese Classics*, Vol V, Part II, pp 666 sq

8 太平御覽, "The Work of Imperial Autopsy of the Tʻai pʻing period", composed by an Imperial committee of thirteen scholars under the presidency of the

in A. D. 741 and was considered to be a good omen for the Emperor. It was spotted blue and red, and covered with scales Its mane resembled that of a dragon, and its neighing was like the tone of a flute It could cover three hundred miles. Its mother was a common horse which had become pregnant by drinking water from a river in which it was bathed. This agrees with the statement of the *Shui ying t'u* quoted above about the dragon horse being the vital spirit of river water. The same horse is described as follows in another work of much later date [1]. "A horse with dragon scales, the tail of a huge serpent, frizzy hair, round eyes and a fleshy crest" When the Emperor fled from the capital to the West, this horse entered a river, changed into a dragon and swam away.

Another dragon horse, which appeared in A. D. 622, had a scaly dragon's body, spotted with five colours, and a horse's head with two white horns. In its mouth it carried an object about three or four ch'ih long. This horse was seen on a river, marching about a hundred steps on the surface of the water, looking about and then disappearing [2].

Finally, we may refer to a passage of the *Shih i ki* [3], where we read that the Emperor Muh of the Cheu dynasty in the thirty second year of his reign drove around the world in a carriage, drawn by eight winged dragon horses [4]

§ 4 Geomancy.

The so-called *fung-shui* (風水, "wind and water") is a geomantical system, prevalent throughout China from olden times down to the present age The tiger and the dragon, the gods of wind and water, are the keystones of this doctrine. I deem it superfluous to treat of it in extenso, because Professor

---

Introd p X, this cyclopedia contains only what the Emperor (T'ai Tsung) reserved for direct publication, whereas the *T'ai-p'ing kwang ki*, 太平廣記, "Ample Writings of the T'ai-p'ing period", republished about 1566, consists merely of such parts of it as were ejected by the Emperor Ch 435, quoting the *Suen shih chi*, 宣室志, written in the ninth century by CHANG TUH, 張讀.

1 The *Yuen kien lei han*, 淵鑑類函, written in 1710 by CHANG YING, 張英, and others; Ch 433

2 *T'ai-p'ing yu-lan*, Ch 435

3 拾遺記, written in A D. 357 by WANG KIA, 王嘉, Ch III, p 1a

4 王馭人龍之駿。 …… 身有肉翅。

De Groot[1] has given already a full account of its origin, elements, meaning and influence. "It is", says he, "a quasi-scientific system, supposed to teach men where and how to build graves, temples and dwellings, in order that the dead, the gods and the living may be located therein exclusively, or as far as possible, under the auspicious influences of Nature"[2]. The dragon plays a most important part in this system, being "the chief spirit of water and rain"[3], and at the same time representing one of the four quarters of heaven (i. e. the East, called the Azure Dragon[4], and the first of the seasons, spring)[5] "The word Dragon comprises the high grounds in general, and the water-streams which have their sources therein or wind their way through them. Hence it is that books on Fung-shui commonly commence with a bulky set of dissertations, comprised under the heading. 'Rules concerning the Dragon' (龍 法), in reality dealing with the doctrines about the situation and contours of mountains and hills and the direction of water-courses"[6].

Finally, we may quote the following passage from the same work[7] "Amoy is unanimously declared by all the wise men of the town to be indebted for its prosperity to two knolls flanking the inner harbour, and vulgarly styled Hó-t'aô soa" (虎 頭 山), or 'Tiger-head Hill', and Lîng-t'aô soa" (龍 頭 山), or 'Dragon-head Hill' The latter, which is situated on the opposite shore, on the islet of Kulangsu, is crowned with huge boulders poised in a fantastic manner, upon which professors have had several blocks of granite arranged for the purpose of helping the imagination to discover the outlines of a dragon on the spot. The costs of these improvements were borne by some well-to do citizens, anxious to promote their own prosperity and that of their fellow townsmen". A "Dragon's head Mountain" is mentioned in the Sin shi San Ts'in ki[8], where we read the following. "The Dragon's head Mountain is 60 miles long, its head enters the water of the Wei (a large tributary of the Yellow River), its tail reaches the Fan river. The height of its head is 20 chang, the tail goes

---

1 *Religious System of China*, Vol III, Ch XII, pp 935—1056
2 P 935   3 P 949
4 P 949 The four quarters are called the Azure Dragon (East), the Red or Vermilion Bird (South), the White Tiger (West) and the Black Tortoise (North) (De Groot, 11, Vol I, p 316)
5 P. 951   6 Ibidem   7 Pp 959 seq

8 辛 氏 三 秦 記' "Annals of the three Ts'in states written by Sin", quoted

gradually down to a height of five or six chang. It is said that
in olden times there was a strange dragon which came from the
southern side of the mountain in order to drink the water of
the Wei The course it followed shaped itself into a mountain
of clay, and therefore (the mountain) was called after it" [1].

As we shall see below [2] also in Japan a great number of
names of mountains point to the same ideas concerning the
connection between mountains and dragons

---

[1] 云昔有異龍從山南出飲渭水、其行道成土山、
故因以爲名。

[2] Book III, Ch IX, § 2, A

CHAPTER III.

§ 1 Enormous light-giving mountain gods.

The *Shan hai king* [1] describes the god of Mount Chung as follows: "The god of Mount Chung is called 'Enlightener of the Darkness'. By looking (i. e. by opening his eyes) he creates daylight, and by closing his eyes he creates night. By blowing he makes winter, by exhaling he makes summer. He neither eats nor drinks nor does he rest. His breath causes wind. His length is a thousand miles. He is in the East of Wu-ki ('Without bowels'). As a living being, he has a human face, the body of a snake and a red colour. He lives at the foot of Mount Chung". The commentator Kwoh Poh [2] explains this passage in the following words. "'Enlightener' is a dragon; he enlightens the nine *yin* (darknesses, i. e. the nine points of the compass at the opposite, dark side of the earth, which is a flat disk; these nine points are North, South, East, West, North-east, North-west, South-east, South-west, and the Centre)". According to the *Hwai nan tsze* it is "a god with a human face and a dragon's body, but without legs" [3].

We may quote here a passage from the *T'ung ming ki* [4], a work of the beginning of our era, to which DE GROOT [5] refers as follows: "The *T'ung ming ki* says, that in the year 99 before our era the emperor Wu convoked a meeting of magicians and

---

1 山海經, a very old classic, Sect 海外北經 (nr 8), p 1b 鍾山之神名曰燭陰。視爲晝、瞑爲夜、吹爲冬、呼爲夏。不飲不食不息。息爲風。身長千里。在無啓之東。其爲物人面蛇身赤色。居鍾山下。

2 郭璞 (who died in A D 322, author of the *Shan hai king t'u tsan*, 山海經圖讚)· 燭龍也、是燭九陰。

3 其神人面龍身而無足 Quoted in the commentary 11.

4 洞冥記 Ch III

learned men, at which Tung Fang-soh spoke as follows: 'I made a journey to the north pole, and came to a mountain planted with fire, which neither the sun, nor the moon ever illumines, but which is lighted to its uttermost bounds by a *blue dragon* by means of a torch which it holds in its jaws'" [1].

The dragon being full of Yang, it is quite logical that he should diffuse light, as we have also seen above (Ch. II, § 1, p. 44). The *Yih lin* [2] says: "A black dragon vomits light and makes Darkness (Yin) turn into Light (Yang)".

§ 2 Nature of the dragons

In KWAN CHUNG's philosophical work entitled *Kwan tszĕ* [3], "The philosopher Kwan", we read the following. "Those who, hidden in the dark, can live or die, are *shi* (蓍, a plant the stalks of which are used in divination), tortoises and dragons. The tortoise is born in the water; she is caused to disclose (what she knows) in the fire, and then becomes the first of all creatures, the regulator of calamity and felicity A dragon in the water covers himself with five colours. Therefore he is a god (*shen*). If he desires to become small, he assumes a shape resembling that of a silkworm, and if he desires to become big, he lies hidden in the world. If he desires to ascend, he strives towards the clouds, and if he desires to descend, he enters a deep well. He whose transformations are not limited by days, and whose ascending and descending are not limited by time, is called a god (*shen*)".

The philosopher HAN FEI [4] says. "Ah, a dragon, as being an

---

[1] 有青龍銜燭火以照山之四極。

[2] 易林, an old divinatory work quoted T S, Sect 禽蟲, Ch 130, 龍部雜錄, p 3a

[3] 管子, ascribed to KWAN CHUNG, 管仲, who died in B C 645 Ch XV, p 4, nr 39, 水地篇: 伏闇能存而能亡者蓍龜與龍是也。龜被于水、發之于火于是爲萬物先、爲禍福正。龍于水被五色、故神。欲小則化如蠶蠋、欲大則藏于天下、欲上則凌于雲氣、欲下則入于深泉。變化無日、上下無時、謂之神。

[4] *Han Fei tszĕ*, 韓非子 (4th century B C), Ch. IV, nr 12, 說難, p. 9a 夫龍之爲蟲也柔可狎而騎也。然其喉下有逆鱗徑尺。若人有嬰之者則必殺人。

animal, is so mild, that one may approach him (be familiar with him, i. e. tame him) and ride on him But under his throat he has scales, lying in a reverse direction, one ch'ih (foot) in diameter. If a man touches them, the dragon is sure to kill him"

The Classics have taught us that the dragon belongs to the four creatures that have the most *ling* (靈), i. e. whose *shen* manifests itself in the most powerful way. The '*Rh ya yih*[1] goes further and states that the dragon possesses the most *ling* of all creatures. According to the *Shui ying fu*[2] "the yellow dragon is the quintessence of *shen*, and the chief of the four dragons. If a king does not drain off ponds and lakes, their water can penetrate into deep pools, and the yellow dragons, following their nature, swim in ponds and lakes".

Lu Puh-wei[3] relates the following "Confucius said: 'A dragon (*lung*) eats what is pure and moves about in what is pure[4]. A *chi* (螭) eats what is pure and moves about in what is muddy. A fish eats what is muddy and moves about in what is muddy. Now I, in ascending do not reach the dragon (i. e. I am not such a high being as the dragon), and in descending do not reach the fishes (i e. I am not such a low creature as the fishes); I am (like) the *chi*'".

Hwai nan tsze[5] goes as far as to declare the dragon to be the origin of all creatures, as we learn from the following passage: "All creatures, winged, hairy, scaly and

---

1 爾雅翼, the Appendix to the '*Rh ya* (a vocabulary probably dating from pre-Christian times, cf De Groot, *Rel Syst* I, p 302), "a broad elaboration of this old dictionary by the hand of Lo Yuen, 羅願, who flourished in the latter half of the 12th century " (De Groot, 11 IV p 166), Section 釋龍．物之至靈者也。

2 瑞應圖, written before the Ch'en dynasty (A D 557—589) by Sun Jeu-chi, 孫柔之, s v 黃龍, Yellow Dragon 黃龍者神之精、四龍之長也。王者不漉池沼、水得達深淵、則應氣而游池沼。

3 呂不韋, the reputed father of Shi Hwang, the founder of the Ts'in dynasty (B.C 249—206), in his work entitled *Lu-shi ch'un-ts'iu*, 呂氏春秋, "Annals of Lu", Section 舉難.

4 龍食乎清而游乎清。

5 淮南子, "The philosopher of Hwai-nan", i e. Liu Ngan, 劉安, (who died

mailed, find their origin in the dragon [1]. Tne *yu-kia* (羽嘉)
~~produced the flying dragon, the flying~~ dragon gave birth to the
phoenixes, and after them the *lwan-niao* (鸞 鳥) and all birds,
in general the winged beings, were born successively. The *mao-tuh*
(毛 犢, "hairy calf") produced the *ying-lung* (應 龍), the ying-
lung gave birth to the *kien-ma* (建 馬), and afterwards the *k'i-lin*
(麒 麟) and all quadrupeds, in general the hairy beings, were born
successively. The *kiai-lin* (介 鱗) produced the *kiao-lung* (蛟 龍),
the kiao-lung gave birth to the *kwun-keng* (鯤 鯁), and afterwards
the *kien-sié* (建 邪) and all fishes, in general the scaly beings,
were born successively The *kiai-t'an* (介 潭) produced the *sien-
lung* (先 龍), the sien-lung gave birth to the *yuen-yuen* (元 黿,
"original tortoise") and afterwards the *ling-kwei* (靈 龜, "divine
power manifesting tortoise") and all tortoises, in general the
mailed beings were born successively". The same author says
that "mankind cannot see the dragons rise; wind and rain assist
them to ascend to a great height" [2].

The *Ta tai li ki* [3] states that "the essence of the scaly animals
is called dragon", and that "the dragon does not ascend if there
is no wind".

In the *Historical Records* [4] we read a quotation from *Chwang
tszĕ* [5], where Confucius after having talked with Lao tszĕ says
"As to the dragon, we cannot understand his riding on wind
and clouds and his ascending to the sky. To-day I saw Lao tszĕ;
is he not like the dragon ?"

According to the *P'i ya* [6] "none of the animals is so wise as
the dragon His blessing power is not a false one. He can be

---

[1] 萬物、羽毛鱗介、皆祖於龍。

[2] Ch. XVII, 說 林 訓. Cf. Ch. IX, 主 術 訓 "The *ying-lung* ascends
riding on the clouds"

[3] 大 戴 禮 記, compiled by TAI TEH, 戴 德, under the reign of the Emperor
Suen of the Han dynasty (B.C 73—49), Ch V, 曾 子 天 圓, p 7b 鱗 蟲
之 精 者 曰 龍 …… 龍 非 風 不 舉。

[4] Ch LXIII, 老 莊 申 韓 列 傳, p 2a 至 於 龍 吾 不 能 知 其
乘 風 雲 而 上 天。吾 今 日 見 老 子、其 猶 龍 邪。

[5] 莊 子 (4th cent B C), Section 天 運, Ch III

[6] 埤 雅, composed by LUH TIEN, 陸 佃 (1042—1102), Ch I, 釋 魚, nr 1
(龍), p 1 蟲 莫 智 於 龍。龍 之 德 不 爲 妄 者。能 與 細

smaller than small, bigger than big, higher than high, and lower than low. Therefore according to the *Yih king*, Kien (乾, the first diagram) by means of the dragon rules Heaven, and *Kw'un* (坤) by means of the horse rules the Earth; the dragon is a heavenly kind of being, the horse an earthly one".

Li Tao-yuen [1], in his commentary on the *Shui king*, states that the expression 'fishes and dragons consider the autumn days as night' means that "at the autumnal equinoctium the dragons descend and then hibernate and sleep in pools".

The *'Rh ya yih* [2] quotes the following passage from a work of Wang Fu [3]· "When rain is to be expected, the dragons scream and their voices are like the sound made by striking copper basins. Their saliva can produce all kinds of perfume. Their breath becomes clouds, and on the other hand they avail themselves of the clouds in order to cover their bodies. Therefore they are invisible. At the present day on rivers and lakes there are sometimes people who see one claw and the tail (of a dragon), but the head is not to be seen In summer, after the fourth month, the dragons divide the regions amongst themselves and each of them has his territory. This is the reason why within a distance of a couple of acres there may be quite different weather, rain and a clear sky. Further, there are often heavy

---

細、能與巨巨、能與高高、能與下下。故易乾以龍
御天、坤以馬行地。龍天類也、馬地類也。

1 麗道元, who lived under the Northern Wei dynasty (A D 386—536), quoted in the *P'i ya*, Ch I, m 1 (龍), p 2a 魚龍以秋日爲夜。按龍
秋分而降則蟄寢於淵。龍以秋日爲夜豈謂是乎。

2 Sect 釋龍, quoted in the T S., Sect 禽蟲, Ch 127, 龍部彙考,
p 6b 將雨則吟、其聲如戛銅盤。涎能發衆香。其噓
氣成雲、反因雲以蔽其身、故不可見。今江湖閒
時有見其一爪與尾者、唯頭不可得見。自夏四月
之後龍乃分方、各有區域、故兩畝之閒而雨暘異
焉。又多暴雨說者云、細潤者天雨、猛暴者龍雨
也。龍火與人火相反、得濕而燄、遇水而燔、以火
逐之則燔息而燄滅。

3 王符, who lived at the time of the Han dynasty He is the author of the *Ts'ien fu lun*, 潛夫論, but this passage is apparently quoted from another of

rains, and those who speak about these rains say: 'Fine moistening rain is heavenly rain, violent rain is dragon rain'. Dragon fire and human fire are opposite. If dragon fire comes into contact with wetness it flames, and if it meets water it burns. If one drives it away by means of fire, it stops burning and its flames are extinguished".

The *P'i ya* [1] states the same fact with regard to the dragon fire, referring to the *Nei tien,* and in the same passage says the following [2]: "The dragons are also born from eggs. When they intend to hatch, the male dragon's cry makes the wind rise, and the female dragon's cry makes the wind abate, and the wind changes....... According to popular belief the dragon's vital spirit lies in his eyes, for this is the case because he is deaf. The 'Discussions on the spontaneous phenomena of Yin and Yang' [3] say 'The *li-lung*'s [4] pupils see a mustard plant or a straw at a distance of a hundred miles'. Further they say 'A dragon can make (litt. change) water, a man can make fire'. Further. 'A dragon does not see stones, a man does not see the wind, fishes do not see the water, demons do not see the earth'. Sun Ch'oh Tszĕ [5] says: 'Kao Tsu (probably the Emperor of the Han dynasty, who reigned B. C. 206—159) drove in a dragon carriage, Kwang Wu (who reigned A. D. 685—717) drove in a tiger carriage' ".

§ 3. What dragons like and dislike

The *'Rh ya yih,* in the passage of Wang Fu above mentioned, says: "As to his character as a being the dragon's nature is rough and fierce; yet he is afraid of iron and likes precious

1 Ch. I (釋魚), nr 1 (龍), p 2b 內典云、龍火得水而熾、人火得水而滅。

2 Ibidem, p 1a, 2a 龍亦卵生。思抱雄鳴上風、雌鳴下風而風化。‥‥‥俗云、龍精於目、蓋龍聾故精於目也。陰陽自然變化論曰、驪龍之眸見百里纖芥。又曰、龍能變水、人能變火。又曰、龍不見石、人不見風、魚不見水、鬼不見地。孫綽子曰、高祖御龍、光武御虎。

3 The same work is quoted in the *Pen-ts'ao kang-muh,* Ch 43, p 40, with the title: *Yin-yang pien-kwa lun,* "Discussions on the phenomena of Yin and Yang" The fact that it is quoted in the *P'i ya* proves that it dates from the eleventh century or earlier.

4 驪龍.   5 A famous poet of the 4th century A D

stones and *k'ung-ts'ing* [1], and is fond of roasted swallow flesh. Therefore persons who have eaten swallows must not cross the sea. Further he (Wang Fu) says. "The *kiao-lung* [2] is afraid of leaves of the Melia Azederach [3], and of five-coloured silk thread. Therefore from the time of the Han dynasty (down to the present day) those who offered to *K'uh Yuen* [4] took five-coloured silk thread and with this tied together the leaves of the Melia Azederach. Among the ancients there were the Dragon-rearer [5] and the Dragon-ruler [6] families, who ruled the dragons only by means of their knowledge of what they desired and disliked" [7].

The *Pen-ts'ao kang-muh* [8], the famous standard work on Natural History and Materia Medica, written in the latter half of the 15th century by Li Shi-chen [9], says. "The small writings (essays) contain the following The dragon's nature is rough and fierce, and yet he likes beautiful gems and *k'ung-ts'ing*, and is fond of (roasted) swallows. He is afraid of iron, of the *wang* plant [10], of

---

1 窑青, i e the *Yin-shih*, 陰石, the "Stone of Darkness".

2 蛟龍.

3 楝, "a tree bearing lilac flowers, the 'Melia Azederach' or 'pride of India', the phoenix likes it, but the dragon abhors it" (WELLS WILLIAMS, *Chin Dict*, p 536, s v.)

4 屈原, i e K'uh Ping, 屈平, a minister of the state of Ch'u (楚), who lived about B C 314, the maker of the famous poem entitled *Li sao*, 離騷. As his royal master would not follow his advise, he drowned himself in the Poh lo river Every year, at the 5th of the 5th month, the anniversary of his death is celebrated and little dumplings wrapped in leaves are offered to him and eaten in his memory Cf DE GROOT, *Fêtes annuelles à Emou*, Vol I, pp 313 sqq The Japanese *Tango no sekku*, 端午の節句, the "Exact moment of the opposition" (of Yin against Yang, i. e the summer solstitium, with which it formerly must have been identical) is originally the same festival It is a dragon festival, at which the dragons by sympathetic magic in the form of dragon-boat races are called up to give fertilizing rains The story about K'uh Yuen is apparently a later explanation of this ancient festival

5 *Hwan-lung*, 豢龍. Cf above, p 50.

6 *Yü-lung*, 御龍. Cf above, p 50

7 其爲性麤猛、而畏鐵、愛玉及窑青、而嗜燒燕肉. 故嘗食燕者不可渡海. 又言、蛟龍畏楝葉五色線. 故漢以來祭屈原者以五色絲合楝葉縛之. 古者有豢龍御龍氏、徒以知其欲惡而節制之.

8 本草綱目, "Collectanea of Plants" 鱗部, Ch 43, p 1.

9 李時珍.

10 莔蓂, *wang ts'ao*, not mentioned in the Chinese dictionaries of WELLS WILLIAMS

centipedes [1], of the leaves of the *lien* tree (Melia Azederach), and of five-coloured silk thread Therefore those who have eaten swallows avoid to cross the water, and those who pray for rain use swallows; those who suppress water calamity (inundations) use iron, those who stir up the dragons (to cause them to make rain) use the *wang* plant, and those who offer to K'üh Yuen use leaves of the Melia Azederach and coloured silk thread, wrapping dumplings in them which they throw into the river Also when physicians use dragon's bones, they must know these particulars about the dragon's nature as to their likings and hatreds" [2].

The beautiful gems remind us of the Indian dragons; the pearls of the sea were, of course, in India as well as in China and Japan, considered to be in the special possession of the dragon-shaped sea-gods. As to the *k'ung-ts'ing*, this is explained to be a hollow stone with water inside, or the vital spirit (精, *tsing*) of copper. Swallows are also mentioned as food of the *shen* (辰) [1]. The same particulars are to be found in the *Nan pu sin shu* [4], where we read that the dragons are afraid of wax, and that their fat makes silk garments impermeable to water.

In regard to the dragons' fear of *iron* we may mention a

GILES and COUVREUR, but found in the Japanese dictionary entitled *Kanwa daijiten*, 漢和大字典, p 1232, where we read "菡, *bō, mō*, a special kind of plant resembling 燕麥 ("swallow-oats", also called *karasu-mugi*, avena fatua), *minogome* - (according to BRINKLEY's dict "Beckmania erucaeformis"), its grains are used as food" The 菡, *kō*, is described there as a special kind of plant with a red stalk and white flowers Its leaves resemble those of the 葵, *aoi* (hollyhock; WELLS WILLIAMS, p 487 "the sunflower, a term for some malvaceous plants, as the Malva, Althea, and Hibiscus, it also includes other large leaved plants")" The 菡草, *kang-ts'ao*, is described by WELLS WILLIAMS (Dict p. 319, s v.) as "a trailing plant, vitis ficifolia, which bears white flowers and small grapes that are said to remove stupidity" But the *Pen-ts'ao kang-muh* gives 菡, not 菡.

[1] 蜈蚣, *wu-kung*.

[2] 又小說載、龍性麤猛而愛美玉、空青、喜嗜燕肉、畏鐵及菡草、蜈蚣、棟葉、五色絲。故食燕者忌渡水、祈雨者用燕、鎮水患者用鐵、激龍者用菡草、祭屈原者用棟葉色絲裹糭投江。醫家用龍骨者亦當知其性之愛惡如此。

[3] See below, p 76

[4] 南部新書, written by Ts'ien Yih, 錢易, in the later Sung dynasty, Ch 辛.

legend to be found in the *T'ien chung ki* [1], where we read the following. In A. D. 762 the dike of a river was broken, and each time when the repairs were nearly finished, it broke again. At last somebody told that in the time of the Emperor Wu of the Liang dynasty (who reigned from A. D. 502 to 549) in a similar case thousands of pounds of iron were buried under the dike, whereupon the work could be completed. On hearing these words the superintendent of the work ordered to do the same, and lo! the thundering noise under the ground was no longer heard on the spot where the iron was laid, but gradually went away, and the dike was soon repaired. "The reason may be", says the author, "that the eyes of the dragons are hurt by the pungent nature (litt. taste) of iron or gold, and that they flee to protect their eyes".

§ 4 Shape of the dragons

WANG FU [2] says: "The people paint the dragon's shape with a horse's head and a snake's tail Further, there are expressions as 'three joints' and 'nine resemblances' (of the dragon), to wit· from head to shoulder, from shoulder to breast, from breast to tail These are the joints; as to the nine resemblances, they are the following· his horns resemble those of a stag, his head that of a camel, his eyes those of a demon, his neck that of a snake, his belly that of a clam (*shen*, 蜃), his scales those of a carp, his claws those of an eagle, his soles those of a tiger, his ears those of a cow. Upon his head he has a thing like a broad eminence (a big lump), called *ch'ih muh* (尺木). If a dragon has no *ch'ih muh*, he cannot ascend to the sky".

The *P'i ya* [3] states that "the dragon's 81 scales form a number

---

1 See above, p 57, note 8, Ch LVI

2 About this author see above, p 66, note 3, this passage, quoted in the *'Rh ya yih*, Sect 釋龍 (T S, Ch 127, 龍部彙考, p 6b), is not to be found in WANG FU's *Ts'ien fu lun* 世俗畫龍之狀馬首蛇尾。又有三停九似之說、謂自首至膊、膊至腰、腰至尾、皆相停也。九似者角似鹿、頭似駝、眼似鬼、項似蛇、腹似蜃、鱗似鯉、爪似鷹、掌似虎、耳似牛。頭上有物如博山、名曰尺木。龍無尺木不能升天。

3 Ch. I (釋魚), nr 1 (龍), p. 1a. 龍八十一鱗具九九之

consisting of nine times nine Nine is *Yang*. The carp's 36 scales form a number consisting of six times six. Six is *Yin*".

In the *Yang kuh man luh*[1] we read: "The dragon has five fingers".

Finally, the *Pen-ts'ao kang-muh*[2] teaches us that "a dragon has whiskers at the sides of his mouth and a bright pearl under his chin, under his throat he has scales lying in a reversed direction, upon his head he has a broad eminence called in writing *ch'ih muh*; if a dragon has no *ch'ih muh*, he cannot ascend to the sky. His breath turns into clouds, and then can change into water and into fire (rain and lightning)" .... "The *Shih tien* says: 'When dragons copulate they change into two small snakes'".

§ 5 Male and female dragons

The difference between male and female dragons is described as follows: "The male dragon's horn is undulating, concave, steep; it is strong at the top, but becomes very thin below. The female dragon has a straight nose, a round mane, thin scales and a strong tail"[3].

The *Shing i ki*[4] relates of a painter, who was very skilled in painting dragons, but whose work one day was critisized by a man and a woman. They said that he did not distinguish male from female dragons, although they were different in reality. When he got angry and asked them how they knew this, they

---

1 賜谷漫錄, Sect 龍, quoted in the T S, Sect 禽蟲, Ch 127, 龍部彙考, p 8a: 龍五指.

2 Ch 43, 鱗之一, 龍, p 4a 口旁有鬚髯、頷下有明珠。喉下有逆鱗。頭上有博山文名尺木。龍無尺木不能升天.呵氣成雲既能變水、又能變火……釋典云、龍交則變爲二小蛇。

3 *Kwang poh wuh chi*, 廣博物志, an "Enlarged *Poh whu chi*" of later times (1607), by Tung Sze-chang, 董斯張 (Cf Wylie, p 187). The *Poh wuh chi* itself is a work of Chang Hwa, 張華, who lived in the fourth century, at the time of the Tsin dynasty (A D 265—420) This passage is quoted in the *Wakan sansai zue*, Ch XLV, p. 674 龍雄者角浪凹峭上壯下殺也。雌者直鼻、圓鬃、薄鱗、壯尾也。

4 乘異記, written by Chang Kiun-fang, 張君房, in the Sung dynasty (960—1280)

answered that they were dragons themselves and were willing to show him their shapes, whereupon they changed into a male and a female dragon.

§ 6 Different kinds of dragons.

The *Shuh i ki*[1] says: "A water snake (水虵, *shui yuen*) after five hundred years changes into a *kiao* (蛟), a *kiao* after a thousand years changes into a *lung* (龍), a *lung* after five hundred years changes into a *kioh-lung* (角龍, "horned dragon") and after a thousand years into a *ying-lung* (應龍)".

Quite different, however, is, as we have seen above (p. 65), Liu Ngan's statement in his work entitled *Hwai nan tsze*[2], according to which the "*flying dragons*" are the offspring of the bird *yu-kia*[3] ("the winged barbel"; this is the reason, says the commentary to this passage, why these dragons have wings); the *ying-lung* are the issue of a quadruped called *mao-tuh*[4]; the *kiao-lung* are the issue of a fish called *kiai-lin*[5]; the *sien-lung*[6] are the issue of a mailed beast called *kiai-t'an*[7], and the *k'uh-lung*[8] are produced by a sea plant called *hai-lu*[9]. When the *yellow dragon*, born from yellow gold a thousand years old, enters a deep place, a yellow spring dashes forth, and if from this spring some particles[10] arise, these become a yellow cloud. In the same way blue springs and blue clouds originate from blue dragons born from blue gold eight hundred years old; red, white and black springs and clouds from red, white and black dragons born from gold of the same colours, a thousand years old.

The *Poh ya*[11] gives the following definition of the principal

---

1 述異記, written by Jen Fang, 任昉, in the sixth century A D (another work of the same name dates from 1701), Ch 上, p. 6a 水虵五百年化爲蛟、蛟千年化爲龍、龍五百年化爲角龍、千年化爲應龍。

2 Ch IV, 地形訓.　　　　　3 羽嘉.

4 毛犢, "hairy calf"　　　5 介鱗.

6 先龍.　　　　　　　　7 介潭.

8 屈龍.　　　　　　　　9 海閭.

10 埃, fine dust

11 博雅, Sect 釋魚, Ch X, p. 6b 有鱗曰蛟龍、有翼曰鷹龍 有角曰虯龍 無角曰螭龍 Although the Poh ya

dragons· "If a dragon has scales, he is called *kiao-lung*, if wings, *ying-lung* (應龍); if a horn, *k'iu-lung* (虬龍); and if he has no horn, he is called *ch'i-lung* (螭龍)". In the Japanese Buddhist dictionary entitled *Bukkyō iroha jiten* [1] we find the same enumeration with the addition of a fifth class, the *p'an-lung* (蟠龍), "coiled dragon", which does not yet ascend to heaven. This dragon is also mentioned in the *Fang yen* [2], where we read. "Dragons which do not yet ascend to heaven are called *p'an-lung*".

In the same passage of the aforesaid Japanese dictionary another division into five classes is given, namely crow-dragons, snake-dragons, toad-dragons, horse-dragons and fish-dragons [3]. This enumeration is to be found in a Buddhist work, the *Su-men ts'ang king* [4], where we read that from these five classes that of the snake-dragons is the principal one, they are the "right kind of dragon".

According to the *Wen-tszĕ tsih-lioh* [5] the *ch'i-lung* (螭龍) [6] is red, white and green, and the *k'iu-lung* (虬龍) is blue. The *k'iu* is mentioned several times in the *Pao P'oh-tszĕ* [7]. "If a pond inhabited by fishes and gavials is drained off, the divine *k'iu* go away" [8]. "As to the flying to the sky of the *k'iu* of the pools,

----

kang-muh, Ch 43, 鱗之一, p 6b, s.v *kiao-lung*, quotes the text in this form (without saying that it is borrowed from the *Poh ya*), the original text of the *Poh ya* gives different characters for the names of the two last dragons These characters are not to be found in the dictionaries, being the 205th radical under the 140th, and 多 combined with 宅; but the pronunciation added to them is *kiu* (巨彪) and *ch'i* (恥支)

1 See above, Introd., p 22, note 1, Vol II, p. 56, s.v 龍.

2 方言. "Local Terms", according to DE GROOT (*Rel Syst.* Vol III, p 1073)· "a small vocabulary composed by YANG HIUNG, 揚雄, an ethical philosopher and statesman who died in A.D. 18" Ch XII, p 7a 未陞天龍謂之蟠龍·

3 烏龍、蛇龍、蝦蟆龍、馬龍、魚龍, *wu-lung*, *shé-lung*, *hia-ma-lung*, *ma-lung*, and *yü-lung*

4 須彌 (Sumeru) 藏經, quoted in the *Ts'ien-k'ioh ku lei shu*, 潛確居類書, a cyclopaedia compiled in 1632 by CH'EN JEN-SIII, 陣仁錫 Cf WYLIE, *Notes on Chinese literature* (2nd ed), p. 187.

5 文字集略, a vocabulary quoted in the *Wakan sansai zue*, Ch. XLV, p 675

6 Cf below, Ch. V (Ornaments)

7 拘朴子, written by KOH HUNG, 葛洪, in the 4th century A D

8 外篇, Ch I, nr 2 (逸民), p 6b 漉魚鼈之池則神虬遐逝。

this is his union with the clouds" [1] "The *ts'ui k'iu* ('kingfisher-*k'iu*') has no wings and yet flies upwards to the sky" [2]. "Place the shape (i e an image of this dragon) in a tray, and the kingfisher-*k'iu* (shall) descend in a dark vapoury haze" [3]. The last sentence points to sympathetic magic which we shall mention below (this Book, Ch. VI).

The *Shui ying t'u* [4] says that the *yellow dragon* is the head of the four dragons, the essence of divine manifesting power [5], and that he can become big and small, appear and disappear in a moment; the *blue dragon* is the vital spirit of water. The azure, blue, yellow, black, white and red dragons as good or bad omens and givers of light or rain are mentioned above.

The legend about the *ying-lung*, the winged dragon, which after having killed the rebel Ch'i Yiu (the first to raise rebellion in B. C. 2637) could not return to the Southern peak where he used to live, for which reason afterwards often drought prevailed, will be given below (Ch. VI).

A nine-headed, eighteen-tailed dragon is mentioned in a passage of the *Lang huen ki* [6], referred to by De Groot [7]. There a Taoist doctor is said to have recited this spell· "I came from the East and found a pond on the road, in its water lived a venerable dragon with nine heads and eighteen tails. I asked what it fed on, it ate nothing but fever-demons".

Further, we read about the "little stone-dragon", or "little mountain-dragon", also called "spring-dragon" [8], the Japanese

---

1 Ibidem, nr 11 (貴賢), p 28a 淵 虬 之 天 飛 者 雲 霧 之 偕 也。T. S Sect 禽 蟲, Ch 130, p 4a, where this passage is quoted, gives 階 instead of 偕, which would mean "this is a flight of stairs formed by the clouds and vapours" But in the *Pao P'oh-tszĕ* itself we read 偕.

2 外篇, Ch III, nr 38 (博喻), p 29a 翠 虬 無 翅 而 天 飛。

3 外篇, Ch IV, nr 39 (廣譬), p 3b 設 象 於 槃 盂 而 翠 虬 降 於 玄 霄。

4 瑞應圖, see above p. 64, note 2, quoted in the *T'ien chung ki*, 天 中 記, Ch LV

5 神 靈 之 精·

6 瑯 嬛 記, "a collection of tales and legends, in three chapters, ascribed to one I Shi-chen, 伊 世 珍, who lived under the Yuen dynasty (*Lang huen* is the Land of Bliss)" (De Groot, *Rel. Syst* Vol. IV, p 105)

7 *Rel Syst*, Vol VI, p. 1053

tokage or *imori* (lizard), which is born between stones in the mountains and has got the name of «little dragon" because it was (and is) believed to cause hail by its breath and to give rain to those who prayed to it [1].

The connection between the snake and the dragon is evident from the description of the so-called *t'eng-shé*, 螣蛇, a wingless serpent, "which can cause the clouds to rise, and, riding upon them, can fly a thousand miles. It can change into a dragon. Although there are males and females, they do not copulate. Their cry forbodes pregnancy" [2]. And KOH HUNG [3] states that "tortoises turn into tigers and snakes into dragons" In the *Yiu-yang tsah tsu* [4] we read: "Dragons and snakes are considered by the learned class to be related".

The gavial [5] also belongs to the dragons. The *Pen-ts'ao kang-muh* [6] describes it as follows: "There are numerous gavials in rivers and lakes. They resemble the class of the *ling-li* [7], and their length is one or two chang Both their backs and tails are covered with scales. By exhaling they can *make clouds* and *cause rain.* It is a kind of dragon. They live in deep holes and can fly only horizontally, not vertically. Their cries are like the

---

山龍子, or *ts'uen-lung*, 泉龍 Cf WELLS WILLIAMS, *Chin -Eng. Dict.*, pp 803 and 1095 "The insect (虫) that changes (易), a small eft or chameleon common in Hukwang, also called 草龍 or grass dragon".

1 *Pen-ts'ao kang-muh*, Sect 鱗魚, nr 1 (龍), Ch. 43 p 12a 此物生山石間、能吐雹、可祈雨、故得龍子之名.

2 *Pen-ts'ao kang-muh*, quoted in the *Wakan sansai zue*, Ch XLV, p 682 In Ch 43, p 40 of the *Pen-ts'ao kang-muh* the text is a little different "The *t'eng-shé* changes into a dragon This divine snake can ride upon the clouds and fly about over a thousand miles If it is heard, (this means) pregnancy. This is borrowed from the *Pien-kwa lun* (i e the *Yin-Yang pien-kwa lun*, mentioned above, p 67) Further, the *Pao P'oh-tszĕ* says 'The *t'eng-shé* do not copulate' "

3 *Pao P'oh-tszĕ*, 內篇, Ch I (金丹)

4 西陽雜俎, written in the ninth century by TWAN CH'ING-SHIH, 段成式, quoted T S, Ch. 130 Sect 禽蟲、龍部雜錄, p 4b. 龍與蛇師爲親家.

5 鼉, cf WELLS WILLIAMS, ll., p. 912, s v. "A large triton, gavial, or water lizard, found to the South of China, ten feet long, of whose hard skin drumheads are made, its gruff voice is heard at night and indicates *rain*" About gavials acting as demons, cf. DE GROOT, *Rel. Syst of China*, Vol, V, pp 625 sq

6 Ch. 43, p 8a. cf. *Wakan sansai zue*, Ch XLV, p 675.

7 鯪鯉, pangolins.

sound of a drum, and when they cry at night, this is called 'the gavial-drum'. When the countryfolk hear it, they predict rain".

About the *shen* (蜃), a huge clam, the same work [1] says the following: "It is a kind of *kiao* (蛟) Its shape also resembles that of a snake, but it is larger. It has a horn like a dragon, a red mane, and the scales under its loins are all lying in a reversed direction It eats young swallows. When exhaling its breath assumes the form of towers and castles, which are seen when it is about to rain, and are called 'clam-towers' [2], or 'sea-markets' [3]. Of its fat, mixed with wax, candles are made, which one may smell at a distance of about a hundred steps. Also in the flames of these candles the shapes of towers and steeples are to be seen. LUH TIEN [the author of the *P'i ya*, who lived during the reign of the Emperor Hwui Tsung (1101—1126)] says. 'If a *kiao* copulates with a tortoise, they produce a tortoise, and when with a pheasant, a clam (*shen*) is produced'".

§ 7 Kiao lung (蛟龍)

The *Shan hai king* [4] describes the *kiao* as follows· "(Out of the Tao Kwo mountains) water comes forth in waves and flows to the South, where it flows into the sea. In this water there are 'tiger-*kiao*'. Their shapes consist of the body of a fish and the tail of a snake. Their voices are like those of mandarin ducks. Those who eat them, have no boils, and they (i e. their flesh) may be used to cure piles". In three other passages [5] of the same ancient work many *kiao* are said to live in special mountain rivulets.

According to the *Yang yu king*, "Classic on the rearing of fishes" [6], "if there are fully 360 fishes, the *kiao lung* is made their chief, and leading the fishes flies away".

---

1 Ch 43, p 7a Cf *Wakan sansai zue*, Ch XLV, p 675.

2 *Shen leu*, 蜃樓, i e mirages.   3 海市.

4) Sect 南山經, Ch I, p 11a (禱過之山)浪水出焉、而南流注于海。其中有虎蛟。其狀魚身而蛇尾。其音如鴛鴦。食者不腫、可以已痔。

5 Sect 中山經, Ch XV, quoted T.S, Sect 禽蟲, Ch. 432, 蛟部彙考, p 2a

6 養魚經, Sect 蛟 quoted T S l.l 魚滿三百六十、則蛟

From the ancient Taoist treatise designated by the name of *Wen tszĕ*[1] we learn the following "As to him who accumulates the virtue of the Tao, phoenixes fly in his court-yard, *k'i-lin* roam about in his suburbs, and *kiao-lung* house in his pond". Further, we read there. "On the highest tops of the mountains clouds and rain arise, and in the deepest depths of the water *kiao-lung* are born".[2].

Kwan tszĕ[3] says. "The *kiao-lung* is the god of the water animals. If he rides on the water, his soul is in full vigour, but when he loses water (if he is deprived of it), his soul declines. Therefore I (or they) say· 'If a *kiao-lung* gets water, his soul can be in full vigour'". The same philosopher states that "when people drain marshes and catch fish, the *kiao-lung* do not dwell in those pools"[4].

Also *Hwai nan tszĕ*[5] mentions the *kiao-lung* with the following words. "The *kiao-lung* lie hidden and sleep in pools, and yet their eggs break up (i. e. the young ones come out of them) on the hills". The commentator remarks: "The *kiao-lung* lay their eggs on hills and hide in pools. Their eggs get life spontaneously"[6].

K'UH YUEN[7], the famous nobleman and poet of Ts'u, who was banished by king Hwai towards the end of the fourth century B C. and about 299 B C. composed his celebrated poem entitled *Li Sao*[8], in the ninth section of this poem describes his journey to the mysterious K'wan-lun mountains in the West, in a car

---

[1] 文子、道德篇· 積道德者鳳凰翔其庭、騏麟游其郊、蛟龍宿其沼。

[2] 上德篇: 山致其高而雲雨起焉。水致其深而蛟龍生焉。

[3] 管子、形勢篇: 蛟龍水蟲之神者也。乘于水則神立、失于水則神廢。故曰、蛟龍得水而神可立也。

[4] 家設困誓篇· 竭澤而漁、則蛟龍不處其淵。

[5] Sect 泰族訓, Ch XX, p 3a 蛟龍伏寢于淵而卵割于陵

[6] 蛟龍乳於陵而伏於淵、其卵自孕.

[7] 屈原, who drowned himself in the Poh-lo river in Hu-nan province, and whose death is commemorated every year on the fifth day of the fifth month (the Festival of the Dragon Boats, cf above, p 68, note 4, and below, this Chapter, § 10)

[8] 離騷, "Dissipation of Sorrows", *Ch'u tszĕ*, 楚辭, Ch I Cf LEGGE, *The Li Sao poem and its author*, Journal of the Royal Asiatic Society, January, July and October 1895

ın the form of a phoenix, drawn by a team of four *kʻiu* (虬) [1].
In the thirteenth section, when proceeding along the Red river,
he says: "I motioned wıth my hand to the *kiao-lung* to brıdge
over the ford". [2] At that tıme his car was drawn by "flyıng
dragons". [3]

The *Ta taı h ki* [4] instructs us that the *kiao-lung* is consıdered
to be the head of the 360 scaly animals, and that "ıf water
accumulates and becomes a river, the *kiao-lung* is born". [5]

The *Poh wuh chi* [6] says: "If a man has eaten swallows [comp.
thıs chapter, § 3, p. 68], he mnst not enter the water; (for ıf
he does so), he wıll be swallowed by a *kıao-lung*".

In the above texts, except in those of the *Shan haı king*, the
words *kiao* and *lung* are combined to one term. The *Shan haı
kıng*, however, speaks of the *kıao* only, and so do a large number
of other works, whıch dıstınguısh the *kıao* from the *lung*. Neither
in the *Shan haı kıng*, nor ın the *Lı kı* [7], which says "(In the
last month of summer) the ınspector of fishıng ıs ordered to kill
the *kiao*", these water animals are mentioned as divine creatures.
The commentator of the former work, Kwoh Pʻoh [8], however,
states the following. "The *kıao* resembles a snake. It has four
legs, and is akın to the *lung*". [9] As we have seen above [10], the
Shuh i ki remarks that a water snake (*shuı-yuen*), when five
hundred years old, changes ınto a *kıao*, and a *kıao* after a thousand
years becomes a *lung*.

---

1 騊玉虬以乘鷖兮。 Legge, 11, pp 844, 855, stanza 47

2 摩蛟龍以梁津兮、 Legge, 11, pp 846, 863, stanza 89

3 爲余駕飛龍兮。 Legge, ıbidem, stanza 86.

4 大戴禮記 (1st cent B C), Ch XIII, nı 81, 易本命, p 7b 有鱗
之蟲三百六十而蛟龍爲之長。

5 Ch VII, nr 64, 勸學, p 7a 積水成川、蛟龍生焉。

6 博物志, a little woık wrıtten by Chang Hwa, 張華, a Mınıster of
State, who lıved ın the fourth century (cf above, p 71, note 3) 人食燕肉
不可入水、爲蛟龍所吞。

7 Sect 月令、Book IV, Ch IV, nr 6 (季夏之月)命漁師伐蛟。
Couvreur, Lı kı, Vol I, p 367

8 郭璞 (A D. 276—324), the famous Taoıstic author and poet, who edıted the
'Rh ya and the Shan haı kıng

9 蛟似蛇、四足龍屬。

The *Shih i ki* [1] (4th century) tells us that the Empeior Chao of the Han dynasty (B. C. 86—74), when angling in the Wei river, "caught a white *kiao*, three chang long, which resembled a big snake, but had no scaly armour. The Emperor said: 'This is not a lucky omen', and ordered the Ta kwan to make a condiment of it. Its flesh was purple, its bones were blue, and its taste was very savoury and pleasant".

The ancient Chinese apparently considered the *kiao* — some four-legged water animal — to be a common, dangerous creature, but afterwards it was believed to be akin to the dragon and called a dragon itself. Thus it became the principal god of rivers and brooks.

According to the *Shuh i ki* [2] "old tiger-fishes become *kiao*", and the author of the *Yiu-yang tsah-tsu* [3] instructs us that "when fishes weigh two thousand kin (catty) they become *kiao*" Another work, however, the *Yuh hu ts'ing hwa* [4], states that eggs left by snakes or pheasants, when having been a thousand years in the ground, become *kiao*.

The *P'i ya* [5] describes this animal as follows· "The *kiao* belongs to the same kind as the *lung*. Its shape resembles that of a snake and yet it has four legs and a thin neck Around its neck it has a white necklace. The big *kiao* are several spans thick. They are born from eggs Their eyebrows are united (交), reason why they are called *kiao* (蛟)".

The *Mih k'oh hwui si* [6] says: "The *kiao*'s shape is like that of a snake, and its head is like that of a tiger. Its length reaches several chang. Many of them live in rivulets and pools and under rock caves. Their voices are like the bellowing of a cow. When people walk on the shore or in the valleys of brooks, they are

---

1 拾遺記, Ch. VI, p 3*b*

2 述異記 (sixth century), Ch 上, p 19*b* 虎魚老者爲蛟。

3 Quoted T. S Sect 禽蟲, Ch 132, 蛟部雜錄, p 1*b* 魚二千 觔爲蛟

4 玉壼清話, quoted ibidem, p 2*a*

5 S v 蛟 Ch I, p 9*a* 蛟龍屬也。其狀似蛇而四足細 頸。頸有白嬰。大有數圍。卵生。眉交故謂之蛟。

6 黑客揮犀, according to DE GROOT (*Rel. Syst.* Vol V, p 864, note 2) "a work in ten chapters by P'ENG SNING, 彭乘, of the eleventh century', quoted in the T. S, Sect 禽蟲, Ch 132, 蛟部雜錄, p 1*b*

troubled by the *kiao* When they see a man, they first surround him with stinking saliva, and after having made him tumble into the water they suck his blood under his armpits. When he has no blood left, they stop sucking".

In the *Pen-tsᶜao kang-muh* [1] Li SHI-CHEN quotes the following passage from the *Pᶜên yuen kwang cheu ki* [2]. "The *kiao* is over a chang long. It resembles a snake but has four feet and its shape is broader, resembling the beam of a railing. It has a small head and a thin neck At its neck it has white tassels (a white necklace [3]) The upper part of its breast is reddish brown, the upper part of its back is spotted with blue, the sides of its ribs (flanks) are like brocade. Its tail has a fleshy ring. Big *kiao* are several span thick, and their eggs are also larger (than those of other *kiao*). They can lead fishes and fly. If people catch turtles, the *kiao* can escape".

As messengers from the River Lord (河伯), the god of the Yellow River, the *kiao* are mentioned in a story to be found in the *Poh wuh chi* (3rd century) [4]. This god wished to deprive an official, who crossed the river with a jade badge of office, of this precious object, and sent two *kiao* to seize the vessel. But both were killed by the audacious man, who after having thrice crossed the river threw the badge into the water as a present to the River Lord, who danced with joy and took it home.

Transformations of *kiao* into human shapes are the subjects of several tales. The *Wu ki* [5] tells the following. "Under the Emperor Ta Ti of the Wu dynasty (A. D. 228—251), in the seventh month of the third year of the Chᶜih-wu era (A. D 240), there was a certain Wang Shuh who gathered medicinal herbs on Tᶜien Tai mountain. At the hottest time of the day he took a rest under a bridge, when suddenly he saw a little blue boy, over a foot long, in the brook The boy held a blue rush in his hand and rode on a red carp. The fish straightly entered a cloud and disappeared little by little. After a good while Shuh climbed upon a high mountain top and looked to all four sides. He saw wind and clouds arising above the sea, and in a moment a thunderstorm broke forth. Suddenly it was about to reach Shuh, who terrified hid himself in a hollow tree. When the sky cleared up, he again saw the red carp on which the boy rode and the

1 Ch 43, 鱗之一, p 7a.   2 裴淵廣州記

3 嬰, probably the same as 瓔 or 纓.   4 Ch VII, p 3a.

5 異記, quoted in the T S Sect 禽蟲 Ch 420 蛟龍部紀 ... 2

little boy returning and entering the brook. It was a black *kiao*!"

In the *Sheu shen heu ki*[1] we read about a *kiao*, who in the shape of a man, about twenty years old, came to a farmer's cottage. He rode on a white horse, under a state umbrella, and was escorted by four followers, all dressed in yellow robes. "They came from the East and arriving at the gate they called. 'Child of Yin (the little son of the farmer, thirteen years old, who was alone at home), we come to sit down for a little while and rest'. Thus they entered the house and sat down on a couch in the lower part of the court-yard. One of them grasped the umbrella and turned it upside down Yin's child looked at their clothes and saw that they were entirely without a seam. The horse was spotted with five colours and looked as if it had a scaly armour and no hair. In a moment a rainy vapour came, whereupon the man mounted the horse and rode away. Turning and looking back he said to the child: 'Tomorrow I must come again'. Yin's child looked where they went and saw them treading the air, turning westwards and gradually ascending. In a moment cloudy vapours assembled from all sides and the daylight was darkened by them. The next day a heavy rain came violently down; the water gushed over mountains and valleys, hills and ravines were overflown. When it was about to overflow the cottage of Yin's child he suddenly saw a big *kiao*, over three chang long, which with its windings protectingly covered the cottage".

The revenge of a *kiao*, transformed into a girl, is told in the *I yuen*[2]. A man who had hit a *kiao* with an arrow met a crying girl with the same arrow in her hand. When he asked her what this meant, she said that she came to return to him the burning pain it had caused her, after which she gave him the arrow and disappeared. Before he reached his house he got a hot fever and died on the road.

The passages mentioned above clearly show that the *kiao*, just as the *lung*, were believed to assume human shapes and to cause rain and thunderstorm. This is not astonishing, for we have seen that the *kiao* were called *lung* themselves.

---

1 搜神後記, written by Ts'ao Ts'ien, 陶潛, in the fifth century. Ch. X, p 1. The *Sheu shen ki*, 搜神記, was written by Yu Pao, 于寶, (or Kan Pao, 于寶) in the first decades of the fourth century

2 異苑, written by Liu King-shuh, 劉敬叔, in the first half of the fifth century; quoted T S., 11, Ch. 132, 外編, p 2b.

§ 8. Rearing and taming dragons.

In Chapter II (pp 50 sqq.) we have referred to the *Historical Records* with regard to the Emperor K'ung Kiah of the Hia dynasty, in whose service Liu Léi tamed two dragons, sent down by Heaven. This Liu Léi had learned the art from the Dragon-rearer family, and he himself obtained the family name of *Yu lung*, "Dragon-ruler"

The *Tso chw'en* [1] gives the same legend in the following passage: "In autumn (of the 29th year of Chao kung, i. e. Chao, duke of Lu, who reigned B. C 541—509) a dragon appeared in the suburbs of Kiang. Wéi Hien tszé asked Ts'ai Mih saying: 'I have heard that none of the animals is the dragon's equal in knowledge, and that for this reason the dragon cannot be caught alive Can we believe that it is right to ascribe this (his not being caught alive) to his knowledge?' Mih replied 'Men really do not know; it is not that the dragon is really knowing. The ancients kept dragons, therefore the State had a Dragon-rearer family (*Hwan-lung shi* [2]) and a Dragon-ruler family (*Yu-lung shi* [3])' Hien tszé said. 'I too have heard about those two families, but I do not know their origin; what is it said to be?' The answer was 'In olden times there was Shuh Ngan of Liu, who had a distant descendant called Tung Fu, very fond of dragons and able to find out their tastes and likings, so as to supply them with drink and meat. Many dragons sought refuge with him and he reared the dragons according to their nature in order to serve the Emperor Shun, who gave him the surname of Tung, and the family name of *Hwan-lung* (Dragon-rearer). He was [also] invested with [the principality of] Tsung-chw'eu, and the family of Tsung I is of his posterity. Thus in the time of the Emperor Shun, and for generations after, dragons were reared. We come [then] to K'ung Kiah of the Hia dynasty, who was so obedient and acceptable to the Emperor of Heaven, that the latter gave him riding dragons, two, a male and a female, from the Hwang-ho, and two from the Han river. K'ung Kiah could not feed them, and had not yet found [members of the] Hwan lung family. T'ao T'ang (Yao)'s family having declined, one of his descendants was Liu Léi, who learned the art of rearing dragons from the 'Dragou-rearer' family With this he undertook to serve K'ung

---

1 LEGGE, *Chinese Classics*, Vol V, pp. 729 sqq ; Book X, year XXIX, par. 4.
2 養龍氏 3 御龍氏

Kiah and could give the dragons drink and food. The Emperor praised him and gave him the family name of Dragon-ruler (Yü-lung)".

§ 9 Dragons ridden by *sien*, or drawing the cars of gods and holy men

The "Traditions on the Files of Immortals", *Lieh sien chw°en* [1], repeatedly mention *sien* who rode away on dragons through the air. We often read also of flying dragons or *ying-lung* drawing the cars of gods or holy men As we shall see below (Ch. VII), Hwang Ti rode on a dragon, and Yu's carriage was drawn by two of these divine animals. In the *Li Sao*, quoted above [2], K°üh Yuen's car was drawn by four *k°iu* or by flying dragons. The Emperor Wu of the Han dynasty (B. C. 140-86) once ascended the Yen ling tower and after the second night watch saw Si wang mu, the "Royal Mother of the West", arriving in a carriage of purple clouds, drawn by nine-coloured, spotted dragons [3]. These ideas are, of course, closely connected with those about dragon-horses, winged and scaly horses of extraordinary size, treated above in Ch. II, § 3, pp. 56 sqq.

§ 10 Dragon-boats.

Dragon-boats are mentioned in the *Hwai nan tszě* [4], where these ships are called "*dragon-boats (and) yih-heads*" (龍舟鷁首). This is explained as follows by the commentator. "Dragon-boats are big ships adorned with carved dragon-ornaments (文), the *yih* is a big bird, the painted shape of which is attached to the prows of ships". WELLS WILLIAMS [5] describes the *yih* as "a kind of seabird that flies high, whose figure is gaily painted on the sterns of junks, to denote their swift sailing; the descriptions are contradictory, but its picture rudely resembles a heron". On these boats, which were used by the Emperors for pleasure

---

1 列仙傳, written in the first century before our era by the famous philosopher LIU HANG, 劉向, quoted T S, Sect. 禽蟲, Ch 131, 外編, pp. 1a, 2b. Cf. the *Shen sien ch°wen*, "Traditions on the divine *sien*", quoted ibidem, p. 3a.
2 This chapter, § 7, p. 77, note 8.
3 *Han Wu-ti nei ch°wen* (attributed to PAN KU, but probably written in the 3rd century), quoted ibidem, p. 3a 王母至乘紫雲之輦駕九色斑龍.
4 About 140 B C, Ch VIII (本經).
5 *Chin. Engl. Dict.*, p. 1092, s v. *yih*.

trips, on which occasions music was made on board, the bird
was painted, not to denote their swift sailing, but to suppress
the water-gods, if we may believe the commentary to a passage
of the *Wen suen* [1]. It seems that the ships represented dragons
with yih-heads, and that the "dragon-ornaments" were the
dragon's scales, carved on the sides of the vessels.

The Japanese courtiers of the eleventh century, however, who
wanted to imitate all the customs prevailing at the Chinese court,
did not understand the words of the *Hwai nan tsze* and had two
kinds of ships made which they called in one term: "*Dragon-
heads (and) Yih-heads*", 龍頭鷁首, "*Ryōtō-gekisu*" The combination of these two words reminds us of the term "*shishi-komainu*",
used at the Japanese Court in the same age to denote the images of
the lion and the unicorn, not separately but as one name for
both together [2]. Therefore I would be inclined to think that the
term *Ryōtō-gekisu* originally denoted one kind of ships, adorned
with a dragon-head in front and a yih-head behind, if a passage
of the *Jikkinshō* [3] did not state that on the occasion of a pleasure
trip in the Emperor Shirakawa's time (1072—1086), "Koresue
played the flute on board of the 'dragon-head', but there was
no flute playing on board of the 'yih-head'". As to MURASAKI
SHIKIBU's *Diary* [4], where we read that the new ships were very
beautiful, and the *Hamamatsu Chūnagon Monogatari* [5], these works
of the beginning and the middle of the eleventh century, as well
as the *Eigwa monogatari* [6] (about 1100), which states that the
Emperor made a pleasure trip with "*ryōtō-gekisu*", seem to speak
of one kind of ships. The *Kagakushū* [7], however, which dates

---

1 文選, Sect 西都賦, compiled in the first half of the sixth century of
our era by SIAO T'UNG, 蕭統, quoted in the *Kokushi daijiten*, 國史大辭
典, p 2338, s v 龍頭鷁首船, *Ryūzu* (mistake instead of *ryōtō*) *gekisu
no fune*

2 Cf my treatise on "The Dog and the Cat in Japanese Superstition", Transactions
of the Asiatic Society of Japan, Vol XXXVII, Part I pp 54—62

3 十訓抄, written shortly after 1252, Ch X, K T K Vol XV, p 823

4 Written from 1008 to 1010, *Gunsho ruijū*, nr 321, Vol XI, p 591

5 濱松中納言物語, written by SUGAWARA KŌHYŌ (菅原孝標)'s
daughter (born in 1008), consort of FUJIWARA NO TOSHIMITSU (俊通 who died in
1058); Ch I

6 榮華物語, Ch. XX (御賀), K. T. K Vol XV, p 1344; Ch VIII, p 1078.

7 下學集, written in 1444 by the Buddhist priest SHAKU NO HATTOTSU,
釋破勒 Ch 器財

from 1444, says: "'Dragon-head' and 'Yih-head' are two different names of ships", which agrees with the words of the *Jikkinshō* [1].

These Chinese ships are different from the "dragon-boats" used in China on the fifth day of the fifth month at the water festival. The latter are real boats used in regatta's, or fancy dragon-boats, carried through the streets and burned at the sea-shore as substitutes which take away all evil influences. No doubt DE GROOT's [2] explanation of this festival, as being based on sympathetic magic, is right. As we shall see below [3], the Chinese used to make clay dragons to cause rain. In the same way their dragon-boat-races are certainly intended to represent fighting dragons, in order to cause a real dragon fight, which is always accompanied by heavy rains. The dragon-boats carried through the streets may also serve to cause rain, although they are at the same time considered to be substitutes.

As to the enormous dragon, made of linen, bamboo and paper, and carried in procession through the streets on the 15th of the first month, a red ball being carried in front of him, this was formerly explained by DE GROOT [4] as an imitation of the Azure Dragon, the head of which (a star) in remotest ages in the beginning of spring rose and set at the same time as the sun (the fiery ball), as if it persecuted this celestial globe and finally succeeded in swallowing it [5]. As to his later explanation concerning the thunder, belched out by the dragon, we may refer to this Book, Ch. IV (Ornaments), § 4.

§ 11. "Dragon-tail-road" and other words connected with the dragon.

The "*Dragon-tail-road*", 龍尾道, *Lung-wéi-tao*, was the road ascending straight southward to the *Shé yuen tien*, 舍元殿, a building belonging to the Chinese Emperor's palace. Along this road the visitors came to be received in audience (北面) by His Majesty, who always faced the South (南面). In imitation the road before the Taikyokuden, a building belonging to the

---

1 Cf the *Nambakō*, 難波江, written by OKAMOTO YASUTAKA, 岡本保孝, who lived 1798—1878, Ch II, 下, *Hyakka setsurin*, Vol. 續下一. p 636
2 *Fêtes annuelles à Emoui*, Vol I, pp 372 sqq
3 This Book, Ch. VI (causing rain).
4 *Fêtes annuelles*, Vol I, p 369
5 Cf. SCHLEGEL, Uranographie Chinoise, pp 55 sqq.

Japanese Palace, was also called *Ryūbidō*, "Dragon-tail-road" [1].

Other words borrowed from China are the following. *Ryūteki*, 龍笛, "dragon-flute"; *ryūbin*, 龍鬢. "dragon's whiskers", a mat woven from rush [2]; according to the *Pao P°oh-tszĕ* (Sect. 登涉, Ch IV, nr 17) it is the name of a kind of grass produced by the whiskers of the dragon ridden by Hwang Ti. The officials who could not ascend the dragon got hold of its whiskers, but by their weight pulled them out Where the whiskers fell down, the "Dragon's whiskers herb" shot up (cf. below, Book I, Ch. VI, § 1); *ryūtan*, 龍膽, pronounced *rindō*, "Dragon's liver", a species of gentian; three of these flowers, together with five *sasa* (笹, a kind of small bamboo), formed the badge of the Minamoto Family (*sasa-rindō*). [3]

§ 12. Dragon-gate.

The *Sin shi San Ts'in ki* [4] says· "*Lung men* (龍門, "Dragon-gate") is another name for *Ho tsin* (河津, "Ford of the Hwang Ho"). Several thousands of big fishes assemble under the Dragon-gate without being able to ascend it (i e to swim against the current). Those which succeed in ascending it become dragons; those which fail remain fishes".

A fish changing into a dragon is represented on the altar table of the Yuh-Fuh-tien in the Fah-yu temple on P°u t°o shan (BOERSCHMANN, *Die Baukunst und religiose Kultur der Chinesen*, Vol. I, p. 65), and dragons trying to grasp the mysterious fiery "pearl", which is hanging in the Dragon-gate, are seen in the same temple (l.l, pp. 46, 87, cf. below, Book 1, Ch. IV, § 4).

As we shall see below (Book II, Ch. XI, § 2, B), there are in Japan several Dragon-gate waterfalls, and also, in the province of Kii, a Dragon-gate mountain. The latter reminds us of the *Lung-men* mountain between the rivers I and Lo, not far from the confluence of these rivers. [5]

---

1 *Ryūan zuihitsu*, 柳菴隨筆, written in 1819 by KURIHARA SHINJŪ (NOBUMITSU), 栗原信充, Ch IX, *Hyakka seisurin*, Vol 續下二, p 488

2 藺, lin, *Kokushi daijiten*, p 2338, s. v *ryūbin*

3 *Ryūan zuihitsu*, l.l, pp. 485 sq

4 辛氏三秦記, written by a certain SIN, 辛, quoted T S, Sect 禽蟲, Ch 128, 龍部 紀事一, p 13a 河津一名龍門。大魚集龍門下數千、不得上。上者爲龍、不上者魚。

5 Cf. ‚‚‚‚‚‚‚ „ ‚ ‚ ‚ ‚ ‚

§ 13 Dragon's dens.

We read in the *Sheu shen heu ki*[1]: "On mount Kʻiu in Wu-
chʻang (in Hu-kwang province) there was a dragon's den Whenever
the inhabitants saw a divine *kʻiu* (虬) fly out of and into the
den, the year was dry, but when they prayed to this dragon
it rained".

Another dragon's den is mentioned in the *Cheh-kiang tʻung-chi*,
"General Memoirs concerning Cheh-kiang",[2] where we read:
"On mount Pien in Hu-cheu there is a Yellow Dragon's Cavern.
At the top there is a spring which dashes forth from the cave,
called the 'Golden Well spring'; the cave is also called the
'Golden Well cave'. The cavern is so deep that one cannot see
its end. At the time of the Liang dynasty a yellow dragon
appeared in it. For this reason King Yueh of Wu erected a shrine
in order to sacrifice to the dragon". Another dragon's den,
mentioned in the *Kwah i chi*, will be treated below in connection
with the Indian Nāga-kings (Ch. IX).

§ 14. Dragon herds.

According to the *Shih cheu ki*[3] herds of dragons assemble at
Fang chang island in the centre of the Eastern sea. The *Luh i
ki*[4] relates about a so-called "Blue smoke temple" situated on
an island. During several days a cloud of smoke hung above the
sanctuary. Suddenly one morning the waves leapt up violently,
a herd of dragons appeared at the surface and entered the Han
river. The big ones were several chang long, the small ones over
a chang. Some were yellow, others black, red, white or blue, and

---

[1] 武昌虬山有龍穴. 居人每見神虬飛翔出入歲
旱. 禱之卽雨.

[2] 浙江通志 (cf. WYLIE, 11, p 45 16th century, revised 1684 and 1736), quoted
T S, 11. Ch 129, 紀事二, p 13*b* 湖州卞山有黃龍洞. 頂
有洞出泉、名金井泉、亦名金井洞. 實穴深邃莫
窺其際. 梁時黃龍見於洞. 吳越王因立宮以祀.

[3] 十洲記, written in the Han dynasty, p 9*a*.

[4] 錄異記, "Writings on Recorded Wonders", written by TU KWANG-TING, a
Taoist priest who lived in the latter part of the ninth century (cf DE GROOT, *Rel
Syst*, Vol. V, p. 630, note 2), quoted T. S 11, Ch 129, 紀事二, p. 14*a*.

they resembled cows, horses, donkeys or sheep. Forming a row
of fifty they followed one another into the mouth of the Han
river; then they returned to the temple. So they went to and
back several miles, sometimes hidden sometimes visible This
lasted for three days and then stopped.

§ 15. Dragon's pearls.

According to *Chwang tsze* [1] a "pearl of a thousand pieces of
gold (*ts'ien kin)"* is certainly to be found in a pool of nine layers
(i. e. very deep) under the throat of a *li-lung* or "horse-dragon".
The *Shuh i ki* [2] (sixth century) states that so-called dragon-pearls
are spit out by dragons, like snake-pearls by snakes. In the *Lung
ch'ing luh* [3] we read about a dragon which in the shape of a
little child was playing with three pearls before the entrance of
his den. When a man approached he fled into the cavern and,
reassuming his dragon form, put the pearls in his left ear. The
man cut off the ear, in order to take possession of the pearls,
but they vanished together with the dragon himself.

Another legend [4] tells us about a man who was very fond of
wine and from a female *sien* in the mountains obtained a pearl
which she said to be kept by the dragons in their mouths in
order to replace wine.

DE GROOT [5] mentions "Thunder-pearls" (雷珠, *léi-chu),* "which
dragons have dropped from their mouths, and which may thoroughly
illuminate a whole house during the night". "Perhaps", says
DE GROOT, "these objects may be the relics of an age of stone".

§ 16. Dragon's eggs.

Dragon's eggs are beautiful stones picked up in the mountains
or at the river side, and preserved till they split amidst thunder,

---

[1] 列禦寇篇: 夫千金之珠必在九重之淵而驪龍
頷下。

[2] Ch 上, p 3b 凡珠有龍珠、龍所吐者、蚖珠蚖所
吐者。

[3] 龍城錄, written in the T'ang dynasty by LIU TSUNG-YUEN, 柳宗元,
Ch II

[4] *Lang hüen ki,* 瑯嬛記 (see above p 74, note 6), Ch 中.

rain and darkness and the young dragon ascends to the sky. Much water comes out of the stones beforehand, and the dragon appears in the form of a very small snake, or water-lizard, which grows larger and larger in a few moments.[1] An old woman, who had found five such eggs in the grass, took the little snakes to the river and let them go, whereupon the dragons gave her the faculty of foretelling the future. This "Dragon-mother", as the people called her, because, when she was washing clothes in the river, fishes (the subjects of the dragons) used to dance before her, became so famous on account of her true prophecies, that even the Emperor wished to consult her She died, however, on her way to the capital, and was buried on the eastern bank of the river; but the dragons made a violent storm arise and transferred the grave to the opposite side of the stream.[2]

The same story is told in the *Nan yueh chi*[3], but there the dragons are said to have several times drawn back the ship by which the old woman against her will was transported to the capital. At last the plan was given up for fear of the dragons. According to the *Kwah i chi*[4] there is always much wind and rain near the Dragon-mother's grave; then people say: "The dragons wash the grave".

In the *Shan-si t'ung-chi*[5] we read about a dragon-woman who jumped out of a big egg, found at the side of a pool. She gave wealth to the house where she lived, but at last she ran away and in the form of a snake disappeared into the crack of a rock in the mountains.

The author of the *Mung k'i pih t'an*[6] says that he often saw a dragon's egg, preserved in a case in the Kin shan monastery in Jun cheu (an old name for Chin-kiang-fu in Kiang-su). It resembled a hen's egg, but it was much larger. Its weight was

---

1 *T'ai-p'ing kwang ki*, Ch 424, *Lang hüen ki*, Ch 下, *Kwai-sin tsah-shih suh-tsih*, 癸辛雜識續集, written by CHEU MIH, 周密, who lived in the second half of the thirteenth and in the beginning of the fourteenth century. Ch 下, p. 23   2 *T'ai-p'ing kwang ki*, ibidem

3 南越志, quoted T S, l.l., Ch 128, 紀事一, p. 5a

4 T S, Ch 130, p. 7a

5 山西通志, quoted T S, Ch. 131, 外編, p 17a.

6 夢溪筆談, written about the middle of the eleventh century by CH'EN KWOH, 沈括 (cf BRETSCHNEIDER, *Botanicon Sinicum*, Journal of the North-China branch of the Royal Asiatic Society, 1881, New series, Nr XVI, Part I, pp 137, 173, nr 510)

very small, and it gave a hollow sound. This egg had been foun
in the T'ien shing era (1023—1032) in the midst of the Grea
River, and by Imperial order had been presented to the monastery
That very year, however, a great flood washed away a larg
number of houses near by, and the people ascribed this to th
dragon's egg.

According to a work of the sixteenth century [1] of our era th
dragon's eggs are found in times of heavy rains. Further, w
read there that in 1469 a fisherman picked up a big egg, a
large as a human head, five-coloured, the lower end pointed an
the upper round. If one shook it, there was a sound as of wate
inside the egg, which was very heavy and luke-warm. Th
people worshipped it, looking upon it as a supernatural thing
A diviner declared it to be a dragon's egg.

§ 17. Dragon's bones, skins, teeth, horns, brains, livers, placentae and foetus, used as medicines.

Among the nine ingredients of spectre-killing pills, mentioned
by DE GROOT [2], we find "Dragon's bones", "certain fossil bones
to be found in the shops of leading apothecaries". There is, indeed
an extensive medical literature on the curative power of these
bones, which are probably remains of prehistoric animals.

The *Pen-ts'ao kang-muh* [3] is, as in all medical matters, the best
source of our knowledge about these bones and the use made of
them by the Chinese physicians. According to some of the authors
referred to by LI SHI-CHEN, the learned author of this medical
standard work, dragon's bones are cast-off skins of living dragons
for these animals are said to cast off not only their skins but
also their bones; according to others they are the remains of
dead dragons. LI SHI-CHEN, on comparing all the different views
and tales, arrives at the conclusion that the dragon, although a
divine being, certainly dies like other animals, and that the
Pen king [4], one of his principal sources, is right in declaring the
dragon's bones to belong to dead dragons.

---

1 *Suh wen hien t'ung k'ao*, 續文獻通考, written by WANG K'i, 王圻
who obtained official rank in 1561, Ch 224

2 *Rel Syst*, Vol VI, p 1087

3 Sect 鱗魚, Ch 43, p, 1 sqq

4 本經 Under this abbreviated title the *Shen Nung Pen ts'ao king*, "Classica
work on Medicines of (the Emperor) Shen Nung", the oldest medical work, is quoted
in the *Pen-ts'ao kang-muh* The work itself is lost Cf BRETSCHNEIDER. *Botanicor*

As to the places where they are found, the *Ming i pieh luh* [1] says: "They come from (litt. are produced in) the valleys of Tsin land (Shansi province) and from spots where dead dragons are lying in caverns on the steep water banks in T'ai Shan. They are gathered at indefinite times" [2]. "Nowadays", says the same author, "many bones are exported from the centre of Liang, Yih and Pa (Sz'-ch'wen province)". [3]

LEI HIAO [4] remarks: "Those from Yen cheu, Ts'ang cheu and T'ai yuen are the best. Among these bones those which are thin and have broad veins are of female dragons, those which are coarse and have narrow veins belong to male ones Those which have five colours are the best, the white and the yellow ones belong to the middle kind, and the black ones are of the most inferior quality. As a rule those with veins lengthwise running are not pure, and those which have been gathered by women are useless."

In WU P'U's [5] opinion the blue and white ones are good, and SU KUNG [6] says· "At the present day all (the bones) come from Tsin land. The fresh and hard ones are not good; those bearing five colours are good. The blue, yellow, red, white and black ones also according to their colours correspond with the viscera, as the five *chih* (felicitous plants), the five crystals (*shih ying*) and the five kinds of mineral bole (*shih chi*)". The meaning of the last sentence is the following The five colours (blue, white, red, black and yellow) correspond to the five viscera (liver, lungs,

1 名醫別錄, written by T'AO HUNG-KING, 陶弘景 (451~536) Cf DE GROOT, *Rel. Syst*, Vol. I, p. 274, BRETSCHNEIDER, l.l., p. 42 GILES, *Bibliogr Dict*, p. 718, s v. "one of the most celebrated adepts in the mysteries of Taoism" Quoted in the *Pen-ts'ao kang-muh*, 11, p 1b

2 生晋地川谷及太山巖水岸土穴中死龍處、探無時。

3 *Pen-ts'ao kang-muh*, ibidem 今多出梁益巴中骨。

4 雷敎, the author of the *Pao chi lun*, 炮炙論, who lived A.D 420—477 Cf BRETSCHNEIDER, 11, p 41, nr 6 "A treatise in 3 books, explaining the medical virtues of 300 drugs and giving directions for the preparation of medicines" Quoted in the *Pen-ts'ao kang-muh*, 11

5 吳普, the author of the *Wu shi Pen-ts'ao*, 吳氏本草, written in the first half of the third century Quoted ibidem Cf BRETSCHNEIDER, 11, p 40, nr 5

6 蘇恭, who with 23 other scholars in the middle of the seventh century A D revised and completed the *T'ang Pen-ts'ao*, 唐本草, thence called the *T'ang Sin Pen-ts'ao*, 唐新本草, "New Pen-ts'ao of the T'ang" Cf BRETSCHNEIDER, 11, p 44, nr 11 Quoted in the *Pen-ts'ao kang-muh*, ibidem

heart, kidneys and spleen) and to the so-called mansions (gall, small and great intestines, bladder and stomach), as we learn from the list given by DE GROOT, *Rel. Syst.* Vol. IV, p. 26. For this reason probably the use of the dragon's bones as medicines was different according to their colours, with regard to the colour of the organ to be cured.

The preparation of the bones is described as follows by LEI HIAO. "For using dragon's bones first cook odorous plants; bathe the bones twice in hot water, pound them to powder and put this in bags of gaze. Take a couple of young swallows and, after having taken out their intestines and stomach, put the bags in the swallows and hang them over a well. After one night take the bags out of the swallows, rub the powder and mix it into medicines for strengthening the kidneys. The efficacy of such a medicine is as it were divine!" [1] In LI SHI-CHEN'S [2] time, however, they were only roasted on the fire till they were red and then rubbed to powder, or fresh bones were used. In the same passage he refers to an author of the Sung dynasty [3], who says that the bones are to be soaked in spirits for one night, then dried on the fire and rubbed to powder. Further, according to CHEN K'UEN [4], some are a little poisonous, and (in preparing and using them) fishes and iron utensils are to be avoided (dragons dislike iron, cf. above, this chapter, § 3, pp 67 sqq.).

As to the illnesses cured by means of dragon's bones, their number is large. Dysentery, biliary calculi, fever and convulsions of babies, boils in the bowels and internal ulcers, paralysis of the legs, illnesses of pregnant women, remittent fever and abscesses are all driven away by this powerful medicine. Bleeding of the nose or ears is stopped by blowing powder of dragon's bones into

---

1 *Pen-ts'ao kang muh*, 11, p 2a· 雷斆曰。凡用龍骨先煎香草、湯浴兩度、搗粉、絹袋盛之、用燕子一隻、去腸肚、安袋於內、懸井面上、一宿取出、研粉、入補腎藥中、其效如神.

2 Ibidem 近世方法但煅赤爲粉。亦有生用者。

3 CH'EN YUEN-TSING, 陳元靚, author of the *Shi lin kwang ki*, 事林廣記 (cf DE GROOT, *Rel Syst*, Vol II, p. 713, BRETSCHNEIDER, 11, p 186, nr 749) Quoted in the *Pen-ts'ao kang-muh*, ibidem

4 甄權, author of the *Yoh sing pen-ts'ao*, 藥性本草, in the first half of the seventh century A D (cf BRETSCHNEIDER, 11, p 44, nr 10). Quoted ibidem,

them, and, when dried on the fire and ground, they are also
used against navel abscesses of babies In short, the strong *Yang*
power of these bones makes, of course, the *Yin* demons which
have comfortably established themselves in the human body take
to their heels as soon as medicine, prepared from the bones, arrives [1].

Apart from the medical works we may mention the following
passages. The *Shuh i ki* [2] (6th century) says: "According to
tradition a dragon, when a thousand years old, casts off his
bones in the mountains. Now there are dragon mounds, out of
which dragon brains are taken". We read in the same work:
"In P'u-ning district (Kwantung province) there is a 'Dragon-
burial islet'. The elders say: 'The dragons have cast off their
bones on this islet. There are at the present day still many
dragon's bones' Thus on mountains and hills, on hillocks and
cavernous cliffs, on all places where the dragons raise clouds and
rain, dragon's bones are found. There are many of them in the
ground, sometimes deep, sometimes near to the surface; teeth,
bones, spines and feet, all are there. The big ones are some tens
of *chang* or fully ten *chang* long, the small ones only one or
two *ch'ih* or three or four *ts'un* The bodies are all complete.
As they had been gathered, I saw them". [3]

At the time of the T'ang dynasty the tribute of the land of
Ho-tung principality, Ho-chung department, in Ho-tung province,
partly consisted of dragon's bones. [4]

---

[1] T S, Sect 禽蟲, Ch 127, 龍部彙考, p. 9, *Pen-ts'ao kang-muh*, 11,
p. 2 sq.

[2] Ch. II, p. 5*a* 傳龍千年則於山中蛻骨。今有龍岡、
岡中出龍腦。

[3] 普甯縣有龍葬洲。父老云。龍蛻骨於此洲。今
猶多龍骨。按山阜岡岫龍與雲雨者皆有龍骨、或
深或淺、多在土中、齒骨脊足宛然皆具。大者數
十丈、或盈十丈、小者纔一二尺、或三四寸。體皆
具焉。嘗因采取見之。We read the same in the *Mao fing k'oh hwa*,
茅亭客話, written by HWANG HIU-FUH, 黃休復, in the Sung dynasty,
Ch. IX (quoted T S, l.1, Ch. 130, 紀事三, p 7*b*), where it is said by a man,
who sold dragon's bones, teeth, horns, heads and spines on the market "Some of
them", said he, "are five-coloured, others white like floss silk, some have withered or
rotten in the long course of the years".

[4] *New Books of the T'ang dynasty*, 新唐, Ch. XXXIX, nr 29, 地理志,
河東道, 河中府, 河東郡, p. 1*a* (anno 760 A D)

Li Chao [1] says in his *Kwoh shi pu* ("Commentary to the Dynastic Histories") [2]: " When the spring water comes and the fishes ascend the Dragon-gate (comp above, this chapter, § 12, p 86), there are a great many of cast-off bones, which are gathered by the people to make medicines from them. Some of them are five-coloured. The Dragon-gate is Tsin land, which agrees with the statement of the *Pen king* (comp above). Are the dragon's bones perhaps the bones of these fishes?" Su Sung [3], who quotes this passage, instructs us that in his time these bones were found in many districts of Ho tung province.

Another work of the eleventh century [4] tells us about a man who in a dark night saw a branch of a tree which spread a brilliant light. He broke it off and used it as a torch. The next morning he discovered that the light was due to a cast-off skin of a dragon, in size resembling a new shell of a cicada, and consisting of head, horns, claws, and tail. Inside it was hollow, yet it was solid, and when he knocked against it, it produced a sound like precious stones The brightness of its light blinded the eye, and in the dark it was a shining torch. He preserved it as a treasure in his house.

The strong light spread by the cast-off dragon's skins is, of course, due to the strong Yang power of the dragons

In 1553, when, the water being very low, a dragon's skeleton was discovered on a small island in a river, the people were all very anxious to get one of the bones. [5]

Also dragon's *teeth* were considered to be a good medicine. The *Pen-ts'ao kang-muh* [6] quotes Su Chi-ts'ai [7], who said: "As a rule

---

1 李肇。

2 國史補, written in the beginning of the ninth century T. S., 1 l., Ch 127, p. 8*b*

3 蘇頌, author of the *Sin i siang fah yao*, 新儀象法要, an astronomic work written at the close of the eleventh century (cf Wylie, p 107), quoted ibidem

4 The *Ch'un chu ki wen*, 春渚紀聞, ten chapters of miscellanies written by Ho Wei, 何薳, who lived in the eleventh century (cf. De Groot, *Rel Syst*, Vol IV, p 110), Ch II, p 11.

5 *Shang han lun t'iao pien*, 傷寒論條辨, written in 1589 by Fang Yiu-chih, 方有執, Sect 本草.

6 L l, p. 4*a*

7 徐之才, a famous physician who lived in the second half of the sixth century, author of the *Lei kung yoh tui*, 雷公藥對 (cf Bretschneider, 1 l, p.

they are good when getting (i. e. being mixed with) *jen-ts'an*
(ginseng) and cow-yellow (cow-bezoar), but they fear (i. e. it is
not good to mix or prepare them with) gypsum and iron utensils".
The illnesses which are cured by means of dragon's teeth are
enumerated as follows in the *Shen Nung Pen-ts'ao king* [1]: "Beings
that kill the vital spirit; when adults have spasms or epileptic
fits, convulsions or madness, when they run as madmen and their
breath is tied under their heart, so that they cannot breathe
(i. e. when they are asthmatic); further, the five (kinds of) fits
and the twelve (kinds of) convulsions of babies".

According to CHEN K'ÜEN [2] they "quiet the heart and calm
down the souls (the *hwun* and the *p'oh*)". CHEN JEH-HWA [3] declares
them to cure head-ache, melancholy, hot fever, madness, and
(possession of) *kwei* and *mei* (demons). They also cure liver diseases,
for "as the *hwun* which is stored away in the liver can change
itself, those whose *hwun* is erring about and is not fixed are
cured by means of dragon's teeth". [4] LI SHI-CHEN gives the following explanation: "Because the dragon is the god of the Eastern
quarter, his bones, horns and teeth all conquer liver diseases" [5].

Dragon's *horns* are used for curing about the same illnesses as
those mentioned with regard to the dragon's teeth. [6]

Dragon's *brains* were believed to stop dysentery [7], and the *liver*
of this divine animal, sometimes of a *living* one, was prescribed
by some physicians in difficult cases. Sometimes a royal patient
for this reason even ordered to kill the dragon of a pond, which
used to hear the people's prayers for rain in times of drought

---

1 Quoted ibidem. 殺精物、大人驚癇、諸痙癲疾、狂走
心下結氣不能喘息、小兒五驚十二癇。

2 Quoted ibidem 鎮心,安魂魄. About the *hwun* and the *p'oh* see DE
GROOT, *Rel Syst.*, Vol. IV, Part I, Ch. I, pp. 4 sqq, p. 23.

3 陳日華, who lived in the Sung dynasty and wrote the *King yen fang*,
經驗方 (BRETSCHNEIDER, l l., p 161, n 338) Quoted ibidem 治煩悶熱
狂鬼魅。

4 HÜ SHUH-WEI, 許叔微, who lived in the time of the Sung dynasty and
wrote the *Pen shi fang*, 本事方 (BRETSCHNEIDER, l l, p. 179, nr 588) Quoted
ibidem 肝藏魂能變化、故魂遊不定者治之以龍齒。

5 L l 龍者東方之神、故其骨與角齒皆主肝病。

6 *Pen-ts'ao kang-muh*, l.1, p. 4b.

7 T'AO HUNG-KING, quoted ibidem The "brain of a dragon a thousand years old" is
mentioned among a hundred medicines in the *Shuh i ki*, Ch II, p 5a.

and guarded the castle of the prince. That very day a terrible thunderstorm broke forth and the dragon flew away; the castle, no longer guarded by its tutelary god, soon fell a prey to the enemy who stormed and destroyed it like in former days[1]. Another time we read about a dragon which by the mighty charm of a Taoist doctor was forced to descend into a jar of water. After having cut out the liver of the living animal he gave it a patient, the wife of a prefect, to eat, and she recovered[2].

Placentae and *foetus* of dragons, found in Pa and Shuh (Sz'-ch'wen province), were said to cure diseases of the blood and those of women after delivery.[3]

§ 18. Dragon's blood, fat and saliva.

The *Yiu-yang tsah tsu*[4] says. "When dragon's *blood* enters the earth it becomes *hu-poh*, amber.

As to dragon's *fat*, we learn from the *Shih i ki*[5] that a tower, lighted by means of it, spread such a brilliant light that it was seen at a distance of a hundred miles. This light was said by some people to be a lucky omen and was worshipped by them from far. The wick was made of "fire-washed cloth" (asbestos cloth which can be cleaned by fire), twined into a rope.

With regard to the dragon's *saliva* we read the following in the *Pen-ts'ao kang-muh*[6]. "WANG KI[7] says: 'From the saliva spit out by dragons perfume is made'. LI SHI-CHEN (the author himself) says: 'Dragon's saliva is seldom used as a medicine; it is only mixed into perfumes. It is said that it can bind camphor

---

1 *Mih k'oh hwui si*, 墨客揮犀, written in the eleventh century by P'ENG SHING, 彭乘 (cf DE GROOT, *Rel Syst*, Vol IV, p. 864, note 2) Quoted T S, Sect 禽蟲, Ch. 130, 紀事三, p 3b

2 *Chao ye ts'ien tsai*, 朝野僉載, "Record of all matters relating to the Court and abroad", ascribed to CHANG SHOH, 張鷟, who probably lived in the first half of the 8th century. T.S., Sect. 神異, Ch. 306, quoted by DE GROOT, *Rel. Syst.*, Vol. VI, p 1031, note 1.

3 *Pen-ts'ao kang-muh*, 11, p. 5a

4 酉陽雜俎 (ninth century), Ch XI (廣知), p. 6b. 龍血入地為琥珀.

5 拾遺記 (fourth century), Ch X, Sect 方丈山, p 3b

6 L l, p 5a.

7 汪機, a celebrated physician of the 16th century, author of the *Pen-ts'ao hui-*

and musk for several tens of years without evaporating.
Further, it is said that, when it is burned, a blue smoke floats
through the air. .... Last spring the saliva spit out by
a herd of dragons appeared floating (on the sea). The abori-
gines gathered, obtained and sold it, each time for two thousand
copper coins."

The *Yiu hwan ki wen* [1] instructs us that the most precious of
all perfumes is dragon's spittle, and that the inhabitants of Ta-
shih land used to watch the vapours arising for half a year or
even two or three years from the same spot of the sea. When they
vanished, this was a token that the dragons which had been
sleeping there all the time had gone away. Then the people went
to the spot in order to gather the saliva of those dragons According to another explanation, found in the same passage, the
dragons lived in whirlpools in the open sea. The spittle which
they emitted was hardened by the sun, and these hard pieces
were blown ashore by the wind. When fresh it was white, gradually
it became purple, and finally black (amber, generally considered
to be the excrements of cachalots, i e sperm whales, is yellowish)

This perfume reminds us of the "Dragon-fight perfume",
mentioned in the *Tsu t'ing shi yuen* [2], which is said to be produced by fighting dragons. One pill of it makes a large cloud of
perfume arise.

According to the *Lang huen ki* [3] the Emperor Shun used the
saliva of a purple dragon as ink in writing the names of holy
ministers on tablets of jade, those of sages on tablets of gold
and those of talentful ministers on tablets of quartz-crystal; those
of ordinary ministers were written with ordinary ink on tablets
of wood. In order to obtain the saliva he ordered Yu Hu to rear
a purple dragon. The latter daily made the animal drop saliva
by holding a swallow, which he had cooked (the favourite food
of the dragons, cf. above, p. 68) before it without immediately
giving it to eat. This made the dragon's mouth water, and
a large quantity of saliva dripped down. Then Yü Hu filled
a vessel with it, whereupon he gave the swallow to the

---

1 遊宦紀聞, written by CHANG SHI-NAN, 張世南, in the Sung dynasty;
Ch VII, quoted T S, l l., Ch 130, 雜錄, p. 5a

2 祖庭事苑, quoted in the Japanese Buddhist dictionary entitled *Bukkyō
iroha jiten*, Vol II, p 63, s v *Ryū-tō*, 龍鬭.

3 瑯嬛記, written by I SHI-CHEN, 伊世珍, in the Yuen dynasty, T S,
l.l, Ch 131, p 1b

dragon. In this way he daily got one *koh* (a gill) of saliva, which was mixed with *hwui shih* (繪實, the "Herb of the *Sien*", 仙草). In the time of Yao this herb grew before the audience hall. It wore flowers in all four seasons. If one rubbed its fruit and mixed it with a purple dragon's saliva, a liquid of a genuine red colour was produced, which penetrated into gold and jade and thus could be used in writing names on the tablets mentioned above.

CHAPTER IV.

ORNAMENTS.

§ 1. Symbols of Imperial dignity and fertilizing rain, represented on garments, honorary gates, coffins etc

As we have seen above (Ch. I, § 2, p. 39), the *Shu king* states that the dragon belonged to the emblematic figures depicted on the upper sacrificial garment of the Emperor.

It is not to be wondered at that this divine giver of rain, at the same time symbol of a good sovereign and his blissful government, should be represented among the Imperial ornaments.

The so-called *shah* (翣) are described by DE GROOT[1] as square boards of wood covered with white linen, with handles five feet long, which in ancient times were carried behind the funeral cars of grandees, and were planted inside the pit when the coffin had been lowered into the grave These *shah* displayed the rank of the grandees by emblematical figures. "The Kien-lung edition of the Three Rituals suggests that the two *shah* which the Son of Heaven had in addition to the six of a feudal prince, were painted with a *dragon*, the characteristic symbol of the imperial dignity"[2].

Four pedestals of the quinquepartite decorative gate at the Imperial Ming tombs "display, on every face, an Imperial Dragon, soaring in the midst of the usual emblems accompanying this divine distributor of fructifying rains, namely clouds and stars"[3]. "The shaft of each (of the four columns in the prolongation of the diagonals of the tablet-house in the avenue leading to the Ming Tombs) is sculptured with a gigantic dragon, coiling itself around it as if climbing the skies"[4].

With regard to honorary gates DE GROOT remarks that the tablet placed perpendicularly underneath their highest roof,

1 *Rel Syst*, Vol. I, pp 185 sqq
2 P. 187, fig 20, a picture of a *shah* adorned with a dragon
3 DE GROOT, l. l, Vol III, p. 1193, plate XL
4 P. 1194.

displaying the characters 御旨, "By Imperial Decree", or 聖旨, "By decree of the Holy One", is supported by a couple of dragons, "the symbols of the blessed reign of the Son of Heaven" [1].

The azure dragon, symbol of the eastern quarter in ancient China, was to be seen on the left side of the coffins of grandees in the Han dynasty, while on the right side a white tiger represented the West. We learn this from a passage of the Books of the Early Han dynasty [2], quoted by De Groot [3], who also refers to the Books of the Later Han Dynasty [4], which state that the imperial coffins "used to be decorated and painted with a sun, a moon, a bird, a tortoise, a dragon and a tiger". This was also the case in T'ang dynasty [5]. At the present day the use of ornamental dragons is not limited to the funerals of Emperors or grandees, but also common people are allowed to enjoy their blessing power. "On the front curtain [6] (of the catafalque) are a couple of dragons rising out of the waves, surrounded by clouds and with a sun between them, the back displays a tiger or unicorn, the top exhibits dragons, sundry ornamental flowers, and figures representing clouds. Thanks to these clouds and to the dragons which produce the same in their quality of watergods, the greatest blessings which the Universe can bestow, viz. fertilizing rains causing crops to grow and so giving food, raiment and wealth, surround the dead" [7]. The grave-clothes for women in Amoy, called "dragon-petticoat" [8], "dragon-mantle" [9], and "clouds-mantilla." [10], are adorned with embroidered dragons amidst clouds, bats, phenixes, stags, tortoises and cranes, emblems of fertilizing rains, old age, joy, pecuniary profits and happiness [11].

The Li ki [12] says that at the great sacrifice to the Duke of Chao in the last month of summer "the ruler (of Lu), in his *dragon-figured robe* and cap with pendants, stood at the eastern

---

1 *Rel. Syst*, Vol III, p 1201   2 Ch 93
3 Vol I, pp 315 sq, cf Vol II, p 699   4 Ch 16 p 2.
5 T S, Sect 禮儀, Ch 56, De Groot, l l, Vol, I, p 317.

6 According to the Li ki (Ch. 58, p 39, quoted by De Groot Vol I, p 182) in ancient times on the side curtains of the catafalque of a Ruler dragons were depicted Cf De Groot, l l, p 183, Fig 18.

7 De Groot, Vol I, p 481

8 蟒裙, bóng-kûn   9 蟒襖, bóng-o

10 霞帔, hê-poe

11 De Groot, Vol I, p 53, Fig III, IV and V.

12 Couvreur, Li ki, Vol I, p 732, Chap XII, Ming T'ang wei, 明堂位, § 11, 君卷冕立于阼阶 Legge Sacred Book Vol XXVIII p 32

steps". A little further [1] we read: "For ladles they (the rulers of Lu) had that of Hia, with the handle ending in a *dragon's* head" and "they had the music-stand of Hia, with its face-board and posts, on which *dragons* were carved" [2]; "they had knee-covers of Cheu, with dragons" [3].

§ 2 Nine different kinds of dragons, used as ornaments.

A well-known work of the end of the sixteenth century, the *Wuh tsah tsu* [4], informs us about the nine different young of the dragon, whose shapes are used as ornaments according to their nature The *p'u-lao* [5], dragons which like to cry, are represented on the tops of bells, serving as handles The *szĕ-niu* [6], which like music, are used to adorn musical instruments. The *ch'i-wen* [7], which like swallowing, are placed on both ends of the ridgepoles of roofs (to swallow all evil influences). The *chao-fung* [8], lion-like beasts which like precipices, are placed on the four corners of roofs. The *ai-hwa* [9], which like to kill, serve as ornaments of sword-grips The *hi-pi* [10], which have the shape of the *ch'i-lung* [11], and are fond of literature, are represented on the sides of grave-monuments. The *p'i-han* [12], which like litigation, are placed over prison gates (in order to keep guard) The *swan-i* [13], which like to sit down, are represented upon the bases of Buddhist idols (under the Buddhas' or Bodhisattvas' feet). The *pa-hia* [14], finally, big tortoises which like to carry heavy objects, are placed under grave-monuments. [15]

---

1 COUVREUR, 1 1, p 736, § 20 其勺、夏后氏以龍勺。LEGGE, l, 1, p 35

2 COUVREUR, 1 1, p 739, § 26 夏后氏之龍簨虡。LEGGE, l 1, p 37

3 COUVREUR, 1 1., p 740, § 29 周龍軬。LEGGE, 1 1., p 38

4 五雜俎, written about 1592 by SIĔ CHAO-CHI 謝肇淛。

5 蒲牢.　　6 囚牛.　　7 蚩吻.

8 嘲風.　　9 睚眦　　10 屓屭

11 螭龍, represented in the T S, Sect 禽蟲, Ch 127, and in the *Wakan sansai zue*, Ch XLV, p. 674 Cf DE GROOT, *Rel. Syst*, Vol III, p 1142, Fig 37, a *ch'i* (or *li*) 螭, carved in the border crowning a sepulchral tablet of stone It is mentioned already in the third century before our era (in the *Lu-shi ch'un-ts'iu*), and described in the *Shwoh wen* as a yellow animal, resembling a dragon, or as a hornless dragon.

12 狴犴.　　　13 狻猊.　　　14 霸下.

15 The same facts are to be found in the *Wakan sansai zue*, Ch. XLV, p 674, and are further explained in the dictionary entitled *Ching tsĕ t'ung* (正字通,

Further, the same author enumerates nine other kinds of dragons — there are so many, says he, because the dragon's nature is very lewd, so that he copulates with all animals [1] —, which are represented as ornaments of different objects or buildings according to their liking prisons, water, the rank smell of newly caught fish or newly killed meat, wind and rain, ornaments, smoke, shutting the mouth (used for adorning key-holes), standing on steep places (placed on roofs), and fire.

§ 3 Ornaments used by Wu-ist priests and mediums.

DE GROOT's description of the religious dress of the Wu-ist priests (the *sai kong* [2] of Amoy) contains the following passage. "On the left and right (of the pile of mountains, representing the continent of the world, embroidered on the back of the principal vestment of the *sai kong*), a large dragon rises high above the billows, in an attitude denoting a soaring motion towards the continent; these animals symbolize the *fertilizing rains*, and are therefore surrounded by gold-thread figures which represent *clouds*, and some which resemble *spirals* and denote *rolling thunder* ... ... There is also a broad border of blue silk around the neck, stitched with *two ascending dragons which are belching out a ball, probably representing thunder*" [3].

A similar, secondary vestment of a *sai kong* is adorned with "an oblong piece of blue silk, embroidered with two dragons which belch out a ball, as also with a continent and waves over which they soar" [4].

"It is then obvious, that the sacerdotal dress of the *sai kong* is a *magical dress*. The priest, who wears it, is invested by it with the power of the Order of the World itself, and thus enabled to restore that Order whenever, by means of sacrifices and magical ceremonies, he is averting unseasonable and calamitous events, such as *drought*, untimely and superabundant rainfall, or eclipses. Besides, since the Tao is the mightiest power against the demon

---

亥集下卷, p. 60, written in the T'sing dynasty by YAO WEN-YING, 廖文英)
In many respects the Japanese have followed these Chinese rules of ornamentation

1 According to the same work (Ch IX), a cross-breed of a dragon ad a cow is a *lin* (麟, a female unicorn), that of a dragon ad a pig is an elephant, and if a dragon copulates with a horse, a dragon-horse (cf above, pp 56 sqq) is born

2 師公.   3 *Rel Syst* VI, p 1265, Plate XVIII.

world, the vestment endows the wearer with irresistable exor-
cising power" [1].

On the so-called "embroidered belly", [2] a piece of red cloth
or silk, suspended on the stomach of the *ki tông* [3], the "divining
youths" used as mediums, possessed by gods, "two dragons are
stitched with gold thread; for dragons are emblems of imperial
dignity, and consequently also those of the Emperor of Heaven,
in whose employ the indwelling spirit of the *ki tông* is, as well
as all other *shen*" [4].

"The *ki* (乩, an instrument for spirit-writing) of a fashionable
club is as a rule clad in red silk or broadcloth, on which dragons
are stitched with gold thread; for it is clear that, having to
harbour so often the spirit of a god, the instrument deserves,
just as well as his image, to wear the dress of divinity, which
is a mantle embroidered with the said imperial animals. Of such
a *ki* of higher order, the end below the vertex is also nicely
carved and gilded, representing the head and scaly neck of a
dragon or snake" [5].

"If the litter (of a *ki tông* deity, whose image is carried about
in it) is fitted out completely, there are inserted behind the back
five thin staffs, to each of which a triangular flag is fastened,
embroidered with the emblem of imperal dignity, viz. *an ascending
dragon which vomits a ball*" [6].

§ 4. The dragons and the ball.

As to the ball, "belched out by the two dragons", this reminds
us at once of the Dragon festival on the 15th day of the first
month; the ball carried in front of the dragon on that day might
be also explained in the same way, i e. as thunder belched out
by the dragon, and not as the sun, pursued by him. This fact
was orally pointed out to me by Prof. DE GROOT himself [7] The
ball between the two dragons is often delineated as a spiral, and
in an ancient charm represented in KOH HUNG's *Pao P'oh-tszĕ*
(17th section) "a spiral denotes the rolling of thunder from
which issues a flash of lightning" [8]. "In the sign expressing
lightning, the projecting stroke signifies the flash; therefore its
effect as a charm is indefinitely increased by lengthening that

1 L.1, p 1266
2 繡肚.   3 乩童.
4 DE GROOT, l.1, Vol VI, p 1275
5 L 1, p. 1297   6 L 1, p 1316
7 See above, this Book, Ch IV, § 10   8 *Rel Syst*, VI, p 1036, Fig 3

stroke so that it looks like a spiral which at the same time represents the rolling of thunder". [1]

This theory agrees with HIRTH's explanation of the "Triquetrum" in connection with the dragon in Chinese and Japanese ornaments [2]. HIRTH identifies the "Triquetrum", i. e. the well-known three-comma-shaped figure, the Japanese *mitsu-tomoe*, with the ancient spiral, representing thunder, and gives a Japanese picture of the thundergod with his drums, all emitting flames and adorned with the *mitsu-timoe* But this ornament is not at all limited to the drums of the thundergod [3]; it is, on the contrary, very frequently seen even on the drums beaten by children at the Nichiren festival in October. At many Japanese temple festivals which have no connection whatever with the thundergod or the dragon, the same ornament is seen on lanterns and flags. HIRTH explains its frequent appearance on tiles as a means of warding off lightning, based on the rule "similia similibus". This is contrary to the use of "sympathetic magic", very common in the Far East [4], according to which the symbol of thunder would not avert thunder but attract it, thus destroying and driving away evil influences. Apparently both ideas are found side by side, for images of dragons were used to attract them, thus causing rain and thunder, but at the same time the thundergod of Mount Atago (with whom Shōgun Jizō was identified as Atago Gongen) was worshipped as the principal protector against fire. But the symbol of thunder on the tiles may also serve to drive away all evil influences from the buildings, like the dragons represented on both ends of the ridgepoles, mentioned above (p. 101).

HIRTH gives a picture from a Japanese work on ornaments, entitled *Nairyu kira ga ōsa*, but the ancient Chinese "Triquetrums", nrs 23, 25, 26, 27, are different from the Japanese forms, as the former have a circle in the centre and five or eight comma's, all placed separately, and turned towards the centre (except in nr 23, where they issue from the centre), while the latter consist of two or three black comma's interlaced with white and often united in the centre. Yet the turning motion is evident in all,

---

1 L l, p 1040

2 *Chinesische Studien*, Vol I, pp 231 sqq. (Verhandlungen der Berl Anthr Ges, Sitzung vom 22 Juni 1889), "Ueber den Maander und das Triquetrum in der chinesischen und japanischen Ornamentik"

3 It is not represented on his drums in the picture of the *Wakan sansai zue*, Ch. III, p 44

4 Cf. below, Book I, Ch V, § 3, and Book II, Ch. III, § 10,

and the more I reflect upon it, the more I feel inclined to accept
HIRTH's explanation of the *mitsu-tomoe* and *futatsu-tomoe* (two
comma's) as the rolling thunder. Its frequent appearance on
lanterns, flags, tiles, and, in olden times, on the *tomo* or
leather shield worn around the wrist by archers, and its frequent
use as a badge of arms may be explained by its magic power,
averting evil and, in some cases, bringing fertilizing rains. I
formerly believed it to be the Yang and Yin symbol, the third
comma being the *T'ai. Kih* (太極, the primordium, from which
Yang and Yin emanate). This primordium, which in China is represented by the whole figure, should by mistake have been represented
by the Japanese by means of a third comma [1]. Yang and Yin, Light
and Darkness, however, are represented by one white and one black
figure, somewhat resembling comma's and forming together a circle.
It would be very strange if the ancient Japanese, who closely
imitated the Chinese models, had altered this symbol in such a
way that its fundamental meaning got lost; for replacing the
two white and black comma's with two or three black ones
would have had this effect. Moreover, in Japanese divination, based
on the Chinese diagrams, the *original* Chinese symbol of Yang
and Yin is always used and placed in the midst of the eight
diagrams. Thus the *futatsu-tomoe* and *mitsu-tomoe* are apparently
quite different from this symbol, and HIRTH rightly identifies
them with the ancient Chinese spiral, representing thunder.
Moreover, I found the same explanation of the *tomoe* in the
Japanese work *Shojiri* [2], which gives a picture of two kinds of
spirals, ancient symbols of thunder and clouds. Finally, on Japanese
prints the dragon ist often accompanied by a huge spiral, representing the thunderstorm caused by him.

Is the ball, so often seen in connection with the dragon, and
often represented as a spiral emitting flames or as a ball upon
which something like a spiral is delineated, identical with the
spiral, denoting thunder? HIRTH and DE GROOT suppose so. The
latter, considering the dragon's nature of a thundergod, arrived at
the conclusion that the dragon must *belch out* the ball instead of
swallowing it, for why should he, who causes thunder, persecute
it and try to swallow it? HIRTH [3] speaks about a dragon which
with his claw is putting the thunder into rotation. This is,

---

1 Cf. FLORENZ, Jap Mythologie, p. 78, note 7

2 鹽尻, written by AMANO NOBUKAGE, 天野信景. who lived 1660—1733,
new edition (1907), Ch. XXXI, p 497.

3 L l p. 233,

however, not the ordinary way of representing the dragon with
the ball or spiral. *Two dragons* flying with open mouths towards
a ball or spiral between them — this is the most frequent and
apparently the most ancient representation. The artists, especially
those of later times, often varied this subject, so that we sometimes see more than two dragons rushing upon one ball, or one
dragon trying to swallow it or having caught it with his claw;
sometimes there are even two balls and only one dragon.
But nowhere they make the impression of *belching out* the ball;
their whole attitude, on the contrary, indicates their eagerness
in trying to catch and swallow it Moreover, how can *two* dragons
belch out *one* ball? And the dragon of the festival constantly
follows the ball with his mouth, apparently in order to swallow
it. Yet I was inclined to accept DE GROOT's theory, although it
was very difficult to make it agree with the eager attitude of
the dragons, when Mr KRAMP had the kindness of pointing out
to me his own opinion on this subject. After having drawn my
attention to HIRTH's paper, mentioned above, he showed me a
little Chinese picture, represented in BLACKER's *Chats on Oriental
China* (London, 1908), on p. 54, where we see two dragons,
rushing upon a fiery, spiral-shaped ball, under which the following
characters are to be read· 兩竜朝月, "A couple of dragons
facing the moon". The moon! These were the first written
characters I ever saw with regard to this interesting subject,
for the sea of texts concerning the dragon, ancient and modern,
did not give a single word. Leaving aside the character 朝,
which is apparently not well chosen to denote the aggressive
attitude of the dragons, we have only to consider the character 月

Would it be absurd to represent dragons trying to swallow
the moon? Not in the least, for the dragons are, as we have
seen above, the clouds, and the ancient Chinese may easily have
fancied that these dragons, quickly approaching and covering the
moon, actually devoured it. When they did so, the fertilizing
rain soon trickled down upon the thirsty earth, a great blessing
to mankind For this reason they might be represented so often
trying to swallow the moon, namely as a symbol of fertilizing
rains. Owing to the close connection between the moon and the
water, the moon, having been swallowed by the dragon, might
have been believed to strengthen the rain-giving power of the
latter. The dragon of the festival, persecuting the moon, might
be carried along the streets in order to cause rain by sympathetic magic.

The Chinese themselves, however, mostly call the ball a *"precious pearl"*. We find it explained in this way in BOERSCHMANN's highly interesting work on *P'u t'o shan* [1], where a gilt ball of glass is said to hang from the centre of the roof of the Great Hall of the Buddhist temple Fa(h)-yu-sze (法雨寺, "Temple of the Rain of the Law"), while eight dragons, carved around the surrounding "hanging pillars", eagerly stretch their claws towards the "pearl of perfection" [2] This term sounds Buddhistic and is appropriate to the Buddhist surroundings, as well as the number eight of the dragons, which is, indeed, fixed by the form of the roof, but is also found on the staircase of the Yü(h)-fo(h)-tien (p. 57). Dragons trying to seize a fiery "pearl" which is hanging in a gate (the Dragon-gate, cf. above, p 86) are represented twice in the same temple (pp. 46, 87). Leaving aside BOERSCHMANN's fantastic ideas about the "dragons playing with the pearl" (p 43), we may be sure that the Chinese Buddhists, identifying the dragon with the Nāga, also identified the ball with their cintāmani or precious pearl which grants all desires. The question rises. "Was the ball originally also a pearl, not of Buddhism but of Taoism?"

Mr KRAMP pointed out to me, that the character 玥, combined from *jewel* and *moon*, though not found in the dictionaries of WELLS WILLIAMS, GILES or COUVREUR, is given in the K'ang-hi dictionary. I found it also in the Japanese lexicon entitled *Kanwa daijiten* (p. 852), explained as a "divine pearl" (神珠), and with the Japanese-Chinese pronunciations *getsu, gwachi.* This is evidently based upon the K'ang-hi dictionary, where we read s v.

魚厥切、音月、神珠也. The same pronunciation and meaning are given in the lexicon entitled *Tszě-wei*. This sacred *yueh* pearl probably dues its holiness to its connection with the moon, for the second part of the character 玥 may not only form the phonetic element, but it may indicate that this is "the pearl of the moon", as there is also a "pearl of the bright moon" (明月之珠, COUVREUR's Dictionary s. v. 月). It is possible that in the little sentence mentioned above: 兩竜朝月, the last character has taken the place of the fuller form 玥, in which case the two dragons would be said to "face the moon-pearl".

---

1 ERNST BOERSCHMANN, *Die Baukunst und religiöse Kultur der Chinesen* Band I *P'u t'o shan*

2 Dragons and pearl pp 18, 35, 57, 59, 77, 124 One dragon with the pearl in his claw, other dragons flying from both sides to the spot, p 35

Difficult points in the moon theory are the *red* colour of the ball and its *spiral*-shaped form. If it is a *pearl*, however, representing the moon or at least closely connected with it, the red colour may mean the lustre of this brilliant, fiery gem, which in the temple on Pᶜu tᶜo shan, mentioned above, is represented by a glass ball covered with gold. The red ball, carried by the Dragon girl in the Hall of the Law of the same temple (BOERSCH-MANN, l. l., p. 122, nr 7) is evidently also a pearl. The spiral is much used in delineating the sacred pearls of Buddhism, so that it might have served also to design those of Taoism, although I must acknowledge that the spiral of the Buddhist pearl goes upwards, while the spiral of the dragon is flat.

We know the close connection of dragons and pearls in both religions. This connection is quite logical, for the masters of the sea are, of course, the possessors and guardians of its treasures. When the clouds approached and covered the moon, the ancient Chinese may have thought that the dragons had seized and swallowed this pearl, more brilliant than all their pearls of the sea.

These are, however, all mere suppositions The only facts we know are: the eager attitude of the dragons, ready to grasp and swallow the ball; the ideas of the Chinese themselves as to the ball being the moon or a pearl; the existence of a kind of sacred "moon-pearl"; the red colour of the ball, its emitting flames and its spiral-like form. As the three last facts are in favour of the thunder theory, I should be inclined to prefer the latter. Yet I am convinced that the dragons do not *belch out* the thunder. If their trying to *grasp* or *swallow* the thunder could be explained, I should immediately accept the theory concerning the thunder-spiral, especially on account of the flames it emits. But I do not see the reason why the god of thunder should persecute thunder itself. Therefore, after having given the above facts that the reader may take them into consideration, I feel obliged to say: "non liquet".

CHAPTER V.

CAUSING RAIN, THUNDER AND STORM.

§ 1. The gods of thunder, clouds and rain

The Classics have taught us that the dragon is thunder, and at the same time that he is a water animal, akin to the snake, sleeping in pools during winter and arising in spring. When autumn comes with its dry weather, the dragon descends and dives into the water to remain there till spring arrives again. When in the first month of the year now and then thunderclaps were heard and a little rain came down, the ancients were convinced that this was the work of the dragons, who in the form of dark clouds appeared in the sky. If our interpretation of the words of the *Yih king* is right, the "advantage" given by them when they were seen soaring over the rice fields, and the "blessing power then, spread by them everywhere", was nothing but the fertilizing rain they poured down upon the earth. In later texts, at any rate, we have seen them clearly qualified as the gods of clouds and rain, whose breath turned into clouds [1] and whose power manifested itself in heavy rains. Koh Hung [2], e.g., in the *Pao P'oh tsze* states the following. "If on a *yin* day there is in the mountains a being who calls himself a "forester", it is a tiger, ... and if on a *ch'en* day a being calls himself "*Rain-master*", it is a dragon..... If one only knows these their animal names, they cannot do him any harm". The tiger, indeed, is the god of the mountains and woods, as the dragon is the divinity of water and rain.

---

1 Cf the *'Rh ya yih*, quoting WANG FU, above, Book I, Ch III, § 2, p 66, HAN YU 韓愈, (A D 768—824), quoted T S, Sect 禽蟲, Ch 127, p 8b, says the same 龍噓氣成雲

2 Ch IV, Sect 登涉, quoted by DE GROOT, *Rel Syst.*, Vol, V, p 801 山中寅日有自稱虞吏者虎也。……辰日稱雨師者龍也。……但知其物名則不能爲害也。

According to the *Kwoh yu* [1], Confucius stated that "apparitions (怪, "strange beings") in the water are called *lung* (龍) and *wang-siang* (罔象), while apparitions between trees and rocks are called *khwei* (夔) and *wang-hang* (蝄蜽)". As to these *khwei*, we learn from DE GROOT [2], who quotes the *Shwoh wen* [3] and the *Shan hai king* [4], that this is a class of one-legged beasts or *dragons* with human countenances, which were fancied in ancient China to be amphibious and to cause *wind and rain*. The *Shan hai king*, as quoted by DE GROOT, describes them as follows· "In the Eastern seas is a Land of rolling Waves, extending seaward over seven thousand miles. There certain animals live, shaped as cows with *blue bodies*, but hornless and one-legged. Whenever they leave or enter the waters, winds are sure to blow, and rains to fall Their glare is that of the sun and the moon, their voice is that of thunder. They are named *khwei.* Hwang the emperor caught some and made drums of their hides, which, when beaten with bones of the 'thunderbeast', resounded over a distance of five hundred miles, and thus struck. the world under heaven with awe". "In this description", says DE GROOT, "we immediately recognize the *lung* or Dragon, China's god of Water and Rain".

Further, DE GROOT [5] quotes the *Tszĕ puh yu* [6], which states the following: "There are three species of drought-causing *pah* (旱魃) Some are like quadrupeds; an other kind are transformations of *kiang shi* (僵尸, corpse-spectres), and both these species are able to produce drought and stop wind and rain. But the principal, superior drought-demons, called· *koh* (or *koh-tszĕ*, 格, 格子), cause still more damage; they resemble men but are taller, and have one eye on the top of the head *They devour dragons*, and all the *Rain-masters* (雨師) fear them much, for when they

---

1 國語, ascribed to Tso K'iu-ming, 左邱明, the alleged author of the *Tso chw'en* Ch V, 魯語, quoted by DE GROOT, *Rel Syst*, Vol V, p 495 丘聞之木石之怪曰夔蝄蜽，水之怪曰龍罔象。
2 L 1, pp 496 sq
3 說文, a dictionary composed in the first century of our era by HU SHEN, 許慎, Ch V, 2.
4 Ch XIV, 大荒東經, p 6b
5 *Rel Syst*, Vol. V, p 761
6 子不語, written in the second half of the 18th century by SUI YUEN, 陸園 Supplement Ch III

(the *koh*) see clouds arise, they raise their heads and disperse them (the clouds) in all directions by blowing, the sun thus increasing in intensity. No man can conquer them. Some say, that when it is Heaven's will that there shall be a drought, the vapours of the becks (山川之氣) condense and become these demons. When the latter suddenly vanish, it will rain".

The term "Rain-master" (*yu-shi*, 雨師) for dragon is also mentioned by Wu Shuh [1]. The Japanese applied it especially to one of their dragon-shaped river gods, most famous for his rain bestowing power [2].

Ascending dragons cause rain, but if they descend from the sky this is not always the case. According to the "Various divinations of farmers" [3], when *black* dragons descend this means drought or at least not much rain, hence a proverb says: „Many dragons much drought". The descending of *white* dragons, however, was explained to be a sure sign of coming rain.

§ 2. Violent rains accompanied by heavy winds and thunderstorms.

In a passage from the *History of the Sung* dynasty, mentioned above [4] with regard to the dragon omens, the appearance of a black dragon above the capital was said to be an omen of big floods which in the next year destroyed the fields and houses in 24 prefectures. We also read there that a dragon, which in the fourth month of the sixth year of the K'ai Pao era (973) rose from a well, caused violent rains to destroy a large number of houses and trees and sweep away the inhabitants. And in the sixth month of the next year, when the tower of a castle gate was struck by lightning, this accident is described as follows: "In Ti cheu there fell a fire from the air upon the tower of the Northern gate of the castle. There was a creature which embraced the eastern pillar. It had the shape of a dragon and

---

1 吳淑 (A D 947—1002), a famous scholar, placed upon the commissions which produced the *T'ai-p'ing yu lan* and the *Wen yuen ying hwa*, and author of the *Shi lei fu*, 事類賦 (Giles, *Biogr Dict*, nr 2345), *Lung-fu*, 龍賦, T S., same section, Ch. 127, p 11a

2 See below, Book II, Ch. III

3 田家雜占, *T'ien kia tsah chen* T S, same section, Ch. 130, p 6b

4 Ch 五行志, see above, p 54

a golden colour; its legs were about three ch'ih long, and its breath smelled very bad. In the morning, when people looked for it, there were on the upper part of the wall thirty six smoky stains, the traces of claws"

Such traces were also seen, much to the astonishment of the people, after a heavy storm accompanied by thunder, which lifted up the tablet of a gate and threw it down at some distance, destroying one of the characters of the inscription. [1]

Another time a white dragon brought heavy wind and rain. The sky was black and it was pitchdark. More than five hundred houses were destroyed; big trees were uprooted and lifted up into the air, from where they fell down quite broken [2]

According to the *Yiu-yang tsah tsu* [3], wind, rain and thunder were caused by a dragon, which in the shape of a white reptile had wound itself around one of the legs of a horse, when this was bathed in a river. The creature had coiled itself so tightly, that the horse lost much blood when the monster was loosened. The general who possessed the horse took the reptile and preserved it in a box. One day some guests advised him to examine its nature by means of water It was laid in a hollow, dug in the earth, and some water was sprinkled over it. After a little while the animal began to wriggle and seemed to grow. In the hollow a well bubbled up, and all of a sudden a black vapour like incense smoke rose and went straight out of the eaves. The crowd beyond was afraid and ran home, convinced that it was a dragon But before they were some miles away suddenly the wind arose, the rain come down, and several heavy thunderclaps were heard

Especially the whirlwinds, called in Japan "*tatsu-maki*" or "dragon-rolls" [4], which form waterspouts and carry heavy objects into the air, were looked upon as dragons winding their way to the sky amidst thunder and rain Holes in the ground, due to volcanic eruptions and emitting smoke, were thought to be the

1 *Lao hioh ngan pih ki*, 老學庵筆記, according to DE GROOT (*Rel Syst*, Vol IV, p 220, note 1) "a collection of notices on miscellaneous subjects, in ten chapters, by LUH YIU, 陸遊, also named WU-KWAN, 務觀, a high officer who lived from 1125—1209". T S, same section, Ch 130, p 7b

2 *Choh keng luh*, 輟耕錄, by T'AO TSUNG-I, 陶宗儀, alias KIU-CH'ING, 九成, published in 1366 (cf DE GROOT, l l, Vol IV, p 346) T S, same section, Ch 130, p 10a

3 *Yiu-yang tsah tsu*, Ch XV (諾皇記下), p 2a

spots from where dragons which had been lying in the earth had dashed forth and flown to heaven [1]

Two boys, born from the marriage of a man with a dragon who first assumed the shape of a snake and then of a woman, suddenly caused a heavy thunderstorm to arise, changed into dragons and flew away. [2]

When in the year 1156 a thunderstorm raged and darkness prevailed, suddenly a cry was heard over an extent of several miles, which repeated itself for more than a month. The people ascribed it to the dragon of a neighbouring pond. [3]

Another time a little snake, which crept out of a small crack of the unplastered wall of a house, became bigger and bigger, changed into a dragon and flew away amidst storm and rain. [4]

How a *kiao* brought heavy rains and inundations was seen above [5], as well as the fact that tempests often were ascribed to dragons fighting in the air. [6]

§ 3 Rain magic and prayers

The dragon being the god of rain, from remote ages his images were used in times of drought in order to cause him to ascend by sympathetic magic. The *Shan hai king* [7] says: "In the north-eastern corner of the Great Desert (Ta hwang) there is a mountain called Hiung-li earth mound; a *ying lung* (according to the commentator a winged dragon [8]) inhabited its southern extremity.

---

1 Cf the *I kien chi*, 夷堅志, written in the twelfth century by Hung Mai, 洪邁, T S, same section, Ch 130, p 9b, *Lung ch'ing luh*, 龍城錄 (Wylie, p 197 "A record of incidents during the earlier part of the T'ang, professing to be written by Liu Tsung-yuen, 柳宗元, of that dynasty It is generally understood, however, that it is a spurious production of Wang Chih, 王銍, of the 12th century"), Ch II

2 *Hoh lin yuh lu*, 鶴林玉露, written by Lo Ta-king, 羅大經, alias King-lun, 景綸, who probably lived in the 12th century (cf De Groot, *Rel Syst*, Vol IV, p 251, note 1) T S, same section, Ch 131, p 16a

3 *Kiang-si t'ung-chi*, quoted T S, same section, Ch 130, p 6b

4 *Fei süeh luh*, 霏雪錄, quoted T S, same section, Ch. 130, p 12a

5 Book I, Ch III, § 7, p 81

6 Book I, Ch II, § 2, A, p 48

7 Sect 大荒東經, Ch XIV, p 6b 大荒東北隅中有山、名曰凶犂土邱、應龍處南極、殺蚩尤與夸父、不得復上、故下數旱、旱而爲應龍之狀乃得大雨。

8 Cf above, this Book Ch IV, § 6, p 72 sqq

After having killed Ch'i Yiu (the first rebel) and Kw'a Fu(?), he (the dragon) could not ascend again, and for this reason often drought prevails on earth. In time of drought an image of a *ying lung* is made and then a heavy rain is obtained". The commentator KWOH P'OH [1] (A. D. 276—324) adds: "The earthen dragons of the present day find their origin in this" [2].

WANG CH'UNG [3] of the Later Han dynasty, who in his work entitled *Lun Heng* [4] severely criticises the superstitions of his time, refers to TUNG CHUNG-SHU'S [5] following statement: "At the rain sacrifices in spring and autumn earthen dragons are set up in order to call down the rain. The idea of this is that by this means clouds and dragons are caused to come. The *Yih king* says: 'Clouds follow the dragon, wind follows the tiger'. They are invited to come by means of their likenesses, therefore when earthen dragons are set up Yin and Yang follow their likenesses and clouds and rain arrive on their own account".

Also the *Lu shi ch'un-ts'iu* [6] states that "by means of dragons rain is made", and LIU NGAN [7] says: "Earthen dragons cause the rain to come". According to a commentary on this passage "the Emperor T'ang (the founder of the Shang dynasty, B. C. 1766) in time of drought made an earthen dragon in order to symbolize the dragon being followed by the clouds" [8]. "The duke of Cheh in the land of Chu", says WANG CH'UNG [9], "liked dragons and had them painted on all his walls and trays, certainly considering

---

[1] 郭璞.

[2] 今之土龍本此。

[3] 王充 (A D 27—97)   [4] 論衡.

[5] 董仲舒, who lived in the second century B, C., author of the *Ch'un-ts'iu fan lu*, 春秋繁露 T S, same section, Ch 127, 龍部藝文一, p. 3b 董仲舒申、春秋之雩設土龍以招雨。其意以雲龍相致。易曰、雲從龍、風從虎。以類求之、故設土龍、陰陽從類、雲雨自至。

[6] 呂氏春秋 (last half of third century B C), Ch XX, under the heading 召類.

[7] *Hwai nan tsze*, Ch. IV, 地形訓. 土龍致雨.

[8] 湯遭旱作土龍以象雲從龍也。

[9] 楚葉公好龍、牆壁槃盂皆畫龍、必以象類爲若

their pictures to be like real dragons Thus there was always rain (i. e. there never was a drought) in the country of this duke".

In the *Supplement of the Books of the Han Dynasty*[1] a description is given of the ceremonies performed when praying for rain; an extensive commentary explains the words. "The underlings raise the earthen dragons". In the first place the passage from the *Shan hai king*, mentioned above, is quoted, and Kwoh P'oh's commentary with regard to the earthen dragons of his days. Then follows a long description of rain ceremonies found in the *Ch'un-ts'iu fan lu*[2] of Tung Chung-shu, the author of the second century B.C. quoted above.

In this passage the rain ceremonies of spring, summer, the last month of summer, autumn and winter are described. The details all agree with the Taoistic system, pointed out by De Groot in his *Religious System*[3], and *wu*-ist priests were the performers of the rites. In the ceremonies of spring, summer, the last month of summer, autumn and winter accordingly the eastern, southern (twice), western and northern gates of the towns and villages are mentioned, and the colours of the silken banners of the altars and the robes of the officiating priests were azure, red, yellow, white and black. Further, the numbers eight, seven, five, nine and six were used with regard to the square altars erected at the five different ceremonies and to the tanks in which shrimps or frogs were placed, as well as to the days during which the different preparations were made[4].

As to the earthen dragons, mentioned in this description, the days on which they were made, their sizes, colours, numbers, the directions in which they were placed and the sides on which they stood, as well as the colours of the robes of those who brandished and erected them, and the numbers and ages of the former, all agreed with the same Taoistic system.

"On *kiah* and *yih* days[5] (in *spring*) one big blue dragon, long

---

1 續漢書, Ch V, p 1 阜與土龍。

2 春秋繁露, Ch XVI, nr 74 (求雨), pp. 3—6.

3 Vol I, p 317, Vol IV, p 26

4 Prayers took place on a day of the Water (水日), it was forbidden to cut down famous trees or trees of the wood, the sacrifices consisted of cocks and pigs, three years old, further, the people roasted pig tails, buried human bones, opened mountain pools, burned firewood, etc, "*in order to open Yin (the water) and close Yang (the sun)*" (開陰閉陽, p. 4b), for the same reason men were forbidden to visit markets.

5 以甲乙日爲大青龍一、長八丈、居中央、爲小

eight chang, is made and stands in the centre; seven small one each four chang long, are made (and placed) on the *east* sid They are all directed towards the *East*, with a distance of *eig* ch'ih between each other. *Eight little boys*, who all have observe religious abstinence for three days and are clad in *blue* robe brandish the dragons. The *T'ien-soh-fu* [1] (Superintendent harvesting), who also for three days has observed religion abstinence and is clad in *blue* robes, erects them".

In the same way in *summer on ping* and *ting* days one big r dragon was made, *seven* chang long, and placed in the centr while six small dragons, each three chang five ch'ih long, stoc on the *south* side; they were all directed to the *south*, with distance of *seven ch'ih* between each other. *Seven fullgrown me* who for three days had observed religious abstinence and wei clad in *red* robes, brandished the dragons, and the *Szě k'ung s fu* [2] (Superintendent of works), who likewise for three day had observed religious abstinence and was clad in *red* robe erected them.

When the mountains and hills were prayed to in the *la month of summer*, on *wu* and *szě* days, one big *yellow* drago *five* chang long, was placed in the centre, and four [3] small one long two chang five ch'ih, stood on the *south* side; they wei all directed to the *South*, with a distance of *five* ch'ih betwee each other. *Five elders*, after three days religious abstinence, an clad in *yellow* robes, brandished the dragons, and five men (c a senior [4]) in yellow robes erected them.

In *autumn*, on *keng* and *sin* days, one big *white* dragon wa made, *nine* chang long, and placed in the centre; eight sma ones, long four chang five ch'ih, were placed on the *west* sid They were all directed to the *West*, and the distance betwee them was *nine* ch'ih; nine old unmarried men (or widowers in *white* robes brandished them, and the *Szě ma* [6] (Inspector c horses), also clad in *white* garments, erected them.

龍七、各長四丈、於東方、皆東向、其間相去八尺 小僮八人、皆齋三日、服青衣而舞之. 田嗇夫刃 齋三日、服青衣而立之.

[1] 田嗇夫.   [2] 司空嗇夫.

[3] The main text wrongly says *five*, but the quotation gives the right number of *fou* [4] The main text gives "five men", the quotation "a senior", 老者.

Finally, in *winter*, when prayers were made to famous mountains, one big *black* dragon, made on *jen* and *kwéi* days, and *six* chang long, was placed in the centre, and five small ones, each three chang long, stood on the *north* side; they were all directed to the *North* and the distance between them was *six* ch'ih. *Six old men*, all clad in *black* robes, brandished the dragon, and a *wéi*[1] (military officer), also wearing *black* garments, erected them[2].

In the ceremonies, used for stopping rain, no dragons are mentioned. We learn from the *Sung-ch'ao shi shih*[3] that in the Sung dynasty the same magic was performed; the dragons were sprinkled with water, and, after the ceremony, thrown into the water.

DE GROOT[4] treats of this custom in order to show that, this kind of rain magic being very common in ancient China, the dragon processions on the 15th day of the first month and the dragon boats on the fifth day of the fifth month may be easily explained in the same way. He also refers to a passage from the *Yiu-yang tsah tsu*[5], where a Buddhist priest, who in the K'ai-yuen era (A.D. 713—742) was ordered by the Emperor to pray for rain, said that he wanted a utensil engraved with the figure of a dragon. Nothing of the kind could be found, till after two or three days an old mirror, the handle of which had the form of a dragon, was discovered in the Emperor's store-house. The priest took it into the chapel and prayed; and behold, that very evening the rain poured down!

The same sympathetic magic is mentioned in the *Pih ki man chi*[6], where a mirror, adorned on the backside with a "coiled dragon", *p'an lung*, 盤龍, is said to have been worshipped (rather used in a magical way) in order to cause rain[7].

---

[1] 尉.

[2] The *Shen-nung k'iu-yu shu*, 神農求雨書, quoted in the *Koh chi king yuen*, 格致鏡原, an extensive cyclopaedia compiled by CH'EN YUEN-LUNG, 陳元龍, and published in 1735, Ch IV, Sect 祈雨, p 5a, gives the same with less details

[3] 宋朝事實, quoted in the same chapter of the *Ch'un-ts'iu fan lu*, nr 75 pp 6 seq, cf the same chapter, section and page of the *Koh chi king yuen*

[4] *Fêtes annuelles a Emoui*, Vol I, pp 375 sqq   [5] Ch III

[6] 碧雞漫志, written in the Sung dynasty by WANG CHOH, 王灼 T S, same section, Ch 131, p 11b

[7] With regard to painted dragons being as powerful as real ones we may refer to the *Yun kih ts'ih ts'ien*, 雲笈七籤, a Taoistic work of the end of the 10th

The aim of this magic was to force the dragons to follow their images and to ascend from their pools. It is no wonder that sometimes drastic measures were taken to cause them to obey this human command, when it failed to have success. Thus in the tenth century of our era the head of two districts did not hesitate to have an earthen dragon flogged in order to force the unwilling dragons to ascend; and he was right, for that very day a sufficient rain came down [1].

As we have seen above, also Buddhist priests used images of dragons in making rain. It is again a story from the Kʻai-yuen era, to be found in the same work [2], which teaches us how they sometimes employed them to stop rain. An Indian bonze was requested by the Emperor to put a stop to the incessant rains, caused by one of his Chinese colleagues, who by order of the sovereign had prayed for rain and had fulfilled his task with so much success that several people were drowned in consequence of the inundations. The Indian priest made five or six dragons of clay, placed them in water and scolded them in his mother-tongue. Then he took them out of the water and laid them somewhere else, laughing loudly. After a little while the rain stopped. The meaning of this magic was apparently different from the ancient Chinese ideas. By placing the dragons in their element, the water, he gave them life, just like a Buddhist priest of the fourth century did with a dead dragon which he had dug up. The latter, however, after having thus made the dragon revive, by means of incantations caused him to ascend to the sky and put a stop to a heavy drought. [3] His Indian colleague of the Kʻai-yuen era, on the contrary, with a scornful laugh removed the dragons after having given them life, in order to cause their counterparts to go away also. We may compare this with several instances of a

---

ci the beginning of the 11th century (cf DE GROOT, *Rel Syst*, Vol IV, p 74), where we read about a dragon painted on a wall, with a well before it, which was prayed to for rain by people from far and near, and used to hear their prayings Once in a time of drought a drunken fellow had the audacity to rail at the dragon. He cried over the balustrade of the well "If Heaven sends a drought like this, what is the use of you?", and with a big stone hit one of the painted dragon's feet The mark was still visible in the author's time When the man came home he suddenly got an unbearable pain in his foot Although he sent a messenger to burn incense before the dragon and to apologize it was all in vain, and he died within a few days T S, same section, Ch 129, p 11b.

1 *History of the five Dynasties*, 五代史 (907—960), *Koh chi king yuen*, 11.

2 *Yiu-yang tsah tsu*, Ch III

3 *Tʻai-pʻing yu lan*, Ch 930 The same priest by his prayers caused two white dragons to descend and to pour down rain over a district of a thousand miles

similar magic, mentioned by FRAZER in his *Golden Bough* [1]. We read there of plagues, caused by vermin, scorpions or serpents, which were stopped by burying or removing the images of these noxious creatures.

A curious prescription for making rain is given in the *Yiu-yang tsah tsu* [2], where we read the following: "Take four water-lizards, and after having filled two earthen jugs with water, put two of the lizards in each. Then cover the jugs with wooden covers, place them on two different quiet spots, prepare seats before and behind them, and burn incense. If you then have more than ten boys, ten years old or younger, day and night incessantly strike the jars with small green bamboo sticks, it certainly will rain". This advice was followed, and after one day and two nights the rain came down. "Tradition says", adds the author, "that dragons and water-lizards belong to the same species". The idea of annoying the dragons by noise and thus stirring them up is also to be found in Japan, where, as we shall see below [3], the Court officials made music and danced on a dragon boat on the pond of the Sacred-Spring-Park, in order to force the dragon to arise and give rain.

Another way of making rain is to arouse the dragons' anger by throwing poisonous plants [4], or ashes [5], or pieces of wood, or stones [6], or tiger bones [7] — the tiger being the dragon's deadly enemy — into their pools, or by pulling a tiger's head by means

---

1 Vol II (sec ed), pp 426 sq Cf Vol I pp. 9 sqq., making rain by magical means, I, pp 82—114

2 Ch XI (ninth century).

3 Ch V It reminds us of the enormous bronze drums, decorated with frogs, the demons of rain, which probably were beaten by the Man tribes in the South of China, when drought prevailed. Cf DE GROOT, *Die -antiken Bronzepauken im Ostindischen Archipel und auf dem Festlande von Südostasien*, Mitth des Seminars f Orient Spr zu Berlin, Jahrg IV, Abth I, pp 76—113

4 *T'ai-p'ing yü lan*, Ch 930.

5 *Weng yuen hien chi*, 翁源縣志, quoted in the Japanese work *Shobutsu ruizan*, 庶物類纂, Section 龍.

6 *Mao t'ing k'oh hwa*, 茅亭客話, quoted T S, same section, Ch 130, p 8a "If one throws a piece of wood or a stone into the dragon pond, this at once causes black vapours to arise, followed by thunder and lightning, rain and hail". On clear days the surface of the water of this pond was five-coloured, a sign of a dragon's dwelling. In time of drought offerings were made and prayers said to him

7 *Chen chu chwen*, 珍珠船, written by CH'EN KIAI-KUNG, 陳屑公, in the Ming dynasty, Ch I

of a rope through a river inhabited by a dragon [1]. As we shall see below [2], the Japanese, following the same methods, threw horse dung, old sandals and other dirty things into dragon-ponds, or stirred the dragons up by means of iron utensils or metal-shaving, for, as we saw above [3], these animals were believed to detest and fear iron

The *Wu tsah tsu* [4] describes the remarkable way in which the people of Ling-nan caused rain. As dragons are very lewd and fond of women, a naked woman was placed on a elevated point in order to attract a dragon. As soon as there came one and flew around her, he was magically prevented from approaching her, so that his anger was aroused and heavy rains came down. The same work [5] says that in the beginning of summer the dragons are divided, so that each of them has his special territory, which he does not exceed. This is the reason why in summer time it rains very much at one place and not at all a little further on.

Apart from these means of stirring up the dragons we often read about *prayers* recited to them, that they might give fertilizing rains. This was done in shrines or at ponds inhabited by dragons, or at the entrances of their dens. The *Mao t'ing k'oh hwa*, e.g., mentions a Dragon-woman's shrine, dedicated to a female dragon which in A. D. 740 appeared in a dream and promised to give

---

1 *Shang shu ku shih*, 尚書故實, written in the ninth century by LI CH'OH, 李綽 "In the South, when there is a long drought, a tiger's head bone is tied at a long rope and thrown into the water on a spot where a dragon is living Then several men pull in an irregular way Suddenly clouds arise from the middle of the pond, and thereupon also rain comes down The dragon being the tiger's enemy, even the latter's dried bones still stir up the dragon like this" 南中久旱即以 長繩繫虎頭骨、投有龍處入水、即數人牽制不定。俄頃雲起潭中、雨亦隨降。龍虎敵也。雖枯骨猶 激動如此. Cf. *Kwah i chi* (13th cent.), quoted T. S, same section, Ch 130, p. 7a In the Shun-hi era (1174—1190) a tiger bone, attached to a long rope, was let down in a "White dragon's pond", near a "White dragon's den" before a Buddhist temple Soon it rained, and as they were slow in pulling the bone out of the pond, a severe thunderstorm menaced the government office, but stopped when the bone was removed

The date shows that we have here a passage from the *Hien ch'wang kwah i chi*, 閑窗括異志, written by LU YING-LUNG, 魯應龍, who lived about the middle of the thirteenth century (cf DE GROOT, *Rel Syst*, Vol IV, p 347, note 1), and not with the *Kwah i chi*, written in the second half of the eleventh century by CHANG SHI-CHING, 張師正, alias POH-I, 不疑 (DE GROOT, 11 , IV, p 210, note 1)

2 Book II, Ch III   3 Book I, Ch III, § 3, pp 67 sqq

4 五雜組 (Ming-dynasty), Ch IX   5 Ch IX,

rain whenever prayers were made to her in time of drought [1]. And in the *Sheu shen ki* we read of a sick dragon, which in consequence of prayers recited before his den, gave a badly smelling rain, which would have spoiled the crops, if a diviner had not discovered it in time and cured the dragon at the latter's request. Thereupon a fertilizing rain fell and a very clear spring dashed forth from a rock [2].

§ 4. Buddhist rain ceremonies.

In the Introduction (§ 4, pp. 25 sqq.) we have dealt with the Buddhist rain ceremonies prescribed in the Mahāmegha sūtra and those described by DE GROOT in his *Code du Mahāyāna*. As we will see below (Book II, Ch. III), also in Japan the Buddhist priests gradually conquered this field, formerly the domain of the Shintōists. They used the same sūtras as the Chinese Buddhists. The latter had a good time in the T'ang dynasty, when sometimes, as we read in the *Tuh i chi* [3], eleven hundred Buddhist priests read sūtras in order to cause rain. As to these ceremonies we may refer the reader to the Introduction.

---

1 Ch 130, p 2a   2 Ch VI, cf Ch. X

3 獨異志, ascribed to LI YIU, 李尤, or LI K'ANG, 李亢, of the T'ang dynasty. T S, same section, Ch 131, p 10b.

CHAPTER VI.

EMPERORS CONNECTED WITH DRAGONS.

§ 1 Hwang Ti rode on a dragon.

The dragon being the symbol of the Emperor and his blissful reign, a large number of legends point to the close connection between this divine animal and the Son of Heaven. In the first place, of course, the holy Emperors of the oldest times are mentioned in this respect.

The *Historical Records* [1] contain the following passage. "The Emperor Hwang gathered copper of Mount Sheu and cast tripod at the foot of Mount King. When the tripod was ready there was a dragon which dropping its whiskers came down to meet Hwang Ti. The latter ascended the dragon and rode on it after which the ministers did the same, more then seventy men in all. Then the dragon ascended and flew away. The remaining lower ministers had no opportunity to climb upon the dragon and all at a time got hold of its whiskers, which (by their weight) were pulled out and fell down".

According to the *Ku kin chu* [2] Hwang Ti was melting cinnabar (in order to prepare the liquor of immortality) in the Tsoh yeh mountains, when he became a *sien* and rode on a dragon to the sky. When the ministers clung to the animal's whiskers, the whiskers fell down. To the question whether they produced the so called "Dragon's whiskers herb" the answer is given that this is a false tradition caused by the other name of the same herb "Red clouds herb". The same monarch made a winged dragon (*ying lung*) attack and ward off the troops of the rebel Ch'i Yiu

---

1 Sect 封禪書, Ch XXVIII, nr 6, p 30a (CHAVANNES, *Mémoires Historiques* Vol III, p 488)

2 古今注, written about the middle of the 4th century by Ts'ui Pao, 崔豹 (cf WYLIE, p 159, DE GROOT, *Rel Syst*, Vol IV, p 244, note 1), quoted T S, Sect 禽蟲, Ch 130, 龍部雜錄, p 4b

3 *Shan hai king*, Sect XVIII, nr 14, 大荒東經, p. 6b. *Bamboo Annals* (*Chuh shu ki nien*, 竹書記年), Ch I, LEGGE, *Chinese Classics*, Vol III, Part

§ 2 Yao and Kao Tsu were sons of dragons.

The Emperor Yao was said to be the son of a red dragon, who came to his mother, bearing on his back the inscription: "You also receive Heaven's protection". Darkness and wind arose on all sides, and the dragon touched her, whereupon she became pregnant and after 14 months gave birth to Yao in Tan hng [1]. A similar story is told about Kao Tsu (B. C. 206—195), the founder of the Han dynasty. T'ai kong, his father, saw a *kiao lung* above his wife amidst thunder and lightning and black darkness, while she was asleep on the bank of a lange pond. She dreamt that she had intercourse with a god, and afterwards gave birth to Kao Tsu. This Emperor, who was very fond of wine, was always protected by a dragon, when he was drunk [2].

§ 3. Shun was visited by a yellow dragon.

The Emperor Shun, Yao's famous successor, was visited by a yellow dragon, which came out of the river Loh. On its scaly armour the inscription: "Shun shall ascend the Throne" was visible [3]. As we have seen above, the same holy sovereign instituted the "Dragon-rearer family", whose members had the task of rearing dragons for the Emperor.

§ 4. Yu drove in a carriage drawn by dragons, and was assisted by a ying lung.

Yü, the celebrated founder of the Hia dynasty, drove in a carriage drawn by two dragons, which had descended in his court-yard, because with him the virtuous power of Hia was at its highest point [4]. When he had completed the regulation of the waters, blue dragons stopped in the suburbs of the capital [5]. According to a later tradition a *ying lung* assisted Yü at the work by marking the ground with its tail [6].

---

1 *Bamboo Annals*, Ch II, LEGGE, l.l, p. 112.

2 *Historical Records*, Ch. VIII (高祖), p 2, CHAVANNES, l l., Vol II, pp 325 sq

3 *Yuh fu shui t'u*, 玉符瑞圖; T S, same section, Ch 128, 紀事二, p 2b 4 *Poh wuh chi*, Ch. II, p. 2a

5 *Bamboo Annals*, Ch III, LEGGE, l.l, p 117 青龍止于郊。

6 *San ts'ai t'u hwui*, 三才圖會, in the *Wakan sansai zue*, Ch XLV, p 675 According to the *Bamboo Annals* (Ch. III, l l.) the spirit of the Ho river, a man with a fish body, gave him a chart of the Ho.

§ 5 Ming Hwang's vessel was moved forward by a dragon.

Also in later times dragons were said to assist Emperors, as
was the case in the T'ien pao era (742—755), when a small
dragon arose from a pond the evening before the Emperor Ming
Hwang, conquered by the rebel Ngan Luh-shan, left the capital
and fled to the South. The dragon went in the same direction
and, when the Emperor crossed a river, the animal appeared in
the water and carried the ship forward on its back. His Majesty,
deeply moved by the dragon's loyalty, thanked it and gave
it wine [1].

§ 6 Two yellow dragons threatened to upset Yu's vessel

Sometimes, however, the dragons of rivers and seas caused
trouble even to Emperors. Thus two yellow dragons threatened
to upset Yü's vessel by taking it on its back, when His Majesty
crossed the Yang-tszĕ kiang; but Yu, not in the least frightened,
laughed and said. "I received my appointment from Heaven
and do my utmost to nourish men. To be born is the course of
nature; to die is by Heaven's decree. Why be troubled by the
dragons?" The dragons, on hearing these words, fled, dragging
their tails [2].

§ 7. Shi Hwang died on account of having killed a dragon

Another Emperor was severely punished for having killed a
dragon. This was Shi Hwang, the founder of the Ts'in dynasty
(246—210 B.C), who was so anxious to have a long life, that
he was highly rejoiced when two *sien* came, pretending to know

---

1 *Ts'zĕ-liu shi kiu wen*, 次柳氏舊聞, written in the T'ang dynasty by
Li Teh-yü, 李德裕 In the same way the vessel of Wu Suh, king of Wu and
Yueh (i e Ts'ien Liu, A D 851—932), which in 909 ran on a rock and could not
advance, was carried forward by two dragons, amidst heavy rain, thunder and lightning
(*Shih-kwoh Ch'un-ts'iu*, 十國春秋, written in the latter half of the 17th
century by Wu Jen-ch'en, 吳任臣, according to De Groot, *Rel Syst*, Vol IV,
p 327, "a rather apocryphical history" (of ten small states which existed between the
T'ang and Sung dynasties) (Wylie, p 44) T S, same section, Ch 129, 紀事二,
p 14a
2 *Bamboo Annals*, Ch. III, Legge, l.l, p. 118, cf. *Hwai nan tszĕ*, Ch. VII, 精
神訓, p 9

how to seek the life-prolonging herb [1]. After having been favoured
with high dignities and salaries, they set sail with a crowd of
six thousand girls and boys, not older than fifteen years, to seek
the island of the blessed [2], but although they sought for it a
long time, it was all in vain. The *sien*, who were afraid of
punishment on account of their lies, now invented a new scheme.
On returning to the Court they advised the Emperor to go on
board himself and set out with a large army. Again the foolish
monarch believed them, and put to sea with not less than three
millions of soldiers, who made a terrible noise by crying in
chorus and beating drums (in order to frighten the sea-gods and
thus be able to reach the island of the blessed). The dragon-god,
aroused by the din, appeared at the surface of the sea in the
shape of an enormous shark, five hundred *ch'ih* (feet) long, with
a head like that of a lion. He was immediately surrounded by
the fleet and killed with poisonous arrows, so that his blood
coloured the sea over a distance of ten thousand miles. That
night the Emperor dreamt that he had a battle with the dragon-
god; and the next day he fell ill and died within seven days [3].

---

1 Cf DE GROOT, *Rel Syst of China*, Vol IV, pp 307 seqq the *chi*, 芝, a branched
fungus, which was said to grow on the isle of Tsu in the Eastern Ocean According
to the *Shih cheu ki* (十洲記, "Description of the Ten Islands", "an account of
fabulous countries which were believed to exist in several regions beyond the oceans,
probably written in the earlier part of the Christian era" [DE GROOT, l l, Vol I, p
272]) the Emperor heard about the existence of this herb on the Tsu island from a
Taoist ascetic philosopher, and then sent an envoy to the island with five hundred
young people of both sexes They put to sea to seek the island, but never came back

2 *P'eng Lai*, 蓬萊, "fairy land, an elysium far from man's abode, some regard
it as denoting Kyūshū in Japan" (WELLS WILLIAMS, *Chin-Eng Dict*, p 661 s v)

3 This version of the tale is to be found in the *Taiheiki*, 太平記, Ch XXVI,
pp 115 seqq

CHAPTER VII.

TRANSFORMATIONS.

§ 1 The dragon's transformations are unlimited

From *Kwan tzĕ* and the *P°i ya*, quoted above [1], we have learned that the dragon's transformations are unlimited. Therefore it is no wonder that Chinese literature abounds with stories about dragons which had assumed the shape of men, animals or objects. When they transformed themselves into human beings, they mostly appeared as old men or beautiful women; the latter remind us of the Nāga maidens of Indian tales. Sometimes fishes, which, when being cooked, spread a five-coloured light, or spoke with human voices, were recognized to be dragons; but also quadrupeds, as dogs, rats or cows, sometimes proved to be the temporary shapes of these divine animals. Snakes, of course, closely akin to the dragons, often served them as metamorphoses to hide their real nature, and new-born dragons were said to creep out of the eggs in this form. Finally, trunks of trees or other objects floating in the water sometimes suddenly resumed their real dragon shapes. One passage [2] says that dragons can always transform themselves except at the time of their birth, when they sleep, or when they are angry or lustful, but this stands alone among the innumerable other statements with regard to their nature and capacities.

§ 2. Appearing as old men or beautiful women

As to their appearing as old men we may refer to the *Suen shih chi* [3], where a yellow dragon is said to have come to a house

---

1 Pp 63 and 65

2 *Chen chu chw°en*, 珍珠船 (cf. above, pp. 119, note 7), quoted T. S., same section, Ch 130, 龍部雜錄, p 8b

3 宣室志, written by CHANG TUH, 張讀, in the ninth century. Quoted

in the mountains in the shape of an old man with a yellow robe
The *Kwang-sin-fu chi*[1] contains a story about a *wu*-sorcerer, who
in the beginning of the Sung dynasty was praying for rain above
a well, when he fell into it in trying to catch the white cow horn
on which he had blown and which suddenly dropped out of his
hands. At the bottom of the well he saw a majestic old man,
sitting in a tower in the water, with the horn in his hands.
This was the dragon of the well, who for this time allowed him
to return and gave him back the horn on condition that he
never should make noise near the well again But at the next
drought the man forgot his promise and blew on the horn above
the well like before. This was too much for the dragon, who
made both horn and man tumble into the water, and this time
the sorcerer was drowned. Afterwards he appeared to one of the
villagers in a dream and at his advice a shrine was erected in honour
of the dragon, who thenceforward heard their prayers for rain.

Also the *Yiu-yang tsah tsu*[2] mentions dragons which assumed
the shapes of old men, as well as of *beautiful women*[3]. Liu
Tsung-yuen[4] tells how a dragon which was punished by the
Emperor of Heaven fell down upon the earth in the shape of a
woman, spreading a brilliant light She had to stay there for
seven days, and then, after having drunk some water, her breath
became a cloudy vapour, she changed into a white dragon, and
flew up to Heaven.

§ 3. Appearing as fishes.

Transformations of dragons into fishes are to be found as well

---

1 廣信府志, "Memoirs of the department of Kwang-sin (in Kiang-si province)", quoted T S 11, p 16*a*

2 Ch II and VI, T S, same section, Ch 131, 龍部外編, p 12*a*

3 Ch VI

4 柳宗元 (A D 773—819), one of the most celebrated poets and essayists of
the T'ang dynasty 謫龍說, T S, same section, Ch 127, 藝文一, p 8*b*
Another punishment of a dragon is mentioned in the *Yun sien tsah ki* (雲仙雜
記, about which work De Groot (*Rel Syst*, Vol IV, p 289) says "Ten chapters
of miscellanies of doubtful authenticity, ascribed to one T'ung Chi, 馮贄, of whom
nothing is known but the name More likely, perhaps, the author was the learned
Wang Chih, 王銍, also named Sing-chi, 性之, who flourished in the middle
part of the 12th century"), where a disobedient dragon is said to have had his ears cut
off by Heaven's punishment, the blood which dripped upon the earth produced a plum
tree with fleshy fruits without kernels T S, same section, Ch 129, 紀事二, p 12*a*

in the Dynastic Histories [1] as in books of tales and legends like the *Lang huen ki* [2] (Yuen dynasty) and even in a geographical work as the *Yih fung chi* [3], where we read about a white eel which was caught by some villagers. They were about to cook it when an old man said. "This is a dragon from the Siang River. I am afraid of calamity" But the others considered this to be foolish prattle and did not listen to his words. The next day the whole village collapsed.

In the *Shwoh yuen* [4] a white dragon is said to have assumed the shape of a fish and to have been hit with an arrow in its eye by a fisherman The dragon accused the man before the Emperor of Heaven, but the latter remarked that it was his own fault because he had been foolish enough to change himself into a fish. The fisherman was not to be blamed for having treated him like other fishes This story is often referred to in Japanese literature, e g. in the *Zoku kojidan* [5], where the fish is said to have fallen into the fisherman's net, and to have lodged a complaint with the *Dragon king* (an Indian conception, cf. the Introduction and the next chapter), who gave him a similar answer and advised him not to do such a foolish thing again. In the *Taiheiki* [6] Nitta Yoshisada, who died in battle, is compared to the dragon of this legend, which, instead of hiding itself in the depths of a pool, came to a shallow place and was caught in the net.

As we have seen above [7], fishes were believed to become dragons when they succeeded in ascending the Dragon-gate (apparently a waterfall), and that old tiger-fishes or fishes weighing two thousand *kin* became *kiao* [8].

---

1 *Books of the Tsin dynasty*, 列傳, Ch VI, 張華傳 (the fish spread a five-coloured light when being cooked)

2 Ch I (the fish spoke with a human voice)

3 一統志, "Memoirs concerning the whole Empire" (1647), T S, same section, Ch 129, 龍部紀事二, p 13a

4 說苑, written by LIU HIANG, 劉向 (who lived B C 80—9), the famous author of the *Lieh sien chw'en* (列仙傳), Sect 正諫

5 續古事談, Ch II, *Gunsho ruijū*, Vol XVII, p. 661

6 Ch XX, p 9a The same comparison is to be found in Ch. XXXI, p 12, of the same work

7 Book I, Ch III, § 12, p 86

8 Book I, Ch. III, § 7, p 79

§ 4. Appearing as snakes, dogs, or rats.

The *Poh mung so yen* [1] relates about a child which in the T°ong-kwang era (923-926) met a white snake on the road, tied it with a rope and swayed its head to and fro till it fell down. In a moment a thunderstorm arose and the child was carried into the air, where it was struck by lightning and dropped dead on the ground. On its back vermilion writing was to be read, announcing that Heaven had punished it for having killed a Celestial dragon.

Two dragons in the shape of *mao* dogs (茅狗), ridden through the air by *sien*, are mentioned in the *Lieh sien chw°en* [2] A *sien* brought them to a diviner, more than 100 years old, and invited him to ride on them together with an old woman. According to the *Lang huen ki* [3] two guardian gods of a cave palace were dragons. The *Kiang-si t°ung-chi* [4] speaks about a very deep "Dragon-rearing pond" near the castle of Kwang ch°ang district in Kien ch°ang fu, inhabited by a dragon. Over the pond there was a stone tray, in which remains of food were always laid for the animal, which used to change into a black dog and eat the food. This pond was still there in the author's time, and a "Dragon-well temple" had been built on the spot.

In the seventh year of the Kia-yiu era (1062) an enormous white rat was seen smelling the sacrificial dishes offered in the temple on the Great White Mountain in Fu fung district (Shen-si province), a mountain with much *ling*, i. e. where the divine power of its god as clearly manifested itself in hearing the prayers of the believers as was the case on the Japanese mountain of the same name (Hakusan). Old people declared the rat, which only smelled the dishes but did not eat them, to be a dragon [5].

§ 5. A cow transformed into a dragon

The author of the *Hwai-ngan-fu chi* [6] tells us how a cow

---

1 北夢瑣言, ascribed to SUN KWANG-HIEN, 孫光憲, also called MENG-WEN, 孟文, a high official under the founder of the Sung dynasty (T°ai tsu, 960—976) (cf DE GROOT, *Rel. Syst.* Vol V, p 527, note 2) T S, same section, Ch 129, p 14a.
2 T S, same section, Ch 131, p 2b   3 Quoted ibidem, p 3b.
4 T S, same section, Ch 129, p 12b

5 *Tung-p°o chi-lin*, 東坡志林, desultory notes by SU TUNG-P°O, 蘇東坡, e SU SHIH, 蘇軾, a famous poet who lived 1036—1101, T S, same section, Ch. 130, p. 4a

6 淮安府志, "Memoirs concerning Hwai-ngan-fu (in the prov. of Kiang su), T S., ibidem, p 12b

became a dragon. A rich farmer who possessed a large herd of
cattle one night dreamt that one of his cows said to him. "I
have become a dragon and have fought with the dragon of the
Sang-k'u lake, but without conquering him. You must bind
small knives upon my horns". The next day he discovered that
an extremely big cow of the herd had scales under its belly.
When he had attached knives to its horns, the cow conquered
the other dragon, which was wounded at the eye and retired
into its lake. The cow itself became the dragon of the Great
Lake. Down to the author's time those who passed this lake
avoided the character 牛 (cow), and those who passed the
Sang-k'u lake avoided the character 瞎 (blind of one or both
eyes); otherwise suddenly a storm burst forth and big waves arose.

§ 6 Appearing as objects.

With regard to *objects* which proved to be dragons we may
refer to the *I yuen* [1], where we read how a man while fishing
in a river found a shuttle and took it home. After a short while
the utensil, which he had hung on the wall, changed into a red
dragon and ascended to the sky amidst thunder and rain.
A dragon which had assumed the shape of a tree growing
under water is mentioned in the *Shuh i ki* [2]. A woman who
touched this tree when going into the water in order to catch
some fish, became pregnant and gave birth to ten male children.
Afterwards, when the dragon appeared in his real form above
the water, nine of the boys ran away in fright, but the tenth
climbed upon his dragon-shaped father's neck and in later years
became the king of the land [3]. The same work tells us about a
girl in the Palace, under the Hia dynasty, who changed into a
fearful dragon and then, reassuming her human form, became a
very beautiful woman, who devoured men [4].

In the *Books of the Tsin dynasty* [5] an astrologer is said to have
discovered the vital spirits (精) of two precious swords among
the stars, and pointed out the spot where they were buried.

---

1 Ch I, p 2 The same work gives a tale about a big piece of drift wood, which
broke the vessel of a man who seized it, turned into a dragon and swam off

2 述異記 (see above, p 72, note 1), Ch 下, p 16*b*.

3 Cf above, Book I, Ch. VI, p 123

4 Ch 上, p 4*a*

5 刭傳 Ch VI 張華傳 These swords which turned into a male and a

There a stone box was dug up, from which a brilliant light shone, but as soon as the swords were taken out of the box their spirits in the sky were extinguished. On one of the swords the characters 龍泉, *lung-ts'uen*, "Dragon-spring", on the other 太阿, *t'ai-o*, were written. According to the astrologer such supernatural swords could not remain for a long time in human hands. Actually one of them soon disappeared, and the other one afterwards jumped by itself out of its sheath into a river, which its owner was crossing When it was sought, nothing was found except two dragons, two or three chang long, wound together and emitting a brilliant light which illuminated the water. Then they vanished, raising turbulent waves by their violent movements. Evidently the swords had changed into dragons and were united again.

CHAPTER VIII.

§ 1 Reborn as a dragon

With regard to the Indian dragon (*Nāga*) in China we may refer to the Introduction and to the following legends.

Buddhist reincarnation into a dragon was said to have been the fate of the Emperor Wu's Consort Kʻih (first half of the sixth century A. D.), who was so jealous that she was reborn as a dragon which lived in a well inside the exclosure of the Palace and frightened her husband in his dreams When he was in love with some woman, the water of the well was violently disturbed. In order to appease the spirit, the Emperor had a palace built over the well and all kinds of clothes and utensils put there, as if she were still a human being; and he never married again [1].

§ 2. Ponds inhabited by Dragon-Kings.

According to another Buddhist legend [2] a Dragon-King, who lived in a palace at the bottom of a pond called *Kwun ming chʻi* [3], appeared as an old man to a hermit who lived in the neighbourhood, and besought this man to save his life, as a Buddhist priest, under pretext of praying for rain by order of the Emperor, made the water of his pond decrease more and more, in order to kill him (the dragon) and to use his brain in preparing some medicine. The hermit advised the dragon to go Sun Szĕ-moh [4], who was studying in the mountains in order to become a *sien*. When the dragon did so, this man promised to

---

1 *History of the South* (南史, *Nan-shi*), 后妃列傳, 下.

2 *Yiu-yang tsah tsu* (ninth century), Ch V (T S, 1.1, 外編, p 11a)

3 昆明池.

save him on condition that he should teach him the way of preparing the three thousand kinds of medicine to be found in the Dragon-Palace at the bottom of the pond. The dragon accepted the condition, whereupon the water of the pond rose more and more, and the bonze died with anger and shame. The dragon kept his promise, and thus Sun Szĕ-moh obtained the knowledge, preserved in his famous medical work, entitled *Ts'ien kin fang* [1].

Other ponds inhabited by Dragon-Kings are mentioned in the *Loh-yang kia-lan ki* [2] and in the *Po-chi kwoh chw'en* [3], but these were in foreign, western countries. Sacrifices were made to them; to the latter by the passers-by (there were three ponds, in the biggest of which lived the Dragon-King himself, in the next his consort and in the smallest his child) because otherwise they were sure to be troubled by wind and snow. The former pond was near a Buddhist monastery in the West of Wu-yih land, and the king of the land prayed to the dragon and threw gold and jade into the pond. When these precious objects were washed out of the pond he ordered the monks to take them

§ 3. Temples of Dragon-Kings

A "Dragon-rearing well" [4] in a "Dragon-King's temple" [5] was said to be inhabited by a dragon. Nobody dared draw water from this well, because if one did so strange things happened, and the person who had ventured to thus arouse the dragon's anger fell ill [6].

Another temple of a Dragon-King on a mountain, near a white dragon's pond and (on the top of the mountain) a dragon's den are mentioned in the *Kwah i chi* [7]. In time of drought the peasants used to pray before the cavern, which always contained water in spring and summer, and when they took this water

---

1 千金方 Dragon's pearls were called 千金珠, cf above, Ch III, § 15 p 88

2 洛陽伽藍記, according to WYLIE (p 55) "a descriptive detail of the various Buddhist establishments in Loh-yang, the metropolis during the N Wéi, written by YANG HUEN-CHI, 楊衒之, an officer of that dynasty"; it was written in the sixth century (DE GROOT, *Rel Syst*, Vol I, p 344) T S, same section, Ch 131, p 5a

3 波知國傳, quoted T S, same section, Ch 129, p 4b

4 縈龍井·   5 龍王廟·

6 *Mih k'oh hwui si* (11th cent.), T S, same section, Ch 130, p 3b

7 括異志, cf DE GROOT, *Rel. Syst*, Vol IV, p. 210, note 1. This must be the later work of this name, dating from the thirteenth century (cf above, p 120, note 1), as the Shun-hi era (1174—1190) is mentioned. T S., 11, Ch. 130, p. 7a.

and worshipped it, abundant rains came down. Near to the same
spot was the Dragon-mother's grave, mentioned above [1].

§ 4. Palaces of Dragon-Kings.

A Dragon-King's Palace is mentioned in the *Luh i ki* [2].
According to a tradition among the sailors it was situated under
a small island about five or six days navigating from Su-cheu
(in Kiang-su province). Even when there was no wind, the waves
were so high there that no vessel dared approach it directly.
At every high tide, however, when the water overflowed the
island and the high waves were not to be seen, the ships could
pass there. At night a red light was seen from afar above the
water on this spot, bright like sunlight, which extended over
more than a hundred miles square and reached the sky.

The *Wuh tsah tsu* [3] describes the same island, but, without
mentioning the light, says that it lies above the water, red like
the sun. Although no human being dared approach it, a sound
was heard on the island as if some thousands of men were busy
there cutting and transporting trees. On clear nights one could
see that all the trees on the mountains were felled. It was said
that this was done for building the Dragon-King's abode. Evidently
the Taoistic ideas concerning the island of the blessed, the land
of the *sien*, are confounded here with the Indian conceptions
with regard to the Nāga palaces.

Finally, we may quote a passage from the *T'ai-p'ing yu-lan* [4],
where a magistrate is said to have often received in his house
a beautiful dragon-woman, who each time arrived in a magnificent carriage, accompanied by female postilions. In his former
existence he had promised to marry her, and now he kept his
word and finally disappeared with her. The people said that he
had gone to the Dragon-Palace and had become a "water-*sien*"
(水 仙).

---

1 Book I, Ch. III, § 16, p 89

2 鰈異記 (ninth century, see above, p 87, note 4). T S same section, Ch
129, p 14a

3 五雜俎 (about 1592), in a passage translated into Japanese in the *Heishoku
wakumonchin*, 秉燭或問珍, written in 1710 by KOJIMA FUKYŪ, 兒嶋
不求, and printed in 1737, referred to by INOUE ENRYŌ, *Yōkwaigaku kōgi*, Vol II,
Ch. XXVII (龍宮仙鄉), p 123 sq

4 Ch 424.

BOOK II.

THE DRAGON IN JAPAN.

CHAPTER I.

When treating of the Japanese dragon legends we have first of all to consider the original beliefs of the natives, and to separate these from the conceptions imported from India and China. In the oldest annals the dragons are mentioned in various ways, but mostly as water-gods, serpent- or dragon-shaped.

§ 1. Okami

In the *Nihongi* [1] we read that Izanagi, when his consort Izanami had died by giving birth to the fire-god Kaguzuchi, cut this child into three pieces each of which became a god The blood which trickled from the upper part of the sword changed into three gods. *Kura-okami* (闇龗), *Kura-yama-tsumi* (闇山祇) and *Kura-mitsu-ha* (闇罔象) Professor FLORENZ gives in his "*Japanische Mythologie*" [2] extensive notes on these three gods. *Kura*, says he, is explained as "abyss, valley, cleft", although the meaning of the character is "dark". The second character, 龗, which in FLORENZ's note 26 consists of the characters indicating *rain* and *dragon*, but in the Japanese text (K. T. K. I, 13) is a combination of the upper part of the character 靈 with dragon, is explained

---

1 Ch I, K T K Vol. I, p 13 復劍頭垂血激越爲神。號曰 闇龗，次闇山祇，次闇罔象。K T. K. is *Kokushi taikei*, 國史 大系, a modern edition of old historical and legendary works, which we quote as K. T. K. Of the same kind are the *Shiseki shūran* (史籍集覽) and the *Gunsho ruyū* (郡書類從) (1795), while the *Hyakka setsurin* (百家說林) contains a great number of works of the Tokugawa period

2 P. 46

as "dragon"; in the *Bungo Fudoki*[1] the characters 蛇龗, "snake-dragon", are read "*okami*". This and the later ideas about Kura-okami show that this divinity is a dragon or snake. He is the deity of *rain* and *snow*, and in the *Manyōshū* (2, 19) he is said to have been prayed to for snow. The *Engishiki* states that this god Okami had Shintō temples in all provinces. In a variant[2] we read that one of the three gods who came forth from the three pieces of Kaguzuchi's body was *Taka-okami*. This name is explained by one of the commentators as "the dragon-god residing on the mountains", in distinction from *Kura-okami*, "the dragon-god of the valleys".[3]

The passage of the *Bungo Fudoki* referred to by FLORENZ says that in the village Kutami in Naori district there was a well, out of which water was scooped for the Emperor Keikō (71—130 A. D.) (not Suinin, as FLORENZ says), when he visited the place. Then a snake-dragon (蛇龗, *okami*, appeared, whereupon the Emperor said "This water is certainly dirty (*kūsai*). Scooping water from it should not be allowed". Therefore the well got the name of Kūsa-izumi.

§ 2. Yamatsumi and Mitsuha

As to the second god mentioned in the *Nihongi, Kura-yama-tsumi*, his name means: "Lord of the Dark Mountains", but one of the commentators explains it as: "Mountain-snake" (*yama-tsu*[之]-*mi*). The name of the third divinity, *Kura-mitsu-ha*, is perhaps to be translated: "Dark-water-snake", or "Valley-water-snake"[4]. FLORENZ thinks that this god is identical with *Mitsuha no Me* in the preceding text (Ch. I, p. 11), although the latter is a female deity. There we read that Izanami, when dying in consequence of the fire-god's birth, gave birth to the earth-goddess Hani-yama-bime and the *water-goddess Mitsu-ha no Me* (水神罔象女). FLORENZ[5] devotes an interesting note to the

---

1 豊後風土記, written in 713, *Gunsho ruijū*, Vol XVII, nr 499, p 1126
2 *Nihongi*, Ch I, p 16, FLORENZ, I I, p 63 高龗。
3 According to ASTON (*Shintō*, p 153) it is simply "*O Kami*", "August god", so that the names Kura o kami and Taka o kami should mean "God of the valleys" and "God of the heights". But in my opinion FLORENZ's arguments are right.
4 FLORENZ translates 'dunkler Wasserdrache' (dark water-dragon), but in note 29 the word *ha* is explained as "snake", not "dragon" Cf my treatise on the *Snake in Jap superstition*, Ch II, A, 2 (Serpent-shaped gods of the water), pp 13 sqq, Mitt. des Seminars f Orient Sprachen zu Berlin, Jahrg XIV, Abt I.

latter, and quotes the *Wamyōshō* [1], which by mistake identifies *Mi-tsu-ha* with the Chinese *wang-liang*, 魍魎, instead of with the *wang-siang*, 罔象. We read in DE GROOT's *Religious System of China* [2] that "the Chinese authors generally do not take the trouble to distinguish between these two terms (wang-liang and wang-siang)". *Wang-siang*, says DE GROOT [3], are *water-ghosts*, as well as the *lung*, or dragons, and he refers to YU PAO's *Sheu shen ki* [4], where a *wang-siang* is described as looking like "a child of three years with red eyes, a black complexion, big ears and long arms with red claws".

A Japanese commentator explains *mitsu-ha* as "Water-snake" (水津蛇), and quotes several names and words in which *ha* means "snake'; if this is true, *Mitsuha no Me* is "Female Water-snake". Another commentary, however, explains the word *ha* as 生, "to produce", so that the name of the goddess would be· "The Woman who produces the water". FLORENZ does not know which explanation is right, nor can I decide.

§ 3. Watatsumi

In another passage of the *Nihongi* [5] Izanami and Izanagi are said to have given birth to "gods of the sea", called "*Watatsumi no Mikoto*" (少童命), or, as in Ch. III, p. 76 (Jimmu Tennō), 海童, "little boys" or "boys of the sea". The Chinese characters with which this name is written agree with YU PAO's abovementioned description of the *wang-siang* as little children; these terms are apparently identical with "sea-gods", 海神 FLORENZ explains the name "*Wata-tsu-mi*" as "Lords of the sea", *wata* being an old word for sea, and *mi* a kind of honorific epithet. The same commentator, however, who saw in *Mitsuha no Me* a "Female Water-snake", considers *Watu-tsu-mi* to be "Snakes of the Sea", *mi* being an old word for *snake*. It is not impossible that he is right, and that the old Japanese sea-gods were snakes or dragons.

§ 4. Mizuchi, the river-gods.

The name of the river-gods, "*mizuchi*", or "water-fathers",

---

1 和名鈔, written by MINAMOTO NO SHITAGAU, 源順, who lived 911–983.
2 Vol V, Ch III, p. 521.   3 Ibidem.
4 Ch. XII See above, p 81, note 1.
5 Ch I, p 12, FLORENZ, l l, Ch IV, p 39, 又生海神等。號少童命。

which is found in Ch. XI of the *Nihongi*[1], is written with
the character 虯, *k͡ŭ*, which means a horned dragon[2]. ASTON[3]
says· "The River-Gods have no individual names. They are called
generally *midzu-chi* or water-father Japanese dictionaries describe
the *midzu-chi* as an animal of the dragon species with four legs.
HEPBURN, in his Japanese-English Dictionary, calls it a large
water-snake. The difference is not material. The dragon-kings of
Chinese myth (of whom Toyotamahiko is an echo) are in India
the Nāga Rāja, or cobra-kings". After having stated that River-
gods are prayed to for rain in time of drought, ASTON gives a
translation of the above-mentioned interesting passage of the
Nihongi, which we may quote in extenso·

"A. D. 379 (67th year of the Emperor Nintoku). This year,
at a fork of the River Kahashima, in the central division of
the Province of Kibi, there was a great water-dragon (*mizuchi*)
which harassed the people. Now when travellers were passing
that place on their journey, they were sure to be affected
by its poison, so that many died. Hereupon Agatamori, the
ancestor of the Omi of Kasa, a- man of fierce temper and of
great bodily strength, stood over the pool of the river-fork and
flung into the water three whole calabashes, saying· 'Thou art
continually belching up poison and therewithal plaguing travellers.
I will kill thee, thou water-dragon (虯). If thou canst sink these
calabashes, then will I take myself away, but if thou canst not sink
them, then will I cut thy body to pieces'. Now the water-dragon
changed itself into a deer and tried to draw down the calabashes,
but the calabashes would not sink. So with upraised sword he
entered the water and slew the water-dragon. He further sought
out the water-dragon's fellows Now the tribe of all the water-
dragons filled a cave in the bottom of the pool. He slew them
every one, and the water of the river became changed to blood.
Therefore that water was called the pool of Agatamori"[4].

ASTON also refers to another passage of the *Nihongi* (Ch. XI,
p. 197), where we read about a similar experiment with two
calabasses, by which a man who was to be offered to a river-god
saved his life. It was in the eleventh year of the Emperor
Nintoku's reign (A. D. 323), and the Emperor had dreamt that
a god pointed out to him two men, who had to be sacrificed to
the god of the Northern river, in order to enable the people to
complete the embankment, which gave way in two places. One

1 K T K, Vol I, p 209   2 See above, p 73

of them plunged into the water and died, whereupon one of the parts of the embankment could be completed. The other man, however, showed the god's powerlessness by means of the calabashes which he (the god) could not submerge; and the remaining part of the embankment was made without the loss of this man's life. From this passage we learn that in ancient times human sacrifices were made to the dragon-shaped river-gods.

§ 5 Oho-watatsumi, the sea-god.

Finally we must mention the sea-god *Oho-wata-tsu-mi no Mikoto*, in whose name we again find the term "Sea-lord" or "Sea-snake", spoken of in the preceding text. He is also called *Toyo-tama hiko no Mikoto* ("Abundant-Pearl-Prince"), and his daughter's name is "*Toyo-tama-bime*" ("Abundant-Pearl-Princess, 豐玉姬). This god had his magnificent palace at the bottom of the sea, and when his daughter announced him that she had seen reflected in the well before the gate the face of a beautiful youth who was sitting in the cassia tree close by, he received Hiko-hohodemi — for this was the youth — in a hospitable way. Afterwards the guest married the princess and lived in the palace for three years Then, however, he returned to the earth (according to the *Kojiki* on the back of a *wani*, 和邇, one fathom long) and was followed by his consort, for whom he had built a "parturition-house" on the seashore. She begged him not to look at her while she was giving birth, but he was too curious and peeped in, whereupon he saw that his wife had become a *wani* (Kojiki), or *dragon* (Nihongi). Angry and ashamed she abandoned her child, Jimmu Tennō's father, and returned to the Sea-god's palace [1].

§ 6. Wani

The word *wani*, which is written either phonetically (和邇) or with the character 鰐, indicating a *crocodile*, is found once more in Chapter I of the *Nihongi* (p 40). We read there. "Further it is said that Koto-shiro-nushi no kami changed himself into a bear-*wani*, eight fathoms long (*ya-hiro no kuma-wani*,

---

[1] *Nihongi*, Ch II, pp. 62 seqq ; *Kojiki*, 上，傳十七，神代下，K T.K Vol VII, p 59 化八尋和邇而匍匐委蛇。*Nihongi*, p 63 化爲龍, p 66 (a variant) 化爲八尋大熊鰐 (wani) 匍匐透蛇。

八尋熊鰐). The epithet "bear" means "strong as a bear" [1].
As to the word *wani*, one version of the Hohodemi legend [2] says
that the sea-princess became a *wani*, and according to another
version she changed into a *dragon*, in the former the same words
are used as in the above-mentioned passage about Koto-shiro-
nushi no kami. "Toyotama-bime changed into a big bear-*wani*,
eight fathoms long, which crept about". Aston [3], in a note to
this passage, supposes that the word *wani* is not a Japanese,
but a Korean word, *wang-i*, which should simply mean: king.
Florenz [4] agrees with him, and they base their opinion upon the
fact that the legend has strong Chinese features. Although the
Indian notions about the Nāga-kings related above (Introduction)
are easily to be recognized in the Japanese legend, yet I think we
must not go as far as to consider the whole story western, nor
have we the right to suspect the old word *wani* on account of
the fact that a *part* of the legend is of foreign origin Why
should the ancient Japanese or Koreans have called these sea-
monsters "kings", omitting the word "dragon", which is the
most important part of the combined term "dragon-king"? And
if the full term were used in Korea, certainly the Japanese
would not have taken up only its last part. In my opinion the
wani is an old Japanese dragon- or serpent-shaped sea-god, and
the legend is an ancient Japanese tale, dressed in an Indian
garb by later generations The oldest version probably related
how Hohodemi went to the sea-god, married his daughter and
obtained from him the two jewels of ebb and flood, or some
other means to punish his brother by nearly drowning him;
afterwards, when having returned to the earth, he built the
parturition-house, and breaking his promise of not looking at
his wife when she was giving birth, saw that she had changed
into a *wani*, i e. an enormous sea-monster As to the pearls,
although mysterious jewels are very common in the Indian tales
about the Nāga-kings, it is possible that also Japanese sea-gods
were believed to possess them, as the sea conceals so many treasures
in her depths; but it may also be an Indian conception When
later generations got acquainted with the Chinese and Indian
dragons, they identified their *wani* with the latter, and embellished
their old legends with features, borrowed from the Indian Nāga
tales. The magnificent palace is of Indian origin, and, as Aston [5]

1 Florenz, 1 1, p 148, note 89   2 *Nihongi*, Ch II, p 66
3 *Nihongi*, Vol I, p 61, note 3.   4 L 1 p 148, note 89

points out, the castle gate and the (cassia) tree before it, as well as the well which serves as a mirror, form a combination not unknown to European folklore. Europe probably also got them from India, the cradle of Western and Eastern legends

After having written this I got acquainted with the interesting fact, pointed out by F. W. K. MULLER [1], that a similar myth is to be found as well on the Kei islands as in the Minahassa. The resemblance of several features of this myth with the Japanese one is so striking, that we may be sure that the latter is of Indonesian origin. Probably the foreign invaders, who in prehistoric times conquered Japan, came from Indonesia and brought this myth with them. In the Kei version the man who had lost the hook, lent to him by his brother, enters the *clouds* in a boat and at last finds the hook in the throat of a fish. In the Minahassa legend, however, he dives into the sea and arrives *at a village at the bottom of the water* There he discovers the hook in the throat of a *girl*, and is brought home *on the back of a big fish*. And like Hohodemi punished his brother by nearly drowning him by means of the jewel of flood-tide, so the hero of the Minahassa legend by his prayers caused the rain to come down in torrents upon his evil friend. In Japan Buddhist influence evidently has changed the village in the sea into the palace of a Dragon king, but in the older version the sea-god and his daughter have kept their original shapes of *wani*, probably a kind of crocodiles, as the Chinese character indicates. An old painting of Sensai Eitaku, reproduced by MULLER, shows Hohodemi returning home on the back of a crocodile. It is quite possible that the form of this Indonesian myth introduced into Japan spoke about crocodiles, and that the vague conception of these animals was retained under the old name of *wani*, which may be an Indonesian word.

On p 149 of the same work ASTON says "There can be little doubt that the *wani* is really the Chinese dragon. It is frequently so represented in Japanese pictures. I have before me a print which shows Toyotama-hiko and his daughter *with dragons' heads appearing over their human ones*. This shows that he was conceived of not only as a Lord of Dragons, but as a dragon himself .. In Japanese myth the serpent or dragon is almost always asso-

1 *Mythe der Kei-Insulaner und Verwandtes*, Zeitschrift für Ethnologie, Vol XXV (1893), pp 533 sqq Dr H H JUYNBOLL kindly pointed out to me the existence of these Kei and Minahassa myths and Dr MÜLLER's interesting article Cf KERN, in the periodical entitled "Bijdragen tot de taal-, land en volkenkunde van Ned Indie", 1893, p 504, JUYNBOLL, ibidem, 1894, p. 712, note 1

ciated with water in some of its forms". He gives the print on
the same page, and we see at once that we are here not so
much on *Chinese*, as on *Indian* territory. In the Introduction (pp.
4 sq.) I have referred to GRUNWEDEL's description of the dragon in
Indian art, so that I need not explain that "the dragon's heads
appearing over the human one" form quite an Indian motive,
transferred to China and from there to Korea and Japan As the
sea-god in his magnificent palace was an Indian conception,
Japanese art represented him, of course, in an Indian way. This
is, however, no proof that the *wani* originally was identical with
the Nāga, or with the Chinese-Indian dragon-kings.

§ 7 The jewels of flood and ebb

In regard to the jewels of flood-tide and ebb-tide we may
refer to the *Mizu kagami* [1], which contains a legend apparently
made in imitation of the Hiko-Hohodemi tale in the *Kojiki* and
the *Nihongi*. It runs as follows In the year 200, when the
Empress Jingō (200—269) arrived in Korea, she took some sea
water in her hand and prayed from far to the god of Kashima
(in Hitachi) and Kasuga (Takemikazuchi, who had a famous old
temple at Kashima and another on the hill of Kasuga at Nara,
under the name of Kasuga-daimyōjin; the latter was, however,
not built before 710). Then came the gods of Kasuga and Sumiyoshi
and Suwa, clad in armour and with helmets on their heads, to the
Empress's ship. Kasuga sent the Great God (Daimyōjin) of Kawakami [2] as a messenger to the Dragon-palace (龍宮, ryūgū) at
the bottom of the sea, and this mighty river-god took the "pearl
of ebb" and the "pearl of flood" from the Great Dragon-king
Sāgara [3] and brought them with him to the surface. While the
Korean warships were put up in battle array, the pearl of ebb,
thrown into the sea, made the water suddenly dry up [4]. Then
the king of Koma entered the sea-bed with his troops in order
to destroy the Japanese fleet; but as soon as he did so the god
of Kawakami, following Kasuga's order, threw the pearl of flood

---

1 木鏡, Ch 上, 神功, K T K Vol XVII, p 351; written in the second
half of the twelfth century

2 河上, the "Rain-Master" (雨師), see below, Ch IV

3 沙竭羅, also mentioned in the *Fusō ryakki*, Shōmu Tennō, K T K Vol VI,
p. 564 He is one of the eight Great Dragon-Kings, cf. above, p 4

4 大龍王沙竭羅龍王ニ干珠滿珠ノ一ノ玉ヲ

into the sea, and behold, all of a sudden the water rose tremendously and filled the whole sea-bed. The frightened troops all prayed for their lives, for the water covered even the whole of Koma land Then the pearl of ebb was thrown into the sea again, and the water sank So the Empress by Kasuga's assistance conquered the enemy's army without shedding a single drop of blood, and obtained three ships laden with tributes and treasures from the king of Koma.

In the *Nihongi* [1] we read that in the second year of the Emperor Chuai's reign (A. D. 193) the Empress Jingō found in the sea a *nyo-i-tama* (如意玉), a "jewel which grants all desires' (*cintāmani*). About such jewels the Indian Nāga tales have taught us above [2]. FLORENZ observes in a note to this passage [3], that the *Usa no miya engi* [4] states that the Empress obtained two jewels from the Dragon-palace, the " *kan-ju*" and the "*manju*", the above-mentioned ebb and flood-jewels, and that this book describes them as being about five *sun* long, the former white and the latter blue.

§ 8. Take-iwa Tatsu no Mikoto, the dragon-god of a sacred pond in Higo province.

The *Sandai jitsuroku* [5] mentions a Japanese dragon in the following passage. "In Jōgwan 6 (A. D. 864), on the 26th day of the 12th month, the *Dazaifu* (太宰府, the Government of Tsukushi, i. e. the present Kyūshū, which had its seat in Chikuzen) reported to the Emperor the following facts. 'In Higo province, Aso district, in the sacred pond of *Take-iwa Tatsu no Mikoto* (健磐龍命), "The Dragon-god of the Strong Rock", a god of the upper second rank and the fifth Order of Merit (勳, *kun*), in the night of the third of the tenth month of last year [i. e. the same year 864, because this would be "last year" at the time when the Emperor received the letter] a sound was heard and a shaking motion observed. The water of the pond leapt up into the air and fell down in the East and West; that which fell in Eastern direction spread like a long strip of cloth, about ten chō broad. The colour of the water was like that of shōyu (red); it stuck to plants and trees, and even after ten days its traces

---

1 Ch VIII, p 156· 是日皇后得如意珠於海中。

2 Introd, p 10   3 L 1, pp 222, note 13

4 *Usa Hachiman no miya engi*, 宇佐八幡宮緣起, copied by USA JŪEI, 宇佐重榮, in 1335

5 三代實錄, written in 910, K.T K, Vol IV, Ch IX, p 167

had not yet vanished. Further, in the same night one of the
three stone gods, about 4 jō high, which from olden times had
stood on the mountain peak of Hime-gami (the "Female Deity"),
was broken. The officials of the Dazaifu, having practised tortoise
divination, positively declared that these occurrences were omens
of (litt. corresponded with) calamity of water [水疫, *sui-eki*,
litt. "water-pestilence"; in the following text, however, *hei-eki*,
"war-pestilence", is said to have been predicted by the diviners]" [1].

On the tenth day of the second month of the following year
(865 A. D.) the Emperor issued a proclamation [2], in which he
said that the aforesaid evil omens were due to his own bad
reign and that he therefore thenceforth would earnestly pray to
the gods and reign better than before. He said that the water
of the sacred pond spoken of by the Dazaifu never increased
even if it rained excessively, nor decreased even in times of
drought (litt. excessive sunshine) [3], and that divination had made
out that the sudden throwing up of its water was an omen of
war [4]. He was much grieved, he said, but hoped to stop these
bad influences by reigning better than before. And seven days
later [5] he despatched two messengers to the Imperial mausolea
at Yamashina and made them read there a written message to
his ancestor Tenji Tennō, by which he communicated the whole
matter to him and besought him to ward off this calamity.

Of so much importance were the "Dragon-god of the strong
Rock" and his sacred pond. It is the first time that we meet
the word *tatsu* used separately] in the sense of *dragon* (in the
Nihongi only to be found in the name *Tatsuta*, "Dragon-field"),
and we may be sure that we meet here with a very old Japanese
dragon-divinity. The same pond is mentioned in the *Nihon kōki* [6],
but without the name of the god to whom it belonged. We
read there in a proclamation of the Emperor Kwammu in the
year 796 A. D. the following: "The Dazaifu has reported that in

---

[1] 府司等決之龜筮云。應有水疫之災。
[2] Ch. X, p 173
[3] 經淫雨而無增。在亢陽而不減。
[4] 龜筮所告。兵疫爲凶。   [5] Ch X, p 174
[6] 日本後紀 written in 841, Ch V, K T. K. Vol III, p 2 大宰府
言。肥後國阿蘇郡山上有沼。其名曰神靈池。水
旱經年。未嘗增減。而今無故涸減二十餘丈。考

Higo province, Aso district, there is in the mountains a water (*numa*, 沼, not only a swamp, but a water bigger than a pond and smaller than a lake) which is called "The Sacred Pond" (神靈池, *Shinreichi*). For many years past even in times of large floods or heavy droughts the water of that pond did not rise nor fall. Now, however, it has, without any reason, decreased more than twenty jō. According to the diviners this means calamity of drought (旱疫, *kan-eki*, litt. 'pestilence of drought')"[1]. In 840 it fell 40 jō[2], and the Emperor ordered the people by proclamation to pray for averting this bad omen[3].

§ 9. An Emperor's dragon-tail.

In the *Ainōshō*[4] a funny explication is given of the use of the word *birō* (尾籠) in the sense of *dōtai* (同躰, "same body"). According to some people, says the writer, this is due to the fact that the Emperor Ōjin (270—310, the Empress Jingō's son, deified as Hachiman in 712) had a dragon's tail, because he was a descendant of the sea-god (Jimmu Tennō, his ancestor, being the grandson of the sea-god's daughter[5]). In order to hide this tail he invented the *suso* or skirt. One day, however, when he left the room, the tail was still inside when a lady-in-waiting shut the sliding-doors and pinched the tail between them. Then the Emperor exclaimed· "Biryū", "(I am) a tailed dragon". Afterwards this word *biryū* was changed into *birō* with the meaning of "same body", because the Emperor had meant to say that what was between the door was also belonging to his body (!). The author of the *Ainōshō* believes the legend of Ōjin Tennō's dragon's tail, because, says he, Toyotamabime's son Ugaya-fuki-aezu no Mikoto married his own aunt, also a daughter of the sea-god, a younger sister of his mother, called Tamayori-hime, with whom he begot four sons, the youngest of whom was Jimmu Tennō. Therefore in his opinion it is quite possible that Jimmu's descendants had dragon-tails!

---

1 The same thing is to be found in the *Nihon isshi*, 日本逸史, Ch. IV and XIII, K. T K Vol VI, pp 39 and 363

2 *Shoku Nihon kōki*, 續日本後紀, written in 869, Ch IX, K T K Vol III, p 285

3 Same work, Ch IX, p 288 Cf Ch X, p 293

4 塙囊鈔, an encyclopaedia written in 1446 by the Buddhist priest Gyōgo, 行譽, Ch. VII, nr 21, p 19   5 See above, p 139

CHAPTER II.

In China the dragon often and the dragon-horse always belong, as we have stated above [1], to the very good omens. The Japanese, who have altogether embraced the opinions of the Chinese upon the subject of forebodings, did not hesitate to believe in the truth of their assertions also in regard to the appearance of dragons.

§ 1 Flying dragon as horse of a ghost or a *sien*

The Chinese dragon, flying through the air, is mentioned in the *Nihongi* [2], where we read: "On the first day of the fifth month of the first year of the Empress Saimei's reign (655) there appeared in the sky a man riding on a dragon. In shape he resembled a Chinese, and he wore a blue (broad-rimmed bamboo) hat (covered with) oiled silk. Galloping from Katsuragi peak he disappeared into the Ikoma mountains; at noon he galloped away from the top of Sumi no e (Sumiyoshi, 住吉) 's Pine-tree Peak in a western direction".

The *Fusō ryakki* [3] gives the same legend and adds "The people of that time said: 'It is the soul of Soga Toyora no Ō-omi Emishi". This was a famous minister who had died in A.D. 645, son of Umako and grandson of Iname, the first protectors of Buddhism; Iname had erected the first Buddhist temple, Kōgenji or *Katsuragi*-dera, which was destroyed in 645 at the fall of the Soga family. Although it is not stated in the text of the *Nihongi*, probably the appearance of this dragon, as horse of a *sien* [4], in the beginning of the Empress's reign was a very good omen, as

---

1 Book I, Ch II, pp 43—59   2 Ch XXVI, p 457

3 扶桑略記, written about 1150 by the Buddhist priest Kwō-EN, 皇圓,

teacher of the f me a Gruwū K T K Vol VI p 548 Ch IV

well as that of the yellow dragon ,which was seen ascending
from the northwestern mountains to the sky in A. D. 887, at the
Emperor Uda's accession to the Throne [1].

§ 2. Dragon-horses.

In the *Nihongi* [2] we read: "The Emperor (Kōtoku Tennō, in
the sixth year of his reign, i. e. 650) said: 'When a holy
sovereign appears in the world and reigns the empire, Heaven
in correspondence therewith gives *good omens*. In olden times,
under the reign of the monarchs of the Western country (China),
Ch'eng Wang of the Cheu dynasty and Ming Ti of the Han dynasty
[in reality of the Tsin dynasty], white pheasants appeared. Under
the reign of the Japanese Emperor Honda (Ōjin Tennō, 270—310
A. D.) a white raven nestled in the Palace, and in the time of
the Emperor Ōsazaki (Nintoku Tennō, 311—399 A. D.) a *dragon-
horse* (龍馬, *ryū-me*, or *tatsu no uma*) [3] appeared in the West
Thus from olden times down till the present day there are many
instances of the appearance of lucky omens in correspondence
with the presence of virtuous men".

Also the *Engishiki* [4] enumerates the dragon-horse among the
lucky omens (祥瑞). It is called there a "divine horse" (神馬),
and is described as follows: "It has a long neck and wings at
its sides. When it treads upon the water it does not sink" [5].
The dragon is mentioned in the same list, with the following
description borrowed from China. "He has five colours and walks
(or flies) about; he can make himself invisible or visible, small
or big".

The *Shoku Nihongi* [6] and the *Shoku Nihon kōki* [7] quote Chinese

1 *Fusō ryakki*, Ch XXII, p 637 即位之間自乾角山中黃龍
騰天。

2 Ch XXV, p. 451 聖王出世治天下時、天則應之示其
祥瑞。

3 See above, pp 56 sqq

4 延喜式, "Ceremonies of the Engi era" (901—922), written in 927 by
Fujiwara no Tokihira and Tadahira (藤原時平 and 忠平), Ch XXI,
Section 治部省, K T K Vol XIII, p 653 神馬 (龍馬。長頸骼
上有翼。踏水不沼。)

5 Cf the *Shui ying fu*, above p 57

6 續日本記, written in 797, Ch IX, K.T K. Vol II, p 145 "The *Hiao
king*, Sect. "Covenants of assisting gods", says 'When the Son of Heaven is obedient

expressions in regard to tortoises and dragons appearing as signs of the reign of a good emperor.

The *Nihon Sandai jitsuroku* [1] compares a cloudy vapour, which hung under the sun on the 27th day of the 7th month of A. D. 883, with a dragon-horse, and states that in A. D. 885 the "dragon-star" (龍星) appeared twice [2], reason why the name of the era was changed (apparently it was considered a bad omen), as the Emperor informed to the people in a proclamation, and Gwangyō 9 was replaced by Ninna 1.

In the *Konjaku monogatari* [3] we find a much mutilated passage about a dragon-horse which flew through the air in Shōmu Tennō's time (724-749).

The *Masu kagami* [4] mentions the dragon-horse only in regard to its capacity of crossing broad rivers. In 1221, when Hōjō Yoshitoki marched from Kamakura to Kyōto against the Emperor Juntoku, the rivers Fujigawa and Tenryūgawa (天龍川, "Celestial Dragon-River") were swollen by the rains to such a degree, "that even a dragon-horse could not have crossed them".

An interesting passage with regard to the dragon-horse is found in the *Taiheiki* [5], where such an excellent horse [6] is said to have been presented by Enya Takasada to the Emperor Godaigo (1318—1339) His Majesty praised it highly, and said that it was certainly a "Heavenly horse" (*temma*, 天馬). At his question whether the fact that such a horse had appeared during his reign, was a good or a bad omen, the answer of the courtiers was, that it was an extremely lucky sign, due to His Majesty's own virtues. As phoenixes appeared at the Chinese Emperor Shun's time

---

to his parents, celestial dragons descend and terrestrial tortoises appear'" (孝經 援神契曰。天子孝、則天龍降、地龜出。) Cf. above, pp. 38, 40, 43 sq

7 續日本後記, written in 869, Ch. XVIII, K.T.K. Vol III, p. 401

1 日本三代實錄, written in 901, Ch XLIV, K T K Vol IV, p 607 Cf the *Fusō ryakki*, Ch XX, K T K Vol VI, p 616

2 Ch XLVII, p 657

3 今昔物語, written by MINAMOTO NO TAKAKUNI, 源隆國, who lived 1004—1077, i e UJI DAINAGON, Ch XI, K T K Vol XVI, p 546

4 增鏡, written in 1340—1350, Ch II, K T K Vol XVII, p 1012

5 太平記, written about 1382, Ch XIII, p 1

6 Excellent horses were often called "flying dragons" (飛龍, *fei lung*) by the Chinese, cf the *Nihon kōki*, Ch XII, K T K III, p 48, and the *Shoku Nihon kōki*,

(supposed to have reigned B. C _2255—2205), and a *kilin* in the age of Confucius, so this heavenly horse was an excellent omen for the period, foreboding at the same time the Emperor's long reign and life, and the glory of Buddhism. They further related how at the time of a Chinese Emperor, Muh Wang of the Cheu dynasty, eight heavenly horses had appeared, all having different names, and how the Emperor, drawn by them all, had visited every place of the world [1]. So all those present congratulated Godaigo with his horse, except Fujiwara no Fujifusa. When his opinion was asked, he declared to be convinced that it was *not* a good omen, and he too referred to Chinese examples to confirm his statement. The houses of two Emperors of the Han dynasty, Wen and Kwang Wu, who had refused such presents, had had a long and lucky reign, he said, while that of Muh, who had used the eight heavenly horses, had soon declined. Those horses were only a metamorphosis of the Fang constellation (房, the eleventh of the zodiacal constellations), and an omen of the fall of the Cheu dynasty. Godaigo, on hearing these words, was angry and put a stop to the festivities of the day. Not believing Fujifusa's pessimistic prediction he accepted the horse, and a few years later (1336) the great schism of the Southern and Northern Courts seemed to prove the truth of Fujifusa's words.

The same work [2] relates how the Emperor Godaigo gave the aforesaid dragon-horse to Nitta Yoshisada, when he despatched him to Owari province (1335) It was expected to cover the distance, which would have required four or five days with an ordinary horse, in half a day, so that he could be back in Kyōto that very evening. In a few hours he arrived in Ōmi province, but there the animal suddenly died, which was, of course, a very evil foreboding.

Finally, we may mention a dragon-horse which certainly was not a harbinger of evil, namely that on which the Empress Jingō after her Consort Chūai's death (200 A. D.) flew through the air to Sugiyama at Ikeda, Buzen province, where she prayed to the gods for assistance with respect to her expedition against Korea. Then the Four Deva Kings, with eight white flags (Hachiman, 八幡) in their hands, descended from Heaven [3]

---

1 Cf above, p 59
2 Ch. XIV, p. 14.
3 *Sansha takusen ryakushō*, 三社託宣略抄, author unknown, the year Keian 3 (1650) is mentioned as date of the epilogue Zoku zoku gunsho ruijū, Vol I, p. 741

§ 3. Carriage of a ghost drawn through the air by eight dragons

In connection with the same Emperor a third tale in the *Taiheiki* [1] may be mentioned. Ōmori Morinaga, who had conquered Godaigo's loyal general, Kusunoki Masashige (1336), one evening saw the latter's ghost appearing in the garden and trying to deprive him of his sword. He questioned the spirit by whom he was accompanied, whereupon Masashige answered that the Emperor Godaigo, that Emperor's son Prince Morinaga (killed at Kamakura in 1335) and Nitta Yoshisada had come with him. Ōmori lighted a torch and, looking upwards, discovered in a big cloud twenty demons carrying on their shoulders the Imperial sedan-chair; then followed the Prince in a carriage *drawn by eight dragons* [2], and Yoshisada rode in front with more than three thousand horsemen. This reminds us of a sentence in the *Gempei seisuiki* [3], a quotation from the *Ba-iku-kyō* [4], which says that "in heaven a horse is made into a dragon and among men a dragon is made into a horse" [5] The number eight is stereotypical in these legends about dragons ridden by kings or gods, or drawing their carriages. So we read about a Buddhistic god with twelve faces and forty two arms brandishing swords and lances, and riding eight dragons in the air amidst rain and wind [6].

§ 4 A dragon appears as a good omen

The *Kanden jihitsu* [7] describes a dragon which was seen under a bridge near Unawa village, Harima province, at the foot of Mount Shiko. It was seven shaku long, had one horn, hands and feet, and its body had the colour of leaves of a tree tinged with a golden lustre. It was a beautiful animal, exactly like the red dragons on pictures. When the villagers descended from the

---

1 Ch XXIII, p 3

2 其次ニハ兵部卿親王。八龍ニ軍ヲ懸テ。扈従シ給フ。

3 Ch XXXVII, p 982

4 馬郁經.

5 天上ニハ馬ヲ爲龍、人中ニハ龍ヲ爲馬。

6 See below, Ch IV, *Taiheiki*, Ch XII, p 9b

7 閑田次筆, written by the same author who wrote the *Kanden kōhitsu*,

bridge and stroked its horn, it was not afraid or angry, but apparently rejoiced. Afterwards the skin of this divine dragon was found near by, on the other side of the river. "This was not an evil dragon or a poisonous snake, but probably a lucky omen of a good reign. The fact that the crop of that very autumn was good, was brought into connection with the appearance of the dragon, which was (therefore) said to be a venerable being" [1].

---

[1] Hyakka setsurin, Vol 續下一, Ch. IV, p 172 The *Gwadan keiroku*, 畫譚雞肋 (written in 1775 by Nakayama Kōyō, 仲山高陽, Hyakka setsurin, Vol 正下, p 419) speaks about the officials appointed in ancient China for rearing dragons (cf above, Book I, Ch III, § 8, p 82), which were not real dragons but horses, further, it treats of dragon pictures

Another work of the Hyakka setsurin (*Konyō manroku*, 昆陽漫錄 written in 1763 by Aoki Konyō, 靑木昆陽, Hyakka setsurin, Vol 正上, p 880) mentions dragon-bones (cf above, Book I, Ch III, § 17, pp 90 sqq) A Dutchman, to whom the author, Aoki, showed such a bone, declared it to be a stone, in agreement with a Chinese work

CHAPTER III.

CAUSING RAIN.

§ 1. Shintō gods.

The ancient annals of Japan very frequently speak of heavy droughts which threatened the country with hunger and misery. They were considered to be punishments, or at any rate plagues, from the gods, which could only be stopped by earnest prayers and offerings to the same divinities. The old, dragon-shaped river-gods (the "river-uncles", 河伯, *kawa no kami*) especially, from olden times believed to be the givers of rain, were besought not to withhold their blessings any longer from the parched and suffering land.

The *Nihongi* [1] tells us that in the first year of the Emperor Kōgyoku's reign (642) there was a long drought which could not be stopped by the Shintō priests. In Aston's translation this passage runs as follows: "25th day. The Ministers conversed with one another, saying: — 'In accordance with the teachings of the village hafuri [Shintō priests], there have been in some places horses and cattle killed as a sacrifice to the Gods of the various (Shintō) shrines, in others frequent changes of the market-places [both old Chinese customs [2]], or prayers to the River-gods. None of these practices have had hitherto any good result'. Then Soga no Oho-omi [Iruka, the last of the Soga's, who was killed in 645, together with his father Emishi, all the Soga's, Iname, Umako, Emishi and Iruka, were mighty ministers and great protectors of Buddhism] answered and said. — 'The Mahāyāna Sūtra ought to be read by way of extract [3] in the temples, our sins repented of, as Buddha teaches, and thus with humility rain should be prayed for'".

---

1 Ch XXIV, K T K Vol I, p 410

2 Cf Aston's note to this passage (*Nihongi*, Vol II, p 174, note 4), and FLORENZ's note 3 (*Nihongi*, *Japanische Annalen*, Book XXII—XXX, sec ed, p 75)

3 轉讀, *tendoku*, ASTON, p 175, note 1 "the reading of passages of a book to

"27th day. In the South Court of the Great Temple, the images of Buddha and of the Bosatsu (Bodhisattvas), and the images of the four Deva Kings, were magnificently adorned. A multitude of priests, by humble request, read the Mahāyāna Sūtra. On this occasion Soga no Oho-omi held a censer in his hands, and having burnt incense in it, put up a prayer".

"28th day A slight rain fell".

"29th day The prayers for rain being unsuccessful, the reading of the Sūtra was discontinued".

"8th month, 1st day The Emperor made a progress to the river-source of Minabuchi Here he knelt down and prayed, worshipping towards the four quarters, and looking up to Heaven [Chinese style, as the Buddhist prayers had been without result]. Straightway there was thunder and a great rain, which eventually fell for five days, and plentifully bedewed the Empire. [One writing has: — 'For five days there was continuous rain, and the nine grains ripened'] Hereupon the peasantry throughout the Empire cried with one voice: 'Bansai', and said 'An Emperor of exceeding virtue'".

Among the eighty five Shintō shrines to which messengers were despatched by the Court to pray for rain, the *Engishiki* [1] mentions several river and water-deities, e g the gods of Kibune [2] and Nibu no kawakami [3], but also the Wind-gods of Tatsuta [4], the Thunder-god of Kamo [5] and many others. The *Nihongi* [6] repeatedly uses the same words in regard to these prayers, namely: "The Emperor sent *daibu* (大夫, officials of a high rank) as envoys to the different Shintō temples in order to pray for rain, he also despatched messengers to pray to the god Ō-imi of Hirose and to the Wind-gods of *Tatsuta* (龍田, 'Dragonfield')". Was it accidental that the Wind-gods, who appeared to be also givers of rain, had their shrine at a place called

---

1 Ch III (神祇三, 臨時祭), K T K Vol XIII, p 142 祈雨神祭八十五座。

2 貴布禰社一座（已上山城國）。

3 丹生川上一座（已上大和國）。

4 龍田社二座。

5 賀茂別雷社一座。

6 Ch XXX, p, 565 遺大夫謁者。詣諸社祈雨。又遺使者祀廣瀬大忌神與龍田風神。

"Dragon-field"? The word *tatsu*, dragon, is, as far as I know, not found in the *Nihongi*, except in this name, but the fact that the ancient Japanese had such a word indicates that they themselves knew a kind of dragons before they were taught by Koreans and Chinese about the existence of the Chinese dragons. They identified these *tatsu* with the *lung* (龍), and, as we have seen above (p. 138), wrote the name of their "water-fathers", *mizuchi*, with the character 虯, *k'iu* (the horned dragon), while the word *okami* was written by means of a character, partly consisting of rain and dragon.

Their dragons were *kami*, gods [1], who lived in rivers and seas, valleys and mountains (in rivulets, lakes and ponds), bestowing r a i n on their worshippers. That those river-gods could also cause w i n d we learn from the above quoted passage of the *Nihongi* [2], where the god of the Northern river is said to have made a whirlwind arise in order to submerge the calabashes So the three kinds of dragons, to be found in Japan, original Japanese, Chinese and Indian, all have one feature in common, i. e. the faculty of causing rain; while the winds belong to the dominion of the former two.

The *Shoku Nihongi* [3] states that in 715 the Emperor Gwammei sent messengers to pray for rain to "famous mountains and large rivers" (名山大川), whereupon the rain came down in torrents within a few days. It is remarkable that he at the same time established religious festivals in the two great Buddhist temples of Nara, Kōfukuji and Hōryūji, and despatched messengers to the different Shintō temples with *nusa* (幣帛, offerings of hemp and bark-fibre [4]). We often observe this dualism in the measures taken by the Emperors to stop drought or too much rain, especially in later times, when Buddhism became more and more powerful [5].

---

1 SATOW, *The Revival of pure Shintō*, Transactions of the Asiatic Society of Japan, App Vol III 1, p 43, ASTON, *Shinto*, p 9

2 Ch. XI, p 197   3 Ch VI, K.T.K Vol II, p 92

4 Cf ASTON, *Shinto*, pp 213 seqq

5 Cf *Sandai jitsuroku*, Ch V, K T K Vol IV, pp 87 seq "On the fifteenth day the Emperor sent messengers to the Seven temples of Famous Shintō gods near the capital in order to offer nusa and to pray for rain. On the sixteenth he invited priests of all the great Buddhist temples, 60 men, to come to the Palace and read there the *Dai Hannya kyō* (Mahāprajñāpāramitā sūtra) by way of extract, this was limited to a space of three days; it is a prayer for sweet rain (in the text three *months* is written, if this is right, the meaning must be that this sūtra in praying for

The Shintō gods who were believed to cause rain were also considered to be able to put a stop to it, and we often read of prayers offered to them to that effect In times of drought mostly messengers were despatched to the different rain-bestowing gods within the so-called *gokınaı* (五畿內), the five provinces adjoining the capital, i. e Yamashiro, Yamato, Kawachi, Izumi and Settsu [1]. The most powerful in this respect was apparently the river-god of *Nibu kawakami* (丹生川上神) mentioned in the *Engishiki* [2] among the ten temples of Yoshino district, Yamato province. Not only hemp and fibre were offered to this river-god, but occasionally also a b l a c k h o r s e in older to cause him to give iain [3]. His dragon-shape is evident from the term "*Rain-master*" (雨師, *U-shı*, by which he was often designated in imitation of the Chinese dragons [4], and which appears to have

---

月 is a misprint for 日) On the eighteenth day it thundered, and a little rain slightly moistened (the earth) On the nineteenth theie was an eaithquake, and the slight rain foithwith stopped The ieadıng of the sūtra was prolonged for two days more, because a good, moistenıng rain had not yet been obtained"

1 *Shoku Nihongi*, Ch. VII, XI, XXXVII, K T. K Vol II, pp 103, 187, 676.

2 Ch IX, K T K Vol XIII, p 291

3 *Shoku Nihongi*, Ch XXXIX, p 739 奉黑馬於丹生川上神。 祈雨也。 *Nihon kōkı*, Ch XVII, K T K Vol. III, p 82. *Engıshıkı*, Ch III, K T. K Vol XIII, p. 144

4 Cf above, Book I, Ch. V, pp 109 sqq We find this term passim in the *Shoku Nihon kōkı* (K. T. K. Vol. III, p 281 雨師俄奔於四溟, "The Rain-Masters suddenly ran on the foui seas" (i e it iained over the whole countiy, p 287 奉授正五位下丹生川上雨師神正五位上, "The highei ordei of the piincipal fifth iank was conferied upon the Rain-Mastei, god of Nibo kawakamı, who (hitherto) possessed the lowei oidei of the principal fifth iank", p 300 (then he was raised to the lower ordei of the secondary fourth rank), p 313 (prayeis for iain havıng been made at the temple of the same Rain-Master by an Imperial envoy, that very evenıng the rain came down), p 397 (nusa were offered to him in oidei to cause him to stop the continuous rains), p 402 "Nusa and silk were offered to the upper and lower shrines of Matsuo and Kamo, and to the shrines of Kibune and the Rain-Master, in oidei to piay foi a sweet rain", in the *Sandaı jitsuroku*, K T K Vol IV, p 41 nusa and a blue (i e daik) horse offeied to the Rain-Master of Nibu kawakamı, in order to stop the continuous iains p 395 nusa offeied with the same purpose, p 465 the same god raised to the principal third rank, and a black horse offeied to him in order to cause iain, etc , and in the *Nihon isshı*, K T K Vol VI, Ch XVIII, p 184 nusa offered to the Rain-Mastei, to stop the iain, Ch XXVI, p. 270 elevated to the secondary fifth iank and piayed foi rain, Ch XXVII, p 285 a black horse offered to him and prayed te for rain, p 286 nusa offeied, Ch XXXI p 334· nusa and a horse offeied, for stoppıng the continuous iains, p 337 nusa offered and prayers made foi iain, Ch XXXVII, p 412 nusa and a white horse from the Imperial stables offered in order to cause the Rain-Master to stop the abundant rains.

been given to him as a special title. He was also prayed to for stopping wind an rain [1].

The *Kimpishō* [2] states that Court nobles had the care of the offerings sent by the Emperor to the Nibu and Kibune shrines in order to pray for rain or to cause the dragon-gods to put a stop to continuous rains. These nobles, however, did not go there themselves, but despatched officials of the Jingikwan, or, on special occasions, Court officials (kurabito). There were sixteen Shintō shrines the gods of which were worshipped for the purpose of causing or stopping rain, namely the seven "Upper shrines" (those of Ise, Iwashimizu, Kamo, Matsuo, Hirano, Inari and Kasuga), and further those of Ōharano, Yamato Ishigami, Hirose and Tatsuta, Sumiyoshi, Nibu and Kibune [3].

Finally, in Buzen province, Kamige district, there was in the so-called *Tatsu no fuchi* (龍の淵), or "Dragon's Pool", an originally Japanese dragon, who was famous for bestowing rain upon those who prayed to him [4] And in Echizen province, Sakai district, there is still nowadays a Shintō shrine of *Kokuryū Myōjin*, 黒龍明神, "the Black Dragon-god", on the bank of the *Kuzuryū-gawa*, 九頭龍川, or "River of the Nine-headed Dragon", also called *Kokuryū-gawa*, or "Black Dragon's Flood". If one prays there for rain, his prayer is certainly heard [5].

§ 2. Horses offered to Shintō gods

With regard to the horses offered to the rain-gods, we may refer to another passage [6], where we read that in 838 white horses were offered twice to the god of *Kibune* (貴布禰), on Mount Kurama near Kyōto, another famous rain-god, and to the afore-

---

1 *Shoku Nihon kōki*, Ch VIII, p 247

2 禁秘抄, a work written in the Kenryaku era (1211—1212) by the Emperor JUNTOKU, *Gunsho ruijū*, Vol. XVI, nr 467, Ch 下, pp 1072 seq See below, Ch. V, § 4.

3 上七社、大原野大神、大和石上、廣瀬、龍田、住吉、丹生、貴布禰。

4 *Buzenkokushi*, 豊前國志, written in 1865 by TAKADA YOSHICHIKA, 高田吉近, Ch IV, 上, p. 31

5 *Nihon shūkyō fūzokushi* (written in 1902, see below, Ch III, § 12), p 325.

6 *Shoku Nihon kōki*, Ch VII, p 247 "Nusa, silk and a white horse were offered

said "Rain-Master", in order to stop the rain. The offering to
the latter of a blue (i. e dark coloured) horse in 859 (for stopping rain) and of a white one in 875 and 883 is stated in the
Sandai jitsuroku [1], while black horses were twice offered to the
same god in 877, as well as in 880 and 885 [2]. It is no wonder
that the Emperor repeatedly elevated this mighty river-god to
a higher rank [3]. The *Kimpishō* [4], a work written in the Kenryaku
era (1211—1212) bij the Emperor JUNTOKU, says that, when at that
time officials of the Jingikwan, the Department of Shintō Rites
and Ceremonies, went to the shrines of Nibu (the "Rain-Master")
and Kibune, in order to pray for rain or to beseech these gods
to stop the too abundant rains, they took a sacred horse with
them from the Imperial stables, and when Kurabito (kurōdo, or
kurando, 藏人, officials of the kurōdo-dokoro, which had the
care of the Imperial decrees) went to those temples, one of the
Emperor's ordinary horses or one taken from the stables of the
retired Emperor was deemed sufficient. In case of stopping rain
a red horse, and when rain was required a white horse was
offered, for the colour red was avoided in praying for rain. The

---

1 Ch III, p 41 "From the fifth month to the present month (the eighth) it had
rained continuously, so that messengers were sent to the shrine of the Rain-Master of
Nibu kawakami in Yamato province, and nusa and a blue horse etc. were presented
to him, this was done in order to supplicate him to stop the rain" Ch XXVII, p
416 · nusa and a white horse offered to the god of Nibu kawakami to cause him to
stop the rain Ch XLIV, p 606 nusa offered to the shrines of Ise, Kamo, Matsuo,
Inari, Kibune and Nibu kawakami, and to the last also a white horse, on account of
the heavy rains and the bad omens
2 *Sandai jitsuroku*, Ch. XXXI, p 464 a black horse offered to the god of Nibu
kawakami, and nusa to the god of Kibune, with prayers for rain Ch XXXI, p 465:
the god of Nibu kawakami raised to the principal third rank, nusa and a black horse
offered to him, and prayers said for rain Ch XXXVII, p 543 nusa offered to the
gods of eleven Shintō shrines (Kamo and others) and prayers said for rain, but a black
horse added to the offerings sent to the temple of Nibu kawakami Ch XLVIII, p
666. nusa and a black horse offered to the Rain-Master-god of Nibu kawakami
3 Comp the above notes *Shoku Nihon kōki*, Ch IX, pp 287, 300 etc
4 禁秘抄, *Gunsho ruijū*, Vol. XVI, nr 467, Ch 下, pp. 1072 seq 神祇
官人參丹生貫布禰之時、神馬召寮、或內野放御
馬。殊時藏人參之、其時被進尋常御馬、或自院
被進之。止雨赤毛、祈雨白毛也。應和御記依式
止雨可奉白馬、而年來赤馬也… ·如延喜式、祈
雨黑毛、止雨白毛也。而先先有沙汰、祈雨白毛、
止雨赤色。

Engishki [1], on the contrary, states that in the Engi era (901—922) a white horse was offered in the former case, a black one in the latter. This may have varied at different times; red (or blue, i. e.~dark coloured), black and white were at any rate the colours, of which red was limited to cases in which the stopping of rain was prayed for

§ .3 Buddhism wins field

Especially in the last of the six oldest Japanese Standard Histories (the *Rikkokushi*, 六 國 史), i. e the *Sandai jitsuroku* (written in 910), we see the Buddhist priests gradually prevailing in their struggle against the Shintōists Whereas formerly in times of drought there was only one way of averting this evil, namely praying and offering to the Shintō rain-gods, and among them especially to the dragon-shaped river-gods, now the Emperors began to employ Buddhistic assistance at the same time, or sometimes even without addressing the Shintō deities.

It is most characteristic that in the seventh month of 877, when such a heavy drought prevailed that the Prime Minister, Fujiwara no Mototsune, tendered his resignation because he considered it a sign of his bad government, nothing was said about prayers or offerings to Shintō gods [2]. The Emperor did not accept Mototsune's resignation, and ascribed the drought to a curse of the Empress Jingō's mausoleum at Tatanami (楯 列) in Yamato, whither he accordingly sent messengers to investigate the matter. They reported that a stag had been cut to pieces and eaten, and that peasants had cut down three hundred and thirty two trees near the mausolea; the guilty officials were punished; but the drought continued. Then one hundred *Buddhist priests* were summoned to the Shishinden (a building of the Palace) and there read the Daihannya (Mahāprajñāpāramitā) sūtra for three days; this was the sūtra to be read in autumn, but at the same time used in causing rain. After two days a thunderstorm arose, and clouds covered the sky. A slight rain fell, but this was not sufficient, so that the sūtra reading was prolonged for two days and the Ni-ō (仁 王) sūtra was read. The next day even the water of the pond in the *Shinsenen*, or Sacred Spring Park (see below, § 4), was required to drain the rice-fields; in one day and one night the pond was quite dry. Then the Emperor sent messengers

---

1 Quoted ibidem

to Jingō's mausoleum, in order to apologize for the cutting of the trees and the killing of the stag. Sūtras were read there for five days without any result whatever, and some of the bonzes were so ashamed that they stole away. One of them, however, the well-known high-priest Dentō Daihōshi [1], gave the advice to have one of his pupils try his magic art of making rain by means of tantras. Then the latter was summoned, and was clever enough to take a limit of five days. The next day an earthquake and a thunderstorm announced the good result of the tantras, the rain poured down for three days, and there was great joy in the Palace and in the land

Two years before, in 875, messengers were despatched to fifteen great Buddhist temples, and the Daihannya sūtra was read in order to obtain rain [2] Sixty Buddhist priests read the same holy text in the Taikyokuden (a building of the Palace), and fifteen others recited the *Daiunrin seiu kyō* (大雲輪請雨經, "Great Cloud-wheel Rainpraying sūtra") [3] in the above mentioned park Shinsenen High officials went to the Imperial mausoleum at Fukakusa and, apologizing for the evil that might have been done, they prayed for benevolence, for the Jingikwan, the Department of Shintō rites and ceremonies, had declared the drought to be a curse on account of the cutting of trees at this mausoleum.

§ 4. The Sacred Spring Park.

The *Shinsenen* (神泉苑, "Sacred Spring Park") was an important place in the days of old, and it is mentioned innumerable times in the ancient annals, from the *Nihon kōki* down to the *Fusō ryakki*. The ways in which it is spoken of, however, are quite different. In the older works the Emperors are said to have visited it many times for their amusement, to see westlers etc., but in the *Sandai jitsuroku* it appears to have become the place where Buddhist services were held in order to obtain rain. Besides in 875 we read about such a ceremony in 877, when Dentō Daihōshi, the same who a month later recommended his pupil for making rain by means of tantras [4], went to the park at the head of twenty one other Buddhist priests, and, practising the method of reciting the "Sūtra of the golden-winged bird-king"

---

1 傳燈大法師, cf *Fusō ryakki*, Ch. XX, K T K Vol VI, p 598
2 Ch XXVII, pp 414 seq
3 This is the *Mahāmegha sūtra*, treated in the Introduction, § 4, pp 25 sqq
4 See above, § 3, this page

(no doubt the Garuda, to frighten the dragon and make him ascend) [1], prayed for rain. The next day another high-priest, the Risshi Enju, and a high member of the Board of Ceremonies, Tachibana Ason, were sent by the Emperor to the Daibutsu of Tōdaiji at Nara, in order to pray there for three days; yet it was all in vain. Then the river-god of Kakō [2] in Hitachi province and Karo [3] in Inaba were elevated to higher ranks, and messengers were sent to all the Imperial mausolea with the announcement that the *nengō* (name of the era) was changed (from Jōgwan to Gwangyō, a means of averting the continuation of the evil, i. e. the drought) [4]. Then followed what is told above (§ 3). It is interesting to observe how the assistance of the ancient Shintō deities was not called in before the Buddhist priests had proved to be unable to cause rain, and even then no prayers or offerings took place, as formerly, but the gods were only elevated to higher ranks, and the change of the *nengō* was only announced to the Imperial ancestors.

It was the pond in the park which made the Buddhists choose it for their rain-prayers. We read in the *Sandai jitsuroku* [5] that on the 23th day of the 6th month of 875 A. D., when all the performances of the Buddhist priests, related above [6], had only caused a slight, insufficient rain to fall, an old man said: "In the pond of the Sacred Spring Park there is a divine dragon. Formerly in times of heavy drought the water of this pond was let out and the pond was dried up, bells and drums were beaten, and when (the dragon) answered (the request), it thundered and rained. This is sure to have a good result". Then the Emperor despatched high officials to the park and had the water let out.

---

1 See above, Introd , p 7, cf Book I, Ch. V, § 3, p. 149

2 河江神 (河江 ("rivers") is in China the Hwang-ho and the Yang-tszĕ kiang)   3 賀露.

4 *Sandai jitsuroku*, Ch XXXI, p 465

5 Ch XXVII, p 445 古老言曰。神泉苑池中有神龍。昔年炎旱、焦草礫石、決水乾池、發鍾鼓聲。應時雷雨。必然之驗也。於是勅遣右衛門權佐從五位上藤原朝臣遠經、率左右衛門府官人儒士等於神泉苑、決出池水。正五位下行雅樂頭紀朝臣有常率諸樂人。泛龍舟陣鍾鼓。或歌或舞。聒聲震天。

Other officials, the Court musicians, took place on a dragon-boat (龍舟, a boat with a dragon-shaped prow, see above, Book I, pp. 83 sqq.) and beat bells and drums, sang and danced, so that their voices "made heaven shake". The next day it thundered and rained a little, but after a short while the sky became clear again, and outside of Kyōto the dust was only moistened a little On the 25th the result was the same, and on the 26th the officials, who incessantly, night and day, had been making music on the pond, were praised by the Emperor and were allowed to stop the work.

From this passage we learn that the dragon of the pond in the Sacred Spring Park was originally not an Indian Nāga, introduced by the Buddhists, but a Chinese, perhaps a Japanese, dragon, which formerly used to be forced to ascend and to make rain by depriving him of his element, the water, or by stirring him up by a terrible noise, according to the Chinese methods described above [1]. The Buddhist priests identified this dragon with an Indian Nāga-king, whom they caused to give rain by reading sūtras. In the seventh century, however, the Chinese ideas prevailed at the Japanese Court, and the Emperor himself sometimes proceeded to a river, and, kneeling and bowing to the four quarters of the compass, prayed to Heaven in the Chinese way. Then it shundered and continuous rains made the crops thrive [2].

In 875 the old Chinese methods of causing rain apparently had sunk into oblivion at the Japanese Court, but were tried again when the old man turned the attention of the Courtiers to them, because the sūtras failed to have any effect.

Like the Shintō dragon-gods the dragon in the Sacred Spring Park was believed not only to be able to make rain, but also to posses the faculty of stopping it, if it was pouring too abundantly. Thus in 880 a Buddhist priest recited the *Kwanchō* (灌頂, washing the head, baptism) *sūtra* there for three days, in order to stop the rain [3].

Also the *Nihon kiryaku* [4] contains several passages relating to Buddhist rain-prayers in the park. In 972 the so-called "Law (method) of the Rain-praying-sūtra" (*Seiukyō-hō*, 請雨經法, i. e. the doctrine of the *Mahāmegha sūtra*, cf. above, pp. 25 sqq.)

---

1 Book I, Ch V, § 3, p 119, cf the Chinese legend concerning the Emperor Shi Hwang, whose soldiers made a terrible noise to frighten the dragon god (Book I, Ch. VI, § 7, p. 125)

2 *Fusō ryakki*, Ch IV, K T K. Vol VI, p 508, the Emperor Kwōgyoku in 642.

3 *Sandai jitsuroku*, Ch XXXVII, p 541.

4 日本紀畧, written after 1036, K T K Vol V

was practised there for nine days with a splendid result, as well as in 982, 985 and 1018 [1].

When leaving the Annals and turning to the legendary works, we obtain the following information. The *Konjaku monogatari* [2] relates how in a time of heavy drought the Emperor ordered KŌBŌ DAISHI (774—835) to cause rain, and the saint for seven days practised the Doctrine of the Rain-praying-sūtra in the Sacred Spring Park. Then there appeared on the right side of the altar a s n a k e [3], five shaku long, carrying a little gold-coloured snake, about five sun in length, and after a while both disappeared into the pond. Only four of the twenty priests who were sitting in a row could see the apparition. One of these elected ones asked what it meant, whereupon another answered that the appearance of the Indian dragon-king Zennyo, 善如, who lived in India in the Anavatapta [4] pond and was now living in the pond of the Sacred Spring Park, was a sign that the doctrine would be successful. And really, a dark cloud rose up in the Northwest, and soon the rain was pouring down. Thenceforth, whenever drought prevailed, the same doctrine was practised in the park, and never in vain.

The *Kojidan* [5] states that this event occurred in the year 824. According to this work the Buddhist priest Shubin (守敏) requested the Emperor to be allowed to practise the Rain-prayer-doctrine himself instead of Kūkai (Kōbō Daishi), as he was as much experienced in such matters as the latter. This was granted, and he succeeded in causing thunder and rain in Kyōto, but not beyond Higashi yama. Then Kōbō Daishi was ordered to make it rain over the whole of the country, which he promised to do within seven days. This limit, however, expired, and the sky was still cloudless as before. The saint, absorbed in meditation (samādhi), arrived at the conclusion that Shubin, his rival,

---

1 Second Part, Ch VI, p 940, Ch VII, p 975, Ch VIII, p 986, Ch XIII, p 1115, at the same time, in 1018, the "Five Dragons Festival", 五龍祭, took place

2 K. T K Vol XVI, Ch XIV, nr 41, pp 812 sq

3 Here we find the snake form of the Nāga, in the *Sandai jitsuroku* and the *Kojidan* the god is called a dragon

4 阿耨達智, translated into 無熱. Buddhist works mention a *female* Nāga, called 善女 Zennyo, "Virtuous Woman", but the same Nāga is represented as a *man* with a dragon's tail, standing on the clouds, in a picture of the ninth century, in Kongōbu-ji on Kōya-san (*Kokkwa*, Nr 227, Pl I) Two other pictures representing this Nāga, also on Kōya-san, have not yet been described Cf PETRUCCI, Les documents de la Mission Chavannes, Revue de l'Université de Bruxelles, Avril—Mai 1910, pp, 495 sq

had caught all the dragons and shut them up in a water-pitcher
by means of magical formulae (tantras). This was the reason
why his (Kōbō's) own prayers were in vain He decided, however,
not to abandon his hope, and continued to recite the sūtra.
During the night of the second day he said "In this pond is a
dragon, called Zennyo, who pities mankind To him I have prayed,
and now I see him rising out of the midst of the lake, gold-
coloured, about eight sun long, seated on the head of another
dragon, eight shaku in length". This was reported to the Emperor,
who soon sent a messenger with offerings for the Dragon-King.
And when the seven days of the new vow had expired, a heavy
thunderstorm broke forth and a torrent of rain came down all
over the country, so that the water of the pond overflowed the
altar. As a reward for having saved the people from starvation,
Kūkai was elevated to the rank of Shōsōzu, bishop [1].

The *Taiheiki* [2] gives another version of the same legend. After
having stated that the park was laid out in the time of the
Emperor Kwammu (781—806) in imitation of the Ling yiu
(靈囿), the park of the Chinese Emperor Wen, of the Cheu
dynasty, the author informs us that the same Japanese monarch
(who built the Palace at Kyōto, the new capital which he
founded and made his residence in 794), had two Buddhist
monasteries built, on the East and West sides of the Sujaku
gate, called Tōji and Seiji, "the Eastern and the Western
Monastery". The former was under the direction of Kōbō Daishi,
who had to guard the Emperor's rank, the latter stood under
Bishop Shubin, who had to protect His Majesty's body. After
Kōbō Daishi's return from China, Shubin, who had been the
great man during Kōbō's absence, was cast into the shade by
his rival. The Emperor, who had been in great admiration for
Shubin's miraculous magic power, now considered Kōbō his
superior. This was more than the ambitious Shubin could bear;
he fostered a deep hatred against his sovereign as well as against
his rival, and in order to revenge himself on the former he
caught all the dragon-gods of the inner and outer seas by means
of the power of his tantras, and shut them up in a water-pitcher.
In this way he caused the terrible drought about which we read
in the *Konjaku monogatari* and *Kojidan*; it lasted fully three
months and made the people suffer immensely. Then Kōbō Daishi
reported to the Emperor that there was only one dragon, a

---

1 The same legend is to be found in the *Genkō Shakusho*, Ch I, K T K Vol,
XIV, p. 651   2 Ch XII, pp. 11 seqq.

Bodhisattva of higher rank than Shubin, namely the Dragon-king Zennyo of the Anavatapta pond[1] in Northern India, who was not in Shubin's power. Immediately a pond was dug before the Palace and filled with pure water, whereupon Kōbō invited the Dragon-king to come and live there. And behold, a gold-coloured dragon, eight sun long, appeared, seated on the head of a snake, more than nine shaku in length, and entered the pond. When Kōbō had reported this lucky news, the Emperor sent a messenger with all kinds of offerings in order to worship the Dragon-king. The result was marvellous, for soon it rained for three days all over the Empire. Since that day the Shingon sect flourished more and more, and Kōbō Daishi was highly revered by high and low. In vain Shubin worshipped Gundari[2] and the Yakshas, to destroy his enemy, for as soon as Kōbō heard this, he began to worship Dai Itoku Myō-ō[3], and there was a violent struggle in the air between these two parties. "In order to make Shubin careless, Kōbō caused the rumour of his own death to be spread, which created great sorrow among all classes of the people, but great joy in his enemy's heart As Kōbō had expected, Shubin broke down his altar and stopped worshipping the demons, but at the same moment Kōbō's power struck him and he fell dead on the floor His monastery soon decayed and disappeared, and Tōji's glory increased yearly. Kōbō made a dragon of so-called *chigaya* (Imperata arundinacea, a kind of reed) and placed it upon an altar[4]. Then he promised to the selected crowd which had assembled, that he would cause the real dragon to stay in the park and protect the country by his doctrine, while the Dragon-king of reed would become a big dragon and go to the Anavatapta pond in India. According to another tradition the reed dragon ascended to the sky and flew away in an eastern direction, but stopped in Owari province, at Atsuta's famous Shintō shrine, a lucky foreboding of the spreading of Buddha's Law to the East. Kōbō said. "When this Dragon-king (i. e. the real one) goes to another country, the pond will dry up, the land will be waste and the world will be in poverty. Then my priests (the Shingon priests) must pray to the Dragon-king to stay, and thus save the country".

So we know that the Buddhist priests, ordered by the different

---

1 無熱池.   2 軍荼利, King of the Yakshas

3 大威德明王, identified with Yamāntaka, a manifestation of Mañjuçrī as "Destroyer of Yama"

Emperors to pray in the park for rain or for stopping rain, always belonged to the *Shingon* sect.

The *Kojidan* [1] relates how in 1016 Bishop Shinkaku (深 覺) prayed for rain in the park and had a splendid success within a few hours, after a very long and heavy drought. The Naidaijin, one of the Ministers, had sent him a message to warn him that he would be derided by the world if he failed, but the bishop answered that it was not for himself, but for the people's sake that he would try. And behold, on the hour of the sheep dark clouds arose, a heavy thunderstorm burst forth and the rain fell down in torrents.

In the *Gempei seisuiki* [2] we read that in 1179 the "Secret Doctrine of the Rain-prayer-sūtra" was practised in vain in the Sacred Spring Park, nor had the prayers of other powerful priests any effect, till at last a secret tune, played on a biwa at the shrine of Sumiyoshi, caused a continuous and heavy rain to fall down. According to the *Hyakurenshō* [3], the same sūtra was read in the park in the years 1215 and 1224; and the *Genkō Shakusho* [4] relates the same thing about the year 1082.

The *Zoku kojidan* [5] mentions a two-storied gate on the southside of the park, which was destroyed by the "Dragon of the Sacred Spring", who in Fujiwara no Saneyori's time (899—970) entered this gate in the shape of a beautiful man. He sat down, and when he was asked from where he came, he answered that he lived in the West and had passed the gate on his way to another place. Then he disappeared, and at the same time the sky became dark and a terrible thunderstorm arose. Tradition said that the Buddhist bishop Genkwa was just reciting the Rain-prayer-sūtra in the park, when the gate was destroyed.

The *Kimpishō* [6] tells us that in case of drought the Court-officials had first of all the task of cleaning the Sacred Spring Park. Then they were ordered by the Emperor to go to the

---

1 Ch III, K.T K Vol XV, p 80

2 源平盛衰記, "Record of the rise and fall of the Minamoto and Taira Families", written by an unknown author about 1250, Ch XVIII, p 471

3 百錬抄, written after 1259, Ch XII and XIII, K T.K Vol XIV, pp 195 and 1212

4 元亨釋書, written before 1346 by the Buddhist priest SHIREN, 師 錬, Ch X, K T K Vol XIV, p. 813

5 續古事談, probably written at the end of the thirteenth century, Ch II, *Gunsho ruijū*, nr 487, Vol XVII, p. 657

6 Cf. above, p. 156, note 2, *Gunsho ruijū*, Vol. XVI, nr 467, Ch. 下, p. 1073

park with some servants in order to sprinkle water on the
stones near the pond (this was, of course, a kind of sympathetic
magic) and to cry with loud voices the following words: "Give
rain, o Sea-dragon-king" [1]. This was the custom in the author's
time, but not before that age. When this ceremony had no
success within seven days, other Court-officials took their place.
When their work was crowned with success, i e. when it rained,
they reported this to the Emperor and obtained food and clothes
as a reward, whereupon they danced in the court-yard or at the
entrance of the Palace. As to other rites, the *Kimpisho* mentions
the praying for rain at the Imperial tombs [2], and the reading
of sūtras in the Taikyokuden, a building of the Palace [3], or in
the seven great Buddhist temples of Nara (Tōdaiji, Kōfukuji,
Genkōji, Daianji, Yakushiji, Seidaiji and Hōryūji), or in the
different Shintō temples In the Buddhist shrines the *Seiukyō*,
i. e. the *Mahāmegha sūtra* [4], in the Shintō sanctuaries the *Kongō-
hannya-kyō*, i. e. the *Vajra-prajñāpāramitā `sūtra* [5], were recited.
Sometimes, for instance in the Ōwa era (961—963), the Great
Bear was worshipped in the Sacred Spring Park, in order to
obtain rain.

An interesting legend is told about the Dragon of the Sacred
Spring Park in the *Taiheiki* [6]. Although it has nothing to do
with rain, we may mention this tale here in connection with
the other stories concerning the same dragon It runs as follows. —
In 1335 the Emperor Godaigo was invited by the Dainagon
Saionji Kimmune, one of the Fujiwara, to come to his house in
order to see a new bathroom. This invitation was given with
the intention to kill His Majesty, who would have stepped upon
a loose board of the floor and dropped down upon a row of
swords, put upright with the points upwards. Fortunately the
Emperor was saved by the dragon of the pond in the park, who
in the night before he intended to go to the fatal house appeared
to him in a dream in the shape of a woman, clad in a red
hakama and light-coloured garments. She said to him · "Before
you are tigers and wolves, behind you brown and spotted bears.
Do not go to-morrow". At his question as to who she was, she
answered that she had lived for many years in the Sacred Spring
Park. Then she went away. When the Emperor awoke, he

---

1 Apparently the legend concerning the Anavatapta pond was forgotten, otherwise
they would not have called him a sea-dragon

2 Cf above, p 158 sq   3 Cf. above, ibidem.

4 Cf. above, ibidem, and p 162   5 Cf above, p 34 (NANJŌ, nrs 10—12).

thought his dream very strange, but, as he had promised to go to Saionji's house, he decided to keep his word. On his way thither, however, he went to the park and prayed to the Dragon-god. And lo! all of a sudden the water of the pond was disturbed, and the waves violently struck the bank, although there was no wind. This agreed so strikingly with his dream, that he did not proceed on his way, but meditated as to what to do, whereupon Kimishige Chūnagon came to warn his Imperial Master against Saionji's treacherous intentions, about which he had heard that very morning. So Godaigo returned to the Palace, and Saionji was banished to Izumo, which he never reached because he was killed on the road.

The *Kimpishō* [1] states the following: "In 1211 the *Onyōshi* (陰陽師, Court diviners) held the festival called *Goryūsai* (五龍祭), the 'Five Dragons Festival', also named '*Amagoi no matsuri*' (雩祭), or 'Rain-praying festival". For three days the onyōshi fasted and kept indoors (i. e. in a temple within the park); the Emperor, however, [did not share the festival, for he] ate fish and offered no clothes or mirrors Sūtras read in the '*Dragon-hole*' (龍穴, *Ryū-ketsu*) were also very successful, or those read in the Sacred Spring Park, or offerings made to *Suiten* (水天, 'Water-Deva', explained by the commentator as '*Tembu no kami*', 'God of the Heavenly Department'), when several persons read these sūtras or made these offerings"

As to the "Five Dragons Festival" [2], we read in the *Fusō ryakki* [3] that this was celebrated in 904, on the eighth day of the seventh month, when a heavy drought prevailed. The Emperor then ordered the Onyōryō (the Department of Divination) to celebrate this festival in Kitayama, a mountain near Kyōto, at a place called *Jūnigwatsu kokkō*. As no Buddhist priests, but the onyōshi were the leaders of this ceremony, it was apparently not practised in honour of Nāgas but of Chinese dragons.

The author of the *Taiheiki* [4] complains that at his time (about 1382) the park was in a deplorable condition on account of the war, and he supposes that this must be very disagreeable for the Dragon-god, who perhaps had left the place because there

---

1 L.l, Ch 下, p 1072

2 Of above, p 162, note 1.

3 Ch. XXIII, K T K. Vol VI, p 669 旱氣尤熾。仍仰陰陽寮。於北山十二月谷口。五龍祭。

4 Ch XII, p 13a.

was very little water in the pond. As to the Rain-prayer-sūtra, i e. the *Mahāmegha sūtra*, this was still in his days considered a powerful means for obtaining rain.

Before leaving this subject we may observe that, according to the *Kokushi daijiten* [1], the park was repeatedly destroyed and restored, but that the pond is still there, and on a small island in the midst of it there are two chapels, one dedicated to Zennyo, the Dragon-king, the other to Benten. So this dragon, identified with an Indian Nāga, has bestowed rain upon Japan for eleven hundred years!

§ 5. The "Dragon-hole" on Mount Murōbu.

The above-mentioned *Dragon-hole* (*Ryū-ketsu*, 龍穴), where sūtras were read in order to cause rain, is spoken of in the *Kojidan* [2], where we read the following details.

The Dragon-hole on Mount Murōbu [3], in Yamato province, is the abode of the Dragon-King Zentatsu (善達, Sudatta? Sudar-çana? [4]), who first lived in the Sarusawa [5] pond at Nara. In olden times, when a harlot had drowned herself in the latter pond, the Dragon-King fled to Mount Kasuga, where he lived till the corpse of a man of low standing was thrown into his pond. Then he fled again and established himself on Mount Murōbu, where the Buddhist bishop Kenkei observed his religious austerities. Another priest, Nittai by name, who for many years cherished the wish of seeing and worshipping the Dragon-King's venerable shape, entered the hole in order to seek him. The entrance was pitchdark, but after having penetrated into the inner part of the hole, he arrived at a splendid palace under a blue sky. Through an opening of a window-blind (sudare), made of pearls, which was moved by the wind, he saw a part of the Hokkekyō, the Saddharma Pundarīka sūtra, lying on a jewel table. Then he heard a voice asking him who he was, and when he mentioned his name and the reason of his entering the hole, the Dragon-King (for he was the invisible speaker) said · "Here you cannot

---

1 國史大辭典, "Great Dictionary of Japanese History" (1908), p. 1338
s v Shinsenen   2 Ch. V, K T. K. Vol. XV, p 119.

3 室生山.

4 Di NANJŌ had the kindness to point out to me, that 善達 may be Sudatta, but that there is no Dragon-king of this name, Sudarçana, however, is found in the list of the Nāga-rājas.

5 猿澤池

see me. Leave this hole and you will meet me at a distance of about 3 chō from the entrance". So Nittai left the hole and actually beheld the Dragon-king, who arose out of the ground, wearing a robe and a cap, and disappeared after having been worshipped by the priest. The latter built a Shintō temple on the spot and erected an image of the Dragon-king, which was still there at the author's time (in the beginning of the thirteenth century). Sūtras were read at this shrine when people prayed for rain; and when the Dragon-king lent a willing ear to the prayers, a dark cloud hung over the hole This cloud spread over the whole sky and the rain came down.[1]

So tells the *Kojidan*; and it strikes us at once that a Buddhist priest erected a Shintō shrine in honour of the Nāga. The legend was apparently invented by the Buddhists to convert this dragon-hole, which probably was the abode of one of the mountain dragons of old Japan mentioned above[2], into a place of Buddhist sanctity. They changed the old Shintō cult into a Nāga worship, without going, however, as far as to replace the Shintō shrine with a Buddhist temple. The *Ryūketsu-jinja*, the "Shintō-shrine of the Dragon-hole", was afterwards called the *Ryū-ō-sha*, or Dragon-king's temple, and was famous for the rain bestowing power of its dragon-god.[3]

The same dragon is called *Zennyo* (善女, "The Good Woman", comp. the Zennyo, 善如, in the Sacred Spring Park, identified with Anavatapta[4]), instead of Zentatsu, in the *Genkō Shakusho*[5], where the Buddhist priest Ringa[6], who died in 1150, is said to have been so powerful that, when he prayed for rain, Zennyo, the Dragon-king, appeared. The same work states that the Buddhist priest Keien[7] lived for a thousand days as a hermit near the Dragon-hole on Mount Murōbu. On his way from there to another place he crossed a bridge over a river, when suddenly

---

[1] 日對件所立社、造立龍王體．于今見在云云．祈雨之時於件社頭有讀經等事云云。有感應之時龍穴之上有黑雲。頃而件雲周遍天上、有降雨事云云。

[2] Pp 135 sqq

[3] Cf YOSHIDA TŌGO (吉田東伍)'s *Geographical Lexicon* (*Dai Nihon chimei jisho*, 大日本地名辭書), Vol I, p 286, s v

[4] See above, p. 162

[5] Ch XI K T K Vol. XIV, p 828.

[6] 琳賀．   [7] 慶圓, who lived 1143—1223

a lady, noble looking and beautifully dressed, came and, without showing her face, politely asked him for the mudrā (mystic finger-charm) used to become at once a Buddha. At his question as to who she was, she answered· "I am the Dragon Zennyo". Then he taught her the mudrā, whereupon she said· "This is exactly the same mudrā as that of the seven former Buddhas"; and when the priest requested her to show him her face, she replied: "My shape is so terrible that no man can look upon it. Yet I cannot refuse your wish". Thereupon she rose into the air and stretched out the little finger of her right hand It proved to be a claw, more than ten shaku long, which spread a five-coloured light. Then she vanished at once. [1]

A dragon of the same name (Zennyo) was said to live in the *Zennyo ryū-ō chi* [2] or "Dragon-king Zennyo's pond" near the "Chapel of the thirty Guardian-gods" [3] on a mountain-peak in Kawachi province, Ishikawa district, called Tōmyō-dake or "Lantern-peak" on account of a Dragon-lantern which was seen there [4], and in a lake on Mount Washio, in the same province, Kawachi district (now Naka-Kawachi), near a Shintō temple. On both these places he was prayed to for rain with much success [5].

§ 6 Reborn as a rain-giving dragon

In the *Kojidan* [6] we read about Bishop Gonkyū. of Kwazan, to whom in the midst of a dense cloud a sacred dragon appeared together with the priest Shōkyū [7], of the Western pagoda [8], on Hieizan. This dragon was the "real shape" of Gobyō (御廟) Daishi, i e. Bishop Jie [9], which Gonkyū had often prayed to see. When he asked why the priest was in the dragon-god's company, he was informed that Shōkyū would become a relative of this god (i. e. a dragon). As soon as Gonkyū awoke, he sent a messenger to the Saitō monastery in order to inquire after Shōkyū's health. On hearing that the priest had been ill for

---

1 *Genkō Shakusho*, Ch XII, p 840

2 善女龍王池·

3 *Sanjū banshin dō*, 三十番神堂·

4 *Yūhō meisho ryaku*, 遊方名所略; written in 1697 by Ryō-ei, 了榮; Ch IV, p 59

5 Ibidem, Ch IV, p 51   6 Ch III, pp 69 sq

7 性救·   8 Saitō, 西塔·

9 慈慧大師, Jie Daishi, a famous Tendai priest who lived 912—985 and

more than ten days, he visited the patient and told him about the dream. Shōkyū shed tears with joy, for now he was sure that his prayer to become a relative of Gobyō Daishı would be fulfilled. After his death he was buried near the latter's tomb. In a time of drought the *Daıhannya kyō*, i. e. the *Mahāprajñā-pāramitā sūtra* (cf. above, p. 34) was recited there in order to avert the calamity, when suddenly a little snake appeared on the stone floor of the tomb, crept slowly behind Shōkyū's grave and entered it A small cloud of smoke arose from the grave to the sky, and, spreading gradually, filled the air, till it became a big cloud; then a thunderstorm raged and heavy rains rejoiced the thirsty earth

A little further [1] we read that Bishop Jıe, at the time of his being abbot (*zasu*, 座主) of Hıeizan, in somebody's dream was said to be a metamorphosis of Utpala, one of the eight Great Dragon-kings [2].

§ 7. Buddhist priests dominating the dragons.

The *Kojidan* [3] mentions the remarkable answer given by Bishop Jōkai [4] to the Emperor when the latter expressed his admiration for the priest's power, because it had rained violently for a couple of hours after Jōkai had been praying for two days. "Your Majesty", said he, "this is not *my* rain, and I cannot accept any reward for it. My rain, however, will arise to-morrow from the Northwest and come down. Then you may reward me". And actually the next day the clouds came from the Northwest, and it rained for three days.

A master in calling up and dominating the dragon-gods was also the Buddhist priest Jōkwan [5], who in the Engı era (901—922) freed the country from a terrible drought by causing the dragons to move about amidst thunder and rain [6]. The same bonze conquered a poisonous dragon on Hıeızan. There was on this mountain a rock in the shape of an open dragon's mouth, and the monks who lived near by in Saitō [7], and especially in a monastery called Senju-ın [8], all died soon. At last is was made

---

[1] Ch. III, p. 70
[2] See above, p. 4, and below, Ch IV   [3] Ch III, p 83
[4] 定海,   [5] 靜觀.
[6] *Uji shū monogatari* 宇治拾遺物語, written 1213—1218, Ch II, K T K. Vol XII, pp 31 seq
[7] 西塔.   [8] 千手院.

out that the rock was the cause of their death, and since that
time it was called the "Poisonous-Diagon-rock" [1]. Nobody would
live there any more, and Saitō and Senju-in became quite
deserted and fell to ruins. Then Jōkwan went to the place and
prayed for seven days and nights before the rock. In the last
night the sky became cloudy and there was a terrible movement
in the air, while Hieizan was covered with clouds. After a while,
however, it cleared up, and behold! the rock had disappeared
and only some rubbish was left. Thenceforth it was safe to live
in Saitō, and Jōkwan's name was kept in grateful memory and
admiration by the monks of the mountain still in the author's
days. Apparently the poisonous dragon had left the place in
consequence of the prayers which were also in times of drought
so powerful in stirring up the dragons and the clouds [2]

According to the *Fusō ryakki* [3], on the 21th day of the second
month of 1065 the priests of Hieizan assembled in the Kamo
temple at Kyōto, where they prayed for rain and recited the
Ni-ō sūtra Then a little snake appeared and spit out some
vapour before the sanctuary, whereupon a little rain fell down.

The *Gempei seisuiki* [4] relates that in 1174 such a heavy drought
prevailed that the rivers dried up and the fields could not be
cultivated Then a priest of Hieizan, Chōken [5] by name, who
had the rank of Gonshōsōzu [6], in order to assist the peasants
wrote a letter to the Dragon-gods and read it aloud, looking up
to the sky. In this letter he reproved and instructed the dragons,
at the same time imploring them to make it rain. Heavenly
men (gods) and dragon-gods, he wrote, ought not to be ashamed
to remedy a wrong they had done, and therefore they, the
dragons, had to cause a "sweet rain" (甘雨) to fall and to
put a stop to this terrible drought. The dragons listened to
these words and gave continuous rains, so that both Emperor
and people were filled with admiration for Chōken's power and
with devotion for Buddha's Law.

§ 8. Dragon-women in ponds.

The *Sanshū kidan* [7] contains the following legends. In the

---

1 *Dokuryū no iwa*, 毒龍ノ岩.　　2 *Uji shūi monogatari*, 11
3 Ch XXIX, K.T K Vol. VI, p 807　　4 Ch III, *Teikoku Bunko*, Vol V, 69.
5 澄憲.　　6 權少僧都, "Vice-bishop".
7 三州奇談, written in 1764 by HOTTA BAKUSUI, 堀田麥水; Ch. I,

neighbourhood of seven ponds in the mountains of Enuma, a district of Kaga province, many strange things happened There were people who said that they had heard there the voices of several hundreds of men in the midst of the night, and that they had seen these men lighting torches upon the ponds Anglers had seen the water rising without any visible reason, and the more they retreated, the higher the water rose, till they at last stopped angling and fled home as fast as their legs could carry them. When looking back at a distance of one or two chō from the ponds, they saw a silver-dragon (銀龍) in the shape of a boy (ginryū no warabegata, 童形) appearing above the water. There was a road between these ponds, from where sometimes a huge face dashed forth; and one night it was as if men were fighting there.

In times of drought the people worshipped these ponds and there prayed for rain. One day a little girl was found there by the inhabitants of a neighbouring monastery. They took her home and educated her, but after twelve years she constantly uttered the wish to make a pilgrimage to Ise, and although she received the answer that this did not agree with the law of the empire (as she was a woman), she persisted in speaking about it. At last her foster-fathers gave in, secretly hired a sedan-chair and let her go to Ise. She went off gladly, but when she came at a lake, she said. "This must be my lake, take me to the bank", and when the sedan-chair carriers did so, she alighted, adjusted her clothes and said· "I am well acquainted here, you can go home". Then with her beautiful garments on she jumped into the water and disappeared in the deep. She was a beautiful girl, but her face was long (a sign of something unnatural [1]). Although the author does not state it, this was apparently a female dragon, temporarily transformed into a girl.

Another dragon-woman lived in the so-called Rope-pond (Nawa ga ike, 繩 が 池) in Etchū province. This was a pond in the mountains, about two ri in diameter. Heavy storms and rains often raged in this vicinity, when everywhere around splendid weather prevailed. Down to the author's time the dragon-woman was said to live in the pond and to cause its never drying up; and his contemporaries still ascribed to her a great influence on the weather [2].

---

1 Bewitching women are often described as having extraordinarily long faces. Cf. *Sanshū kidan*, Ch I, p 673, where a gigantic woman with a huge face is supposed to be a fox or a tanuki, at any rate the vital spirit (精) of an old creature

2 Ibidem, Ch. V, p. 839.

A similar pond is spoken of in the *Sanshū kidan kōhen* [1]. An evil snake (*akuja*, 惡蛇) was believed to have there her abode and to commit all kinds of strange things. When one stood on the bank of the pond and looked over the water, such a dreary wind was blowing, that most people fled home. If one prayed there for rain, his prayer was usually heard. The author was in doubt whether a terrible looking woman, who one night appeared on a neighbouring bridge to a man returning from a festival in a slightly tipsy condition, was the snake of the pond or a transformed wind-tanuki [2]. She stood on the balustrade of the bridge, binding up her hair and laughing loudly with open mouth, so that all her black teeth were visible. Her malicious face was square and very ugly, and it seemed as if she had but one leg. When people approached with torches, she flew away. Another time she attacked a man who had also enjoyed a good cup of sake and who was on his way home in the dead of night. She flung him from the road into the grass and then disappeared, but the poor fellow was ill for a whole month. As the water of the pond was flowing around the village and under this bridge, it is possible, says HOTTA, that the woman was the snake of the pond, although her body, which she moved so easily in flying away, did not remind one of a *dragon-snake* (龍蛇) (which always wants a cloud as vehicle). The name of the pond, "Shiroshūto (白醜人) no ike", or "Pond of the White and Ugly Person", had perhaps something to do with the transformation of the snake into an ugly woman.

§ 9. Stirring up the dragons by throwing iron or filth into their ponds.

If an iron utensil was thrown into the Rope-pond, mentioned in § 8, suddenly darkness covered the land and a hurricane devastated the ricefields. For this reason the villagers strictly forbade other people to approach the pond without a special reason It was said that greedy merchants, who had bought rice, threw metal shavings into the pond in order to cause storm and rain, which would destroy the crop and thus make the price of the rice run up [3]. This way of stirring up the dragons by means of

---

1 三州奇談後編, written in 1779 by the same author; Ch V, p 952.

2 風狸, *kaze-danuki*, cf my treatise on "*The Fox and Badger in Japanese Folklore*" Transactions of the Asiatic Society of Japan, Vol XXXVI, Part III, p 403

iron which they disliked very much was borrowed from China, as we have seen above [1]; it was practised also at the «Pond of the Ugly Woman", mentioned in the *Sanshū kidan kōhen* (above, § 8), where within a day after one had thrown metal shavings into the pond certainly a heavy storm arose and the rain came down in torrents.

We may compare with this a passage of the *Matsunoya hikki* [2], where we read that the inhabitants of Tsukui-agata [3] (district), Sagami province, used to throw horse dung, old sandals and other filth into a pond in the neighbouring Toyama, when drought prevailed After having done this they rapidly fled for fear of the angry dragon, which certainly arose, causing a terrible hurricane and heavy rains. As we have stated above [4], the idea of causing rain by arousing the dragons' anger is quite Chinese.

It was certainly also a pond, inhabited by a dragon or a snake, which we find mentioned on p. 653 of the *Sanshū kidan* (Ch. I). In summer, when the people wanted rain, they went thither, cut a mackerel to pieces and threw these into the mountain pond, at the same time praying for rain. If they did so, their prayer was always heard, and the rain came down at once. This seems to be an offering to the dragon, but it might be another way of stirring him up by ill-treating one of his subjects, the fishes, before his eyes.

§ 10 A dragon engraved on an incense pot believed to cause rain. Pine trees cause clouds to rise and rain to fall.

The dragon was so much connected with rain, that even an incense pot, decorated with a "cloud-dragon", *unryū* (雲龍), was supposed to be the reason why it always rained on the day of an Inari festival. This pot was preserved among the precious objects of a temple, dedicated to the Rice-goddess, but was hidden when the suspicion rose that it caused the annoying rain on Inari's day [5]. This appeared, however, not to be the case, for the rain poured down as well after this measure as before.

---

1 Book I, Ch V, § 3, pp 119 sq , cf pp 67 sqq.

2 松屋筆記, written by TAKADA TOMOKIYO, 高田與清, who lived 1782—1847, Ch. 109, p. 23 (new printed edition, Vol III, p 411)

3 津久井縣.

4 Pp 119 sq

5 Comp above, p 117, where we have read about an old murō with a dragon-shaped handle, used in China as a magical instrument for causing the dragons to give rain.

as soon as the day arrived, fixed for the dances of children,
clad in festive dresses in honour of Inari. On the days devoted
to Sannō, Suwa and Tada Hachiman the weather was all right,
but Inari's festival was always spoiled by rain. At last the reason
was found out. The boards of the stage, on which the dances
were performed, were made of the wood of some sacred pine
trees which had belonged to a neighbouring Shintō temple but
were sold by the villagers at a time of pecuniary distress. The man
who bought these trees placed them in the compound of the
Inari temple, and as the wood was very strong, it was used in
building the stage for the sacred dances of this sanctuary Now
it struck the people that every time when this timber was used
(such stages are always temporarily built, and broken down after
the festival), and the sun shone upon the boards, it began to
rain. On account of this fact a messenger was despatched to
the village whence the wood had come, in order to make inquiries
as to the trees in question. The man came back with the news
that the two woodcutters who had cut those trees had died within
a few days in a state of madness, as if they were possessed by
some evil spirit. This confirmed the people's opinion as to these
pine trees being the cause of the rain at Inari's festival, therefore they took them away and laid them near the worshipping-
hall (instead of using the wood for building the dancing stage).
They said: "We have heard that in China, in olden times, under
the reign of the Emperor Shi Hwan, of the Ts'in dynasty (B. C.
246—210), a pine tree suddenly became a big tree and kept off
the rain. How is it that these pine trees are causing rain nowadays?
It is said that pine trees, being covered with a scaly armour,
change into d r a g o n s when they become old. This may be the
reason why they always had the miraculous power of calling
up the clouds and the rain" Thus spoke the people, and they
all admired the wonderful influence of the pine trees [1]

§ 11 The eight Dragon-kings.

A *Shintō* (!) temple, dedicated to the eight Dragon-kings, is
mentioned in the *Seki no akikaze* [2]. The author of this work

---

[1] *Sanshū kidan*, Ch II, p. 712

[2] 關ノ秋風, written by SHIRAKAWA RAKUŌ, 白川樂翁, "The merry
old man of Shirakawa" (i e MATSUDAIRA SADANOBU, 松平定信, who lived

prayed there for rain himself, and his prayer was heard Then he ordered the villagers to repair the shrine. Afterwards, when the sluices of heaven were opened too long, he successfully prayed to the dragons again, this time for stopping the rain.

§ 12 A Buddhist dragon's suicide.

The *Nihon shūkyō fūzokushi* [1] gives an old tradition explaining the names of three Buddhist temples in Shimōsa province. In 730 A. D., when the priest Shaku-myō by order of the Emperor prayed for rain, he had a splendid success, and at the same time a dragon appeared in the air, who cut his own body into three parts and died. The middle part fell in Imba district, where the temple called *Ryūfukuji*, 龍腹寺, or "Shrine of the Dragon's Belly", is to be found. The tail came down in Katori district (also in Shimōsa), and caused the shrine *Ryūbyi* (龍尾寺, "Temple of the Dragon's Tail") to be built, while the head descended on the spot where the aforesaid priest had been praying and where still nowadays the name of the sanctuary, *Ryūkakuji*, 龍角寺, or "Temple of the Dragon's Horn" (at Sakai village, Shimohabu district) reminds the believers of the dragon of old.

A similar legend is to be found in the *Yūhō meisho ryaku* [2], where the *Shasekishū* [3] is quoted A blue dragon, on having heard a priest explaining Buddha's Law, was so full of emotion that his body divided itself into three parts. Where the head came down, Ryūtōji, "the Temple of the Dragon's Head", was built (at Nara); in another place in Nara, where the dragon's tail fell down, Ryūbyi was erected; and his trunk gave origin to the name of Ryūfukuji, also in the old capital, the only one of the three shrines which still existed in Mujū's time (i. e. in the beginning of the fourteenth century).

§ 13 Conclusions.

The passages, referred to in this chapter, have clearly taught us that there were from ancient times in Japan three methods of causing or stopping rain. The oldest, probably originally

---

[1] 日本宗教風俗志, written in 1902 by KATŌ KUMAICHIRŌ, 加藤熊一郎, p. 247.

[2] Ch. III, p 54. Cf above p 170, note 4.

[3] 沙石集, written by the Buddhist priest MUJŪ, 無住, who died in 1312

Verh Kon Akad v Wetensch. (Afd Letterk.) N R Dl XIII, N° 2. 12

Japanese, although at the same time Chinese, way was offering white or black or red horses to the dragon-shaped river-gods (red horses only for stopping rain). Then followed the Chinese custom of the Emperor's praying to the four quarters of Heaven, and the, also quite Chinese, idea of stirring up the dragons by great noise (as was done by the Court officials in 877 on the pond of the Sacred Spring Park). The same thought is found in the custom, prevalent in much later times, of throwing iron into a dragon's pond. The snake, and therefore also the dragon, which is considered to belong to the same species, is believed to hate and fear iron very strongly [1], and many a mighty serpent is said to have been killed or driven away by means of a single needle. Therefore, when iron is thrown into a pond, inhabited by a dragon, this rain-god is sure to get angry and to arise from his abode to the sky, which is in a moment covered with clouds. Then the dragon gives vent to his anger in a terrible thunderstorm accompanied by heavy rains, and the aim of the person who threw the iron utensil or the metal shavings into the pond, is reached.

The third way of causing rain, i. e. the Buddhist method, started from an opposite point of view. Instead of making the dragons rise by annoying them, the Buddhist priests recited sūtras which made such an impression upon the devout minds of the Nāgas, that they at once used to assist mankind and to liberate the people from the terrible sufferings caused by a long drought. Sometimes a sūtra was read concerning the Garuda-kings, the deadly and much dreaded enemies of the Nāgas, probably in order to make the latter feel quite dependent on Buddha's mighty protection. As Buddhism flourished more and more, this kind of rain-prayer soon became by far predominant in Japan In the eighteenth century, however, the Chinese methods of stirring up the dragons seem to have revived. Nowadays, when in the seventh and eighth months a continuous drought prevails and the peasants anxiously look up to the sky, fearing that the crops may be spoiled, they often go about in processions, beating drums and making noise, just as the Court-officials did in the year 877 A. D. So deeply rooted are the old Chinese ideas in the minds of the people.

---

1 Cf above, pp 67 sqq

CHAPTER IV.

THE INDIAN NĀGA IN JAPAN.

As we have seen above [1], the Indian Nāga legends served already in the time of the *Nihongi*, i. e. in the beginning of the eighth century, to embellish the old tales concerning the Japanese sea-gods. The magnificent palace of Oho-watatsumi no Mikoto at the bottom of the sea, and the "Jewel which grants all desires" of the Empress Jingō left no doubt about their Indian origin. It is no wonder then, that the more Buddha's Law flourished in Japan, the more the original Japanese sea and river-gods had to give way to the Indian conquerors; therefore most of the dragons, mentioned in later works, are Nāgas. In Chapter III we have seen that the rain-prayers, first offered exclusively to different Shintō gods, especially to the dragon-shaped river-deities, from the ninth century were also addressed to the Nāgas. In times of drought the Buddhist priests were more and more looked upon by the Emperors as the most powerful rescuers of the country, and large crowds of Shingon priests recited their sūtras in the Palace as well as at the Dragon pond of the Sacred Spring Park, in order to cause the Nāgas to make it rain all over the country.

As to the legends, referred to in this Chapter, many of them, although relating to Nāgas, at the same time have Chinese features. This is quite clear, for it was via China that all the Indian tales came to Japan. Moreover, many originally Japanese dragons, to which Chinese legends were applied, were afterwards identified with Nāgas, so that a blending of ideas was the result.

§ 1. The Dragon-kings revere Buddha's Law.

The *Sandai jitsuroku* [2] (901 A.D.) quotes a written supplication of the Lord of Harima, Sugawara no Koreyoshi (812—880), to

---

1 Book II, Ch. I, §§ 5 and 6, pp 139 sqq

2 Ch. V, p. 82. 眈動幽明。龍王移水府之深。星容布天圖之賚。 Another text gives 琛 instead of 深; then it would mean "The Dragon-kings transpose the precious stones of the water regions"

the Great Buddha of Nara (in 861), in which we read these words: "You give motion to the Darkness and the Light; the Dragon-kings retreat into the depths of the water regions, and the stars spread all over the sky (i. e. by the influence of your Law)". In the same supplication [1] we find the well-known term "*Ryūjin hachibu*", 龍神八部, "Dragons, Spirits, (or Dragon-gods), and (other beings of) the eight departments", a variant of *Tenryū hachibu*, 天龍八部, or *Ryūten hachibu*, 龍天八部 [2]

The *Shasekishū* [3] (before 1312 A. D.) refers to a sūtra entitled *Shinchikwan-kyō* [4], where we read: "If one wears only one Buddhist sacerdotal robe, he can cross the sea without being annoyed by poisonous dragons". So great is the reverence, even of these dangerous creatures, for Buddha and his believers.

§ 2. Dragons appear at the dedication of Buddhist temples

The *Fusō ryakki* [5] (about 1150 A. D.) relates how in 596, when the Buddhist temple called Hōkōji [6] was dedicated at Nara, a purple cloud descended from the sky and covered the pagoda as well as the Buddha-hall, then the cloud became five-coloured and assumed the shape of a dragon or phoenix, or of a man or an animal. After a while it vanished in a western direction [7].

A work of much later date, the *Yūhō meisho ryaku* [8] (1697), contains a legend about a Buddhist temple named Unryūzan, "Cloud-dragon-shrine", in Fuwa district, Mino province. When the abbot Ryūshū [9], who lived 1307—1388, was erecting this sanctuary, on the day of his starting the work a dragon appeared with a pearl in its mouth, a very good sign indeed. For this reason he called the mountain *Ryūshuhō*, "Dragon-pearl-peak" (龍珠峯). When the temple was ready, a rain of flowers fell from heaven.

---

1 P. 85
2 Cf above, Introd, § 1, pp 1 sq, note 5
3 Ch VI, 上, p 17 See above, p 177, note 3
4 心地觀經.
5 Ch III, K. T. K. Vol VI, p. 497.
6 法興寺.
7 變爲五色。或爲龍鳳。或如人畜。良久向西方去。
8 Ch VI, p 47. See above, p. 170, note 4.

§ 3. Dragons living in ponds or lakes, mostly near Buddhist shrines

In the history of Shitennō-ji, the "Monastery of the Four Deva-kings", the Buddhist monastery built by Shōtoku Taishi at Namba (the present Ōsaka), we read that in the compound of one of the buildings of this monastery, called Keiden-in, there was a deep pond, named Kōryōchi [1], in which a *blue dragon* was supposed to live [2].

At a distance of 36 chō from the temple of *Hakusan Gongen*, "The Manifestation of Mount Hakusan" (the Buddhist name of the ancient Shintō god of this holy mountain, which lies on the frontiers of Mino, Hida, Echizen and Kaga provinces) there was, according to the *Kojidan* [3] (1210—1220 A. D.), a sacred pond called *Mikuriya no ike*, or "August Kitchen Pond". All the Dragon-kings were said to assemble there and to prepare their food (供養, *kuyō*, food for offerings). Human beings could not approach it, for as soon as they had the audacity of doing so, a violent thunderstorm burst forth and killed the culprits [4]. Yet two holy men prayed to Hakusan Gongen to allow them to scoop a little water out of this pond. Another priest, who heard this, stayed for thirty seven days in the temple, continually repeating the same prayer. Then he went to the bank of the pond and earnestly practised the *kuyō-hō* or "food-offering-method". The sky was clear and there was no thunder or rain to drive him away. No sooner, however, did he scoop a little water into a pitcher, than his mind became confused and he felt as if he were dying. Yet he was able to return home after having concentrated his thoughts. Sick people who drank this water or rubbed themselves with it, were sure to be cured by the power of Buddha's Law.

The *Uji shūi monogatari* [5] (1213—1218) contains a tale about a young Buddhist priest who lived in the Nara period (719—784) and made the following practical joke. On the bank of the Sarusawa pond (near the Kōfuku temple) he put up a placard, announcing that on a special day and hour a dragon would arise from the

---

1 號荒陵池。其底深。青龍恒居處也。
2 *Fusō ryakki*, Ch III, p 495
3 Ch V, K T K Vol XV, p 119
4 號曰御厨池。諸龍王相集備供養之池也。件池人敢不能近寄。若有近寄人之時。雷電猛烈害人云云。
5 Ch. XI, K T K Vol XVII, p. 225 See above, p 171, note 6.

pond. As the passers-by, who read this, all believed it, on the
indicated day an immense crowd flocked together from Yamato,
Kawachi, Izumi and Settsu provinces, in order to see the miracle.
The priest himself, standing at the gate of the Kōfuku temple,
was highly amused by the success of his joke and laughed in
his sleeve when seeing the crowd on the tiptoe of expectation.
When the evening fell and no dragon appeared, they all went
home greatly disappointed.

The *Gempei seisuiki* [1] (about 1250) tells us how in 717 A.D. the
Zen priest Shinyu was invited by an unknown goddess, who said
to have always protected the Emperor and the people, to come
to the top of Mount Hakusan, in order to worship there her
"real shape". When he went there, and prayed near the pond
on the mountain, at the same time uttering incantations (*kaji*)
and making three sacred mudrās (mystic finger-distortions), there
arose from the midst of the pond an enormous nine-headed,
serpent-shaped dragon. The priest, however, declared that this
was not the deity's real shape, and increased the power of his
mantras (magical formulae), till he at last beheld the august
form of the Eleven-faced Kwannon.

When connecting this legend with the passage of the *Kojidan*,
referred to above, we may easily conjecture that the sacred pond
on Mount Hakusan had been from olden times the abode of an
original Japanese dragon, which gave rise to different Buddhist
dragon legends in regard to this pond

In the *Genkō Shakusho* [2] (before 1346) we read that the day
before the priest Jitsuhan's [3] arrival at Daigoji (in Kyōto), Genkaku [4],
the abbot of this monastery, saw in a dream a blue dragon
arising from the pond in the garden, lifting up his head and
spouting clear water from its mouth. As he understood the
meaning of this dream, the abbot the next morning ordered his
pupils to clean the monastery thoroughly in order to graciously
receive the venerable pupil, who actually arrived.

In a much later work, the *Sanshū kidan kōhen* [5] (1779), we find
the following particulars about an old woman who could cure
all kinds of diseases. She was believed to be possessed by the god
of the neighbouring pond, be it a river-otter (*kawa-oso*, 水獺),
or a *dragon-snake* (龍蛇). She was a strange, poor old woman,

---

1 Ch XXXIX, p 742. See above, p 163, note 2
2 Ch XIII, p 853.
3 實範.   4 嚴覺

who ate nothing but boiled flour, and refused to accept money from her patients Her fame was so great, that hundreds of people came from far and near to obtain some medicine from her. And queer medicine it was, for in reality it was nothing at all. After a patient had told her his complaint, she went inside, put a rush mat upon her head, and after having thus meditated for a while she came out of the house and gave an imaginary medicine to the patient, saying. "Here are doses for seven days. Only if you believe in me and think that you swallow medicine, it certainly shall have a good effect. If it has no result within seven days, you must come back". If the person followed her advice, he actually recovered. It was no wonder that the patients flocked together from all quarters. As she was busy from morning till night, she distributed charms, with "Namu Amida Butsu" or something of the kind written on them and marked with her stamp, instead of keeping the longer procedure which she had followed in the beginning. If anybody tried to deceive her, she immediately discovered this. She was such a wonderful being, that there were people who proposed to buy her for seven hundred ryō (from the villagers?) and to take her to the capital, but this was prevented by the authorities. Her strange food gave rise to the suspicion as to her being possessed by a tanuki, especially because she used to eat with her face hidden in the vessel. Others supposed her to be the mother of Hō-kun (鮑君, Lord Salted Fish [?]), or the wife of the "Great King with the straw sandals" [1], i. e. one of the Ni-ō [2]. But the physician of the place was of another opinion He said to Hotta, the author of the *Sanshū kidan kōhen*: "This old woman is assisted by some water-demon. I have often heard the villagers tell that she 'purifies herself' [3], as she calls it, twice a day, going into the pond and repeatedly diving under water, so that even her head is not visible. After having spoken with several patients she washes her head with well water, and if her head is not wet, she cannot see her patients. She certainly is a creature connected with the pond, be it a river-otter or a dragon-snake Some thirty or forty years ago, when her husband was still alive, one winter there came a Buddhist nun and lodged in their house, who washed clothes and served not only for herself but also for others. Thenceforth she stayed there every month for

---

1 草鞋大王, *Sō-ai tai-ō*

2 仁王.　　3 垢離ヲ取ル, *kori wo toru.*

three or four days, and then went home. At last the man, warned by a neighbour, watched her from the upper story of the latter's house, and saw her coming out of his house. After having walked some distance in human shape, she was transformed into a line of white vapour (白氣), flew to the pond, and disappeared under the water. The man, very much frightened by this sight, went to a neighbouring Buddhist temple and requested the priest to recite prayers on his behalf. Moreover, he pasted holy Buddhist texts and charms on the walls of his house, in order to avert the evil This was sufficient, for the nun never returned. Within a couple of years, however, the man died, and now, after more than thirty years, again such strange things happen in the same house. Probably the old woman is possessed by the Master (主, *nushi*) of the pond". So spoke the physician, no doubt jealous of the woman on account of her medical fame, but at the same time clearly expressing the superstitious ideas of the people. The term "dragon-snake" seems to indicate the Nāga, a serpent identified with a dragon; moreover, Buddhism plays a predominant part in this story.

Before the Restoration a so-called "Dragon-god festival" (*Ryūjin-sai*, 龍神祭) used to be yearly celebrated by the priest of the Gongen shrine at Hakone, the well-known mountain village in Sagami province. Three hundred thirty three gō (合) of "red rice" (*sekihan*), in a new wooden rice bowl, were offered to the Dragon-god of Hakone lake in the following way The Buddhist priest (now Ieyasu's shrine belongs to Shintō) went in a boat to the middle of the lake and there placed the bowl on the water, whereupon the boat went on, neither the priest nor the boatmen looking back Then they heard a sound as of a whirlpool on the spot where the offering had been made, and the bowl disappeared under the water [1]

§ 4. Reborn as dragons.

In the *Taiheiki* [2] (about 1382) we read the following legend. The second son of the Emperor Godaigo, Prince Takanaga, also called Ichi no Miya, who had been banished to Hata in Tosa province, longed so much for his consort, who had remained in Kyōto, that he despatched his faithful vassal, Hada no Takebumi,

---

1 *Nihon shūkyō fūzoku shi*, 日本宗教風俗志 (written in 1902), p 213.

to the capital in order to take her to his place of exile. When
the latter was on his way to Tosa with the lady, and they were
waiting for a propitious wind at Ama ga saki in Settsu province,
there was a samurai, Matsuura Gorō by name, who fell in love
with the beautiful woman, stole her and after having taken her
on board his ship, set sail at once. No sooner had Takebumi
perceived this trick, than he called the vessel back with a loud
voice, but the only answer he received was an outrageous laughter,
and the vessel pursued its course. Then poor Takebumi, at his
wit's end, said· "To-day I will become a dragon-god at the
bottom of the sea, and check that ship". With these words he
disemboweled himself and jumped into the sea. There is a well-
known whirlpool, called Uwa no Naruto, the "Sounding door
(i. e. eddy) of Uwa", between Shikoku and Awaji, which was said
to be the Eastern Gate of the Dragon-palace. It was there that
Takebumi's revenge revealed itself in a terrible way, for the vessel,
caught by the eddy, was turned about for three days, and in
vain all kinds of precious things, as bows and swords and clothes,
were flung into the sea as offerings to the Dragon-god. Then
the crew arrived at the conclusion that the dragon wanted the
woman herself, and Matsuura was about to throw her into the
furious waves, when a Buddhist priest advised him not to arouse
the Dragon-god's anger by making to him a human offering
which he, the dragon, certainly disliked, being a pure being and
a believer in Buddha. It is better, said the priest, to recite
sūtras and pray. So the whole crew prayed to Kwannon, and lo!
there appeared on the waves Takebumi's spirit, still beckoning
the vessel as he had done before his death, and preceded by
several retainers on horseback. Although there often happened
mysterious things on that spot, this time it was certainly
Takebumi's angry soul which caused the calamity. Therefore they
placed the woman, together with one sailor, in a small boat,
hoping to satisfy the ghost in this way and to get rid of her
without causing her death. As soon as they had done this, the
ship was at once driven out of the whirlpool and disappeared
in a western direction; it was never heard of again. As to the
lady, she safely arrived at an island, where she was kindly
received by the inhabitants, and where she remained for the rest
of her life, not daring to run the risk of being stolen again.

In the Fuse lake in Etchū province, so tells us HOTTA, the
author of the *Sanshū kidan* and the *Sanshū kidan kōhen* [1], a

---

1 Ch VII, pp 988 seqq

disappointed lover was said to have drowned himself, and his
passion (執念, shūnen) was believed to have condensed into
the form of a white dragon (with other words, his soul, on
account of its passionate condition at the time of his death,
was reincarnated in a dragon). This was in HOTTA's days
(eighteenth century) an old tale, and the lake had become ten times
narrower than before, so that the dragon was no longer supposed
to live in the water, but in a so-called "dragon-hole" (ryū-kutsu,
龍窟) under the ground, where "dragon-vapours", or "dragon-
breath", (龍氣) used to rise as a sign of the demon's presence
(these are Chinese ideas). In the beginning of the Anei era
(1772—1780) people who crossed a neighbouring ferry of the
river which flows into the lake, saw a long, white monster
swimming from the lake into the river mouth. When it was
at the bottom of the stream the water became quite white.
Sometimes the dragon showed his snow-white back, but not his
head or tail. Some people, who had seen his head, which seldom
was visible, said that it was square. After having enjoyed himself
in swimming along the coast for one day, he disappeared.
This dragon was said to have lived in that vicinity for a long
time, and as he was called "the white man" (白男, shiro-otoko),
HOTTA supposes him to be the same person who once drowned
himself and took this shape after having been deceived by his
sweetheart, "the white girl", and was afterwards living under
the ground because the lake had become too narrow. As he could
not immerse the land and destroy the fields, he from time to
time simply made an excursion to the neighbouring sea coast.
At the same ferry there was a creature called "shiga", which
stretched itself and checked the boats when the snow began to
melt; this was also some "breath" (氣), probably, says HOTTA,
the same "dragon-breath" which was examined by a wonder-
fully daring man during the Keichō era (1596—1614) according
to the work entitled "Chūgwaiden"[1]

According to a modern work, the Nihon shūkyō fūzoku shi
mentioned above[2], there is in Kasahara village, Tōtōmi province,
a pond called "Sakura ga ike", "Cherry-tree Pond". It is the
abode of a huge dragon, to whom those who have a special wish
pray on the middle day of higan (彼岸, "yonder shore", a
period of seven days in either equinox; the middle day is the

---

[1] 中外傳 (time and author?).
[2] P. 117, note 1, p 204

equinoctial day), at the same time making an offering to him
consisting of a bucket of hard boiled rice (*kowameshi*, 強 飯,
i. e. *sekihan*, 赤 飯, "red rice", rice boiled with red beans), which
they cause to float on the water. If they afterwards find the
bucket empty, this is a sign that the dragon has eaten the rice,
accepting the offering and hearing the prayer, but if the rice is
still in the bucket, the prayer will not be fulfilled. This dragon
is the reincarnation of the Buddhist priest Genkō, 源 皇, a Tendai
priest of Hieizan, teacher of Hōnen shōnin, 法 然, who lived
1132—1212. Genkō wished to become a dragon, because his life
was too short to obtain a sufficient knowledge of Buddha's
doctrine One day he heard from one of his disciples that the
above mentioned pond was an excellent place for a dragon to
live in. Then he sat down in religious meditation (samādhi), put
one drop of water in his hand, by means of which he made
clouds and rain, and flew through the air to the pond There
he died in meditation, and when his disciple came and called
him, an enormous dragon appeared above the water and wept.
At the pupil's request he assumed his former human shape and
talked with him for a long time.

We may make mention here of an old legend, to be found in
the *Gukwanshō* [1], which told that *Inoue no Naishinnō*, the Imperial
Princess Inoue, daughter of the Emperor Shōmu and Consort of
the Emperor Kōnin, had become a dragon even before her death.
She was accused of having practised *wu-ku*, 巫 蠱, a Chinese
magic art exercised by means of small reptiles and insects [2], in
order to have her son made Crownprince. For this reason she
was imprisoned in a hole in 772 by order of the Prime Minister
Fujiwara no Momokawa, and three years later both she and her
son died. According to popular tradition, however, she had turned
into a dragon even before her death.

§ 5 Dragon-kings of the sea check the course of vessels in order to obtain special Buddhist treasures as offerings

The *Fusō ryakki* [3] (1150) relates the following legend concerning
the abbot Dōshō (道 昭), who went to China in 651 and,

---

1 愚 管 抄, probably written by Bishop Ji-en, 慈 圓, who died in 1225,
K T K Vol. XIV, Ch VII, p 597
2 Cf. De Groot, *Religious System of China*, Vol. V, Ch. II, pp 826 seqq
3 Ch IV, K. T. K Vol. VI, p 514

when he returned to Japan, obtained from Hüen Tsang, the
famous pilgrim who went to India in 629 and returned in 645,
besides a relic of Buddha and sūtras a small kettle for preparing
medicines. Hüen Tsang had brought this kettle with him from
India and said that it was of the utmost value, because all
diseases could be cured by means of the medicines cooked in it.
This proved to be true, for one of Dōshō's companions, who fell
ill before they left China, was cured at once thanks to this
marvellous utensil On their way to Japan, in the midst of the
ocean, the ship suddenly stopped and did not move for seven
days, while wind and waves were raging around it in a terrible
way. Then a diviner said: "There is something on board which
is wanted by the Sea-god. I think it is the kettle". First the
abbot refused to give up his treasure, and said that there was
no reason why the Dragon-king should ask for it. But when the
others, afraid for their lives, urgently begged him to follow the
diviner's advice, the priest gave in and threw the kettle into
the sea. Immediately the storm and the waves abated, the ship
could continue its course, and soon they arrived in Japan.
Apparently the Dragon-king had actually wanted the offering of
the sacred kettle.

The *Konjaku monogatari* [1] describes how a Prime Minister, who
for his king transported a precious Buddha image across the sea,
was overtaken by a terrible storm. It was in vain that he threw
all kinds of precious things into the sea, the Dragon-king apparently wanted something else. At last the minister understood
what would appease him, and, praying for his life, he offered
the pearl from between the eyebrows of the Buddha image.
The Dragon-king stretched out his hand and took the pearl,
whereupon the storm calmed down. Although this danger was
over, the minister. who was convinced that he would be decapi-
tated when he confessed to his sovereign the loss of the
pearl, wept bitterly and besought the Dragon to return the
treasure. Then the Sea-god appeared to him in a dream and
promised to restore the pearl to him, if he would stop the nine
tortures which were inflicted upon the dragons. Rejoiced the
man awoke and, addressing the sea, answered that he was willing
to free the dragons from their tortures by copying and offering
holy Buddhist texts. And when he had done so, the Dragon-king
kept his promise and returned the pearl; but it had lost its
lustre. The Sea-god again appeared to the minister in a dream

---

1 Ch. XI, K T K Vol XVI, pp. 571 seq

and said that the pearl had freed him from the tortures of the serpent-road (蛇道), but that the *Kongō-hannya-kyō* (*Vajra-prajñāpāramitā sūtra*, cf. above, p. 34), which he had copied on his (the dragon's) behalf, had been still more powerful, as it had removed all his sufferings.

§ 6. The "jewel which grants all desires" (cintāmaṇi)

There lived in Northern India a Buddhist abbot, "Buddha's vow"[1] by name, who for the sake of mankind sought the "Precious pearl which grants all desires"[2]. He went on board a ship and, when in the midst of the sea, by Buddha's power called up the Dragon-king. After having bound him by means of mystic formulae (tantras), he required the pearl from him, whereupon the dragon, unable to escape, took the pearl from his-head and prepared to hand it over to the priest. The latter stretched out his left hand, at the same time making the "sword-sign", a mudrā (mystic finger-twisting), with his right hand. The Dragon-king, however, said: "In former times, when the Dragon-king Sāgara's daughter gave a precious pearl to Çākyamuni, the latter received it with folded hands; why should a pupil of the Buddha accept it with one hand?" Then the priest folded his hands, giving up the mudrā, and was about to take the pearl, when the Dragon-king, no longer suppressed by the mystic sign, freed himself from his bands and ascended to the sky, leaving the abbot behind with empty hands, and destroying his boat. The only man who was saved was the priest himself. Afterwards the same abbot met Bodhidharma[3], the patriarch, who came across the sea from Southern India (in 526), and together they went to Japan[4].

§ 7. The eight Dragon-kings.

At the time of Bishop Jie[5] being head-abbot (zasu, 座主) of Hieizan, somebody saw in a dream seven of the eight Great

---

1 佛誓, Bussei

2 如意寶珠, *nyo-i hōju, cintāmaṇi*, comp. above, p. 10

3 波羅門, Baramon, the "Wall-gazing Brahman".

4 *Fusō ryakki*, 扰萃 (Shōmu Tennō), K. T. K Vol. VI, p. 584.

5 Jie lived 912—985, cf. above, Book II, Ch. III, § 6, p. 170, note 9.

Dragon-kings [1] crossing a large sea in ships; on the eighth vessel no dragon was to be seen. When the man asked the reason of this Dragon-king's absence, he received the answer that the absent dragon was at present head-abbot of Hieizan. Evidently Jie was a metamorphosis of Utpala [2], the last of the eight Dragon-kings. That a dragon was his "real shape" we have seen above [3].

In the *Taiheiki* [4] an exile on Sado island prays to different gods to make a ship approach his lonely place. Among these deities are· "Gongen (Manifestations), Kongō dōji (*Vajra kumāra*), Tenryū (Heavenly Dragons), Yasha (Yakshas), and the eight Great Dragon-kings" [5]. Apparently the Nāgas last-mentioned were considered to be different from the Heavenly Dragons, which formed one of the four classes of Nāgas, mentioned above [6]. The eight Dragon-kings probably belonged to the second class of Nāgas, the "Divine Dragons" (神龍).

§ 8. The Dragon-gods of the inner and outer seas.

The *Gempei seisuiki* [7] says that Fujiwara no Yasuyori, banished to the island called Kikai ga shima, invoked the compassion of "the dragon-gods of the inner and outer seas, and (the other beings of) the eight departments" [8]. The same expression, i. e. "dragon-gods of the inner and outer seas", is found in the *Taiheiki* [9], where we read how in the year 1333 Nitta Yoshisada, Godaigo's faithful general, invoked them. He was marching towards Kamakura in order to punish the Shikken Hōjō Takatoki, and when he arrived at Inamurazaki, a cape between Enoshima and Kamakura, he prayed to the "Dragon-gods of the inner and outer seas" to make the sea retreat, that he might be able to pass with his troops along the shore and thus easily reach Kamakura. They apparently heard his prayer, for that night the tide suddenly became so low, that Takatoki's ships could not approach the coast, and the arrows of his soldiers could not reach Nitta's troops, which marched along the dry shore straight

---

1 Cf. above, Introd , § 1, p 4
2 優鉢羅龍王, Uhachira Ryū-ō
3 Book II, Ch. III, § 6, p 170
4 Ch II, p 9a.
5 權現金剛童子天龍夜叉八大龍王。
6 Introd , § 3, p. 21   7 Ch VII, p 183
8 內海外海龍神八部 Cf above, Introd ; § 1, pp 1 sq , note 5.
9 Ch X, p. 7b

to Kamakura. There they forced their way into the town and
caused Takatoki to disembowel himself.

§ 9. Dragon-palaces

According to the *Genkō Shakusho*[1] the Chinese bonze Kien
Chen[2], when crossing the sea on his way to Japan, was invited
by a dragon-god to come to his palace and preach for him[3].
After having complied with the request the priest continued his
journey and at last (in 762) arrived in Kyūshū (then called
Dazaifu).

The famous legend concerning *Tawara Tōda*, which is found
in the *Honchō kwaidan koji*[4], is a blending of Chinese and Indian
ideas. It runs as follows In the Hidesato temple, a Shintō shrine
near the Seta bridge in Ōmi province, Tawara Tōda[5], "Rice
bag Tōda", is worshipped together with *Suifushin*[6], the "God of
the Water Department". If one takes a centipede (*mukade*) to
this shrine, the animal immediately dies for the following reason.
In olden times, when Fujiwara no Hidesato (who lived in the
first half of the tenth century) crossed the bridge, a big serpent
lay across it. The hero, however, was not at all afraid, and
calmly stepped over the monster which at once disappeared into
the water and returned in the shape of a beautiful woman. Two
thousand years, she said, she had lived under this bridge, but
never had she seen such a brave man as he. For this reason
she requested him to destroy her enemy, a huge centipede[7],
which had killed her sons and grandsons. Hidesato promised
her to do so and, armed with a bow and arrows, awaited the
centipede on the bridge. There came from the top of Mikami
yama two enormous lights, as big as the light of two hundred
torches. These were the centipede's eyes, and Hidesato sent three
arrows in that direction, whereupon the lights were extinguished

---

1 Ch I, K T. K Vol XIV, p 642

2 鑑眞, Kanshin

3 The text says only "he went to the Dragon-palace", but the commentator explains
the reason why he did this

4 本朝怪談故事, written in 1711 by the Buddhist priest Kōso, 厚譽;
Ch I, m 16, p 29

5 俵藤太.   6 水府神.

7 The centipede is, according to *Chinese* belief, the snake's deadly enemy, whose
ability in killing snakes is so great, that it is considered to be an excellent charm
against them, and used in order to cure diseases caused by *ku*-sorcery. Cf De Groot,
Religious System of China, Vol V, pp 863 seqq

and the monster died. The dragon woman, filled with joy and gratitude, took the hero with her to the splendid Dragon-palace, where she regaled him with delicious dishes and rewarded him with a piece of silk, a sword, an armour, a temple bell and a bag (*tawara*) of rice. She said, that there would always be silk left as long as he lived, however much he might cut from it; and the bag of rice would never be empty [1]. As to the temple bell, this was the most precious treasure of the Dragon-palace.

After his return to the world of men Hidesato offered the bell to Miidera, the famous Buddhist monastery near Ōtsu in Ōmi province. One day a priest of Hieizan stole it, but as it did not produce any sound but the words: "I wish to go back to Miidera", he angrily threw it into the valley, where it was found and taken back to Miidera by the monks of this monastery. Then a small snake appeared and, stroking the cracks of the bell with its tail, made them vanish at once, so that the precious object was uninjured as before.

The *Taiheiki* [2], which also tells Tawara Tōda's legend, says that the bell was stolen during the war between Miidera and Hieizan, when the former monastery was on fire, and that it fell to pieces in the valley, but was restored by the snake in one night. The snake was probably the dragon woman herself or a messenger from the Dragon-palace. In the version of the *Taiheiki* the serpent which Hidesato met on the bridge did not change into a woman, but into a strange small man; it was the Dragon-king himself. On account of the miraculous rice bag the hero was thenceforth called Tawara Tōda, "Rice bag Tōda" [3].

The *Yūhō meisho ryaku* (1697) [4] mentions a Buddhist priest, Nanzō by name, who lived in the Enkyū era (1069—1073) and who for three years prayed in the temple of Kumano Gongen

---

1 In a later version of the legend he got a box of white wood, three or four sun square, called *debebako*, 出米箱, "Rice supplying box" This was put above the ceiling, and if one placed a rice box beneath and pointed at the box above, saying, "Rice for to-morrow for so many persons", the next morning certainly such a quantity of rice was in the box beneath This miraculous box remained in the family for many generations, and retained the same faculty of giving rice, till it was taken down to be cleaned and by mistake was dropped on the stones in the garden Then it broke, and a dead little white snake fell out of it. After that no rice was provided any more, but the box and the snake are still preserved by the family.

2 Ch XV, p. 5.

3 In reality the name Tawara was written 田原, not 俵 Tawara, 田原, is the name of a noble family at Aki (Bungo province), and of a place in Mikawa

4 Ch X, p 39, see above, p 170, note 4 This passage is quoted in the *Nihon shūkyō fūzoku shi* (1902), p 247

for a long life, that he might be able to thoroughly study Buddha's doctrine. At last he learned by a divine revelation in a dream that, if he went to a large, deep lake on Mount Koto-wake, on the frontiers of Hitachi and Mutsu provinces, he would become a dragon and have a very long life. Highly rejoiced at the success of his prayers he followed the god's advice and took up his abode in a hole near the lake, where he spent his days in reading sūtras and leading a strictly ascetic life But a female dragon, who daily visited him in the shape of a beautiful woman, in order to hear him reciting the sūtras, fell in love with him and invited him to go with her to the dragon-palace at the bottom of the lake He followed her, carrying eight sūtra rolls, and forthwith lived with the woman in the luxurious mansion, where he changed into an eight-headed dragon (on account of the eight sūtra rolls). His voice is often heard, reciting the sūtras in the lake. About three ri from this spot there is another lake on Nuka ga take, which formerly was inhabited by a nine-headed male dragon. This was the above-mentioned dragon-woman's husband, and when his place was taken by his eight-headed rival (the transformed priest), he went to the other lake and had a fight with the obtruder, but was beaten and killed. For this reason no longer a dragon lives in the lake of Nuka ga take.

Finally, we may refer to a name, formerly given to the seastar on account of its resemblance to the common spools for winding thread on, i. e. *Ryūgū no itomaki*, "spool of the Dragon-palace"[1].

§ 10. Dragons connected with Buddhist priests

The *Genkō Shakusho* says that a blue dragon appeared to the Tendai priest Eisai (榮西), when he in 1168 ascended the Chinese T'ai (台) mountain, the holy ground of the Tendai sect[2].

In the same work we read how the Dragon-king Kwō-taku (廣澤) announced in a dream to the Chinese teacher of Fang-Ngau (方巷) and Enji (圓爾, i e. the Japanese priest Ben-en, 辯圓), that these two pupils were now ready to become priests. In consequence of this dream the master sent the latter back to Japan, in order that he might preach the Law there[3]

A third legend found in this work speaks of a daughter of the Emperor Sujaku (930—946), who went mad and, clad in

---

1 *Inter zakko*, 筠庭雜考, Ch IV, written by Kᴉᴛᴀᴍᴜʀᴀ Sʜɪɴsᴇᴛsᴜ, 喜多村信節 (1783—1856), Hyakka setsurin, 續下一 p 520
2 Ch. II, K. T K. Vol XIV, p. 658   3 Ch VII, p. 747

scanty garments, visited the cottage of a Buddhist hermit, to beseech him to hold incantations on her behalf (i. e to exorcise the evil spirit which was possessing her). The hermit agreed and the Princess returned home. In the middle of the night she (i. e. the evil spirit within her) suddenly exclaimed: "Help, help! a dragon is about to cut my throat with a sword, and a boy is tying me with a rope!" The ladies in waiting were very much frightened, but the next morning the patient was cured. A dragon and an angel, invoked by the priest's incantations, had driven out the evil demon [1].

§ 11. Eight dragons ridden through the sky by a Buddhist deity.

The *Taiheiki* [2] describes the vision of a man who passed the night praying before the Outer Shrine (Gegū) at Ise. He saw a gigantic god with twelve faces and forty two arms, brandishing swords and lances and riding eight dragons through the air amidst rain and wind, at the head of many others who drove in carriages above the clouds. They came from all sides, two or three thousand in all, in carriages or on horseback, while a brilliant palace, made of precious stones and silver, glittered in the sky.

§ 12 Curses wrought by dragons

The *Shinchomonshū* [3] mentions curses of dragons in the following passages. "An old tradition said that the guardian-god of the Ryūmon temple [4], a Buddhist sanctuary especially devoted to the religious services for the deceased relatives of Mr Mogami Gengorō, in Dewa province, was a dragon. One day the stone wall of this shrine had fallen to ruins, and a large number of men were working there together and had piled up stones, when a snake, about six or seven inches long, appeared from under the stones, was pursued and killed Those who had killed her, became at once giddy and died on the spot; the others, who had only pursued her, were ill for about fifty or sixty days. The body of this snake, tradition says, is now in the Keiyō temple opposite Asakūsa in Yedo".

---

1 Ch XI, p 822   2 Ch XII, p 9b

3 新著聞集, written by an unknown author about 1700, Zoku Teikoku bunko, Vol XLVII, Ch. IX, p. 126

4 龍門寺, "Dragon-gate temple"

No less severe was the curse of another snake-shaped dragon. The house of the head of a village called "*Ryō no ike*" or "Dragon's pond", in Uma district, Iyo province, was said to be built on a pool, inhabited by a dragon in remote ages. A pond in the garden, three or four shaku square, which was the remainder of this pool, was never dry, not even in times of drought On the 15th day of the 7th month (Ullambana, the Bon-festival for the dead) of the year 1638 the villagers were dancing (the "*bon-odori*", or "bon-dance") in this garden and making such a noise, that it lasted a while before they heard the master of the house crying for help. When they ran into the room, they found him standing in the dark, holding an animal by the throat which had swallowed one of the arms of his child, about eight years old. They cut the beast to pieces, but it became larger and larger and at last filled the whole room. It appeared to be an enormous serpent, yet it had evidently entered the house through a very small opening, only sufficient for an earthworm. Upon the sand of the pond a trace was visible, only a thin line, which showed that the dragon had crept out of the pond in the shape of an earthworm. The curse of the monster soon followed in a terrible way, for the whole family, more than seventy persons, died one after the other, except one blind minstrel who escaped this fate and told the story afterwards [1]

A man whose ship knocked against a huge snake, thirteen ken long, killed the monster with his sword, and, in order to escape its curse, cut its trunk into three pieces, buried these together with the head, and had masses said for the animal's soul. But this was all in vain, for thirteen years later, on the same day of the same month, nay even at the same hour, he exclaimed: "I drink water", was choked and died. The people were convinced that his death was caused by the snake. This water-serpent was, of course, a dragon [2].

§ 13. Relics of dragons preserved in Buddhist temples.

At Noda, in Mikawa province, there is a Buddhist shrine called *Senryū-in*, or "Spring-dragon-temple" (泉龍院), where three dragon's scales are preserved. Before the temple was built, its founder, Mōrin Shōnin, preached there every night, and each

---

1 Ch IX, p 128 The same legend is to be found in the *Yamato kwai-i-ki* (大和怪異記, written by an unknown author in 1708), Ch III, p 13b
2 Ch. IV, p 48.

time a beautiful woman came to listen, till she finally assumed her original shape, that of a huge serpent, which jumped into a pond near by and disappeared. The priest, who pitied the creature, filled up the pond and built a temple over it. Three scales, left by the dragon, are preserved in the sanctuary [1].

One of the treasures of another Buddhist shrine, called *Ryūgenji*, or "Dragon-spring-temple" (龍源寺), in Hagi village, Mikawa province, is the tooth of a "hidden dragon" (潛龍, *senryū*), subdued by the priest Shūtei [2].

§ 14 The "Dragon-flower-meeting".

In MIURA KENSŪKE'S *Bukkyō iroha jiten* [3], s. v. *Ryūge-e*, 龍華會, or "Dragon-flower-meeting", we read that, when Maitreya shall "forsake the world and find the truth of Buddha", he shall assemble a large crowd and expound his doctrine. All the trees on earth shall then assume the shapes of golden dragons and shall open their flowers. This is the meaning of the name of the religious meeting, mentioned above

---

1 *Nihon shūkyō fūzoku shi* (1902), p 197
2 Ibidem
3 Vol II, p 63, cf above, Introd., § 3, p 22, note 1

CHAPTER V.

The Chinese and Indian ideas on dragons having so thoroughly
pervaded the Japanese mind as we have seen in the preceding
chapters, it is not astonishing that many an ancient Shintō god
was identified or connected with them. Sea-gods or serpent-shaped
mountain-deities were especially liable to be considered in this
light, and the thirteenth and later centuries did not hesitate to
explain old legends of the gods in their own way, making abundant
use of the words "Dragon-god" and „Dragon-king". The following
passages are specimens of this tendency

§ 1. Sāgara, the Dragon-king, the Yamato no orochi, Antoku Tennō and the Kusanagi sword.

The *Gukwanshō* [1] (before 1225) tells us that *Itsŭkushima no
Myōjin* (嚴島 ノ 明 神, the goddess of the island Itsŭkushima
in the Inland sea) was according to tradition a Dragon-king's
daughter, reborn as Antoku Tennō, the unhappy Emperor
who was drowned in his seventh year in the battle of Dan-
no-ura (1185). His grandmother, Nii-no-ama, Kiyomori's widow,
jumped over board with the little Emperor, when she saw that
the battle was lost. So the Dragon-king's daughter returned to
her father.

Details of this legend are found in the *Gempei seisuiki* [2] (about
1250), which relates that this goddess was a grandchild of
Amaterasu, the Sun-goddess, and the daughter of the Dragon-
king Sāgara [3]. The same work gives, in another passage [4], the

---

1 Oh V, K T K. Vol XIV, p. 533 About the *Gukwanshō* cf above, p 187, note 1
2 Ch. XII, Teikoku Bunko, Vol V, p 323

3 婆 竭 羅, Shakatsura, i e Sāgara, one of the eight Great Dragon-kings Of
above Introd, § 1, p 4, Book II, Ch IV, § 6, p. 189 According to EITEL, *Handbook
of Chinese Buddhism*, Sāgara's daughter, eight years old, became a Buddha under
Mañjuçrī's tuition   4 Oh XLIV, p. 1158

reason why the dragon was reborn as Antoku Tennō. The retired Emperor Go-Shirakawa, thus we read there, sought in vain the Kusanagi sword [1], one of the three treasures of the Imperial family, which Susanowo no Mikoto had found in the tail of the eight-headed serpent Yamato no orochi. After having prayed for seven days in the temple of Kamo, he received a divine revelation in a dream, to the effect that the sword was to be found at the bottom of the sea at Dan-no-ura, and that two female divers of that place, Oimatsu and Wakamatsu, a mother and her daughter, were to be ordered to seek it. In consequence of this dream Yoshitsune was despatched to Dan-no-ura, and the two women were told to dive for the sword They obeyed and remained under water for a whole day (!) Then they returned to the surface, and the mother said that down there was a very strange place, which she could not enter without Buddha's powerful assistance; therefore she wanted the *Nyohō-kyō* [2], a sūtra, to be copied and wound around her body. Immediately a large number of venerable priests assembled and copied the sūtra, the woman wound this round her body and dived again. This time it lasted no less than one day and one night before she came up, without the sword. Yoshitsune asked her what she had seen, but she answered that she could tell only the Emperor himself. So he took her to Kyōto, where she reported the following to the Emperor She had entered the gate of a magnificent building, apparently the Dragon-king's palace, and when she had told that she came as a messenger from the Emperor of Japan, to ask for the precious sword, two women led her into the garden, to an old pine tree, where from under a half-raised blind (sudare) she could look into a room. There she saw a big serpent, twenty shaku long, with a sword in its mouth and a child of seven or eight years within its coils. The monster's eyes were large and glittered like the sun and the moon, and its red tongue incessantly moved up and down. The serpent said to the woman "Tell the Emperor, that this sword does not belong to Japan, but to the Dragon-palace. My second son [3], driven out of my palace on account of some evil deed, changed into the eight-headed serpent of the head-waters of the River Hi in Izumo (the Yamato no orochi), and was killed by Susanowo, who took the sword out of the snake's tail and gave it to Amaterasu. Under the reign of the Emperor Keikō (71—130 A. D.), when Prince Yamato-dake

---

1 *Kusanagi no tsurugi*, 草薙劍. 2 如法經.

3 In the other versions of the legend it was his daughter

---

subjected the barbarians, Amaterasu handed over the sword to
Utsuki no miya[1], who gave it to the Prince. Then my second
son assumed the shape of a big snake, ten shaku long, and lay
down in Yamato-dake's way at the foot of Ibukiyama (in Ōmi
province), in order to frighten the Prince and take back the sword.
The Prince, however, was not afraid of the snake and stepped
over it, thus frustrating my son's design[2]. Finally, the latter
reincarnated himself as the Emperor Antoku and jumped into
the sea with the sword, which he returned to me. This child
here is my son in his human shape, and the sword which I am
holding in my mouth is the one you ask for. But I cannot give
it to the Emperor". On receiving this message, Go Shirakawa
was very much distressed and thought the precious object was
lost. This was, however, not the case, for the real sword was
preserved in the Great Shrine (Daijingū) at Ise, and Antoku's
sword was only a counterfeit. How strange that the Dragon-god
did not know this!

Another legend in a different way connected the Kusanagi
sword with a Dragon-king. In 674 A.D a Korean bonze stole
the sword from the Shintō temple at Atsuta in Owari province,
and hid it under his mantle. But a dark cloud descended before
the shrine, took the treasure and placed it back into the sanctuary.
Then the priest, after praying there for a hundred days, again
stole the sword and fled to Ōmi province. Once more the black
cloud appeared, deprived the thief of his prey and flew away
with it an eastern direction (to Atsuta). A third time the theft
seemed to be crowned with success, for the priest had succeeded
in secretly carrying the sword on board a ship bound for Korea,
when a severe storm arose and checked the vessel in its course.
In despair the Korean threw the sword into the sea, and the
Dragon-king took it and returned it to Atsuta[3].

§ 2 The Thunder-god caught by Sukaru and identified with a Dragon-king

In the *Gempei seisuiki*[4] we find the following remarkable story.

---

[1] 嚴宮 According to the ordinary legend Amaterasu gave the sword to her
grandson Ninigi Yamato-dake used it afterwards against the barbarians, and after his
death it was placed in the Shintō temple of Atsuta in Owari province
[2] Cf. *Nihongi*, Ch VII, K T K Vol I, p 148 The god of Mount Ibuki took the
shape of a great serpent, but the Prince strode over it and passed on Then the god
"raised up the clouds and made an icy rain to fall" (Aston, *Nihongi*, Vol I, p 209)
[3] *Gempei seisuiki*, Ch. XLIV, pp 1157 seq
[4] Ch XVII, p. 451, under the heading "How Sukaru caught the Thunder"

"At the time of the Emperor Yūryaku (the twenty second Emperor, 457—479), there was an important vassal of His Majesty, Oshibe Sukaru by name. One day when this man entered the palace of Hatsuse Asakura and the apartments of the Emperor, who was staying there, the latter was just in intimate intercourse with the Empress. As just then a thunderstorm was raging, the monarch, for shame at having been surprised, ordered Sukaru, in order to get rid of him, to invite the roaring thunder (to the palace) The vassal, on having received the Imperial command, left the palace and rode on horseback from the road of Abe no Yamada to Toyora-dera, looking up to the sky and crying. 'Thou, Thunder-god who art roaring in the sky, His Majesty commands thee to fall down'. The thunder, however, continued going away and making the air resound with its echoes. Then Sukaru again set spurs to his horse and exclaimed: 'Although thou art a Thunder-god, thou art roaring in the air of Japan. How shouldst thou be able to disobey the Emperor's order?' Then with a loud noise the *Dragon-king* returned and dropped on the earth between Toyora-dera and Iioka. Sukaru at once called Shintō priests, caused them to place the Dragon-god in a sedan-chair, and returned to the palace. When he reported the matter to the Emperor, the Thunder erected his scales, stared with eyes dilating and watched the Palace, while his radiance illuminated the whole building. This spectacle frightened His Majesty, and, after having made all kinds of offerings to the Thunder-god, he quickly sent him back to the spot where he had fallen down. This spot is now called 'The Thunder's Hill' (Ikazuchi no oka)".

This is a very old legend, found in the *Nihongi* and the *Ryō-i-ki*. The version of the *Nihongi*[1] is as follows. — "In the seventh year of the Emperor Yūryaku's reign (463), on the third day of the seventh month, His Majesty said to Oshibe no Sukaru, Minister of State (Muraji, 連) 'I wish to see the shape of the god of Mimoro hill (Mimoro no oka, also called Mount Mimoro) As you excel others in strength, you shall go and after having caught him yourself, you must bring him here'. Sukaru answered. 'I will try to do so', and ascending Mimoro hill he caught a *big serpent* (大蛇), which he showed to the Emperor. As the latter had not practised religious abstinence (in honour of the god),

---

1 Ch XIV, p. 242. Cf. Aston's translation (*Nihongi*, Vol I, p. 347), where the name is written *"Sukaru Chihisako Be no Muraji"* In the *Gempei seisuiki* (Ch XVII, p 451), however, at the side of the characters 少子部 is written in kana. *Oshibe.*

the deity's thunder rolled and his eyes flashed. The Emperor was frightened, covered his eyes and did not look upon the god, but hid himself in the interior of the Palace and ordered the snake to be released on the hill. For this reason the Emperor altered the deity's name into 'Ikazuchi' ('Thunderbolt')".

As to the *Ryō-i-ki* [1], this gives the same details as the *Gempei seisuiki*, which apparently borrowed the legend from it. Instead of "Dragon-king", or "Dragon-god", however, the ancient work simply calls the deity "Thunder-god" (雷神), which shows that the identification of this divinity with a Dragon-king dates from later times. The author of the *Gempei seisuiki*, translating the old text into modern Japanese, followed the ideas of his age, and, changing the word "Thunder-god", which he once retained, the two other times into "Dragon-king" and "Dragon-god", he added the words: "erected his scales and dilated his eyes". The fact that the *Nihongi* spoke of a *serpent*-shaped mountain god made the identification with a dragon quite logical. The author of the *Gempei seisuiki* omitted the last part of the legend, which in the *Ryō-i-ki* runs as follows. "Afterwards, when Sukaru had died, the Emperor by decree ordered to delay the funeral for seven days and seven nights. He praised his loyalty and had his tomb made on the same spot where the Thunder had fallen down. Over the grave he erected a stone monument with the following inscription: 'This is the Thunder-catcher Sukaru's tomb' The Thunder, angry at this insult, came down with a loud roar and trampled upon the stone monument, but while he was smashing it, he was seized (by Sukaru's ghost). When the Emperor heard this, he released the Thunder, who was not dead, but, being quite perplexed, remained there for seven days and seven nights. The Emperor ordered another stone monument to be erected with the following inscription: 'This is the tomb of Sukaru, who in life-time and after death caught the Thunder'. This is the reason why at the time of the old capital (i. e. Suiko Tennō's capital, Owarida no miya, 小治田宮; the Empress Suiko reigned 593—628) this spot was called 'Thunder-hill'".

§ 3. **Watatsumi no kami, the Sea-god, identified with a Dragon-king.**

A similar alteration of an old text by the author of the *Gempei seisuiki* is to be found in the legend about Prince Yamato-dake,

---

1 靈異記, written by the Buddhist priest KEIKAI about 750 A D Ch I, Gunsho ruiju, nr 447, Vol XVI, p. 23.

who, when his ship was tossed about by wind and waves on its
way from Musashi to Kazusa province, was saved by his talented
concubine Otōto Tashibana hime, who jumped into the sea in
order to sacrifice herself on behalf of the Prince to the *Dragon-
god*, and thus appeased the turbulent waves [1]. This legend is
borrowed from the *Nihongi* [2], but there we read only about
Watatsumi no kami [3], the "God of the Sea" (海神).

§ 4 The dragon-hole in the Gion shrine.

A dragon's hole in a Shintō temple is mentioned by the *Zoku
kojidan* [4]. This hole was said to be in the hōden ("treasure-hall",
where the shintai or "god-bodies" of the gods are preserved) of
the Gion shrine at Kyōto. In 1221, when the temple was destroyed
by fire, Nashimoto, the Buddhist head-abbot (zasu) of Hieizan,
tried to measure the depth of the hole, but even at a depth of
fifty jō (five hundred shaku) the bottom was not yet reached.

§ 5 The dragon-snake offered by the Sea-god to the Sada shrine.

The *Shokoku rijindan* [5] says the following: "In the Shintō
temple of Sada, in Akika district, Izumo province, worship is
performed in several ways. Between the eleventh and the fifteenth
day of the tenth month there comes from the open sea a small
snake, about one shaku long, floating on the waves and approaching
the shore. It is a beautiful, gold-coloured animal, called *dragon-
snake* (龍蛇, *ryūja*). The priest of the shrine, after having
purified himself, goes to the beach and awaits the snake, which
he carries, coiled up upon some seaweeds, to the temple. It is a
present from the Sea-god to the shrine".

§ 6 A dragon-snake as a tree-sprite on Kōya san

Another tale in the same work [6] refers to a serpent-shaped
tree-sprite, the spirit of a willow called *ja-yanagi*, 蛇柳, or
"snake-willow", on Kōya san. This was a big serpent or dragon,

---

1 Ch XLIV. p 1157   2 Ch VII, K T K Vol I, p 146
3 Cf above, Book II, Chap I, § 3, p 137

4 續古事談, probably written at the end of the thirteenth or in the beginning of the fourteenth century, Ch. IV, Gunsho ruijū, nr 487, Vol XVII, p 681

5 諸國里人談, written in 1746 by KIKUOKA SENRYŌ, 菊岡沾凉;
Ch I, Zoku Teikoku Bunko, Vol. XX, p. 879

6 Ch. I, p. 891

which from remote ages lived on this sacred mountain, till it was forced by Kōbō Daishi to retreat to a spot about half a mile distant. He made the demon promise to do so by causing poisonous snakes to appear on his (the demon's) body, so that he suffered immensely and at once was willing to go away. Thenceforth Kōbō Daishi forbade to bring flutes on the mountain, for fear that the sound of a flute, by its resembling a dragon's cry, might attract the serpent and cause it to return to its former abode. This was told by one of the monks to Hideyoshi, when the latter, staying as a pilgrim on the mountain, had ordered a famous nō-actor, whom he had taken with him, to give a performance. The monk warned him, not to arouse the dragon by flute playing, but Hideyoshi laughed at him. But no sooner had the tones of the flute resounded on the mountain, than dark clouds arose in the clear sky and covered the earth. A severe thunderstorm shook mountains and valleys, trees were uprooted and the rain poured down in torrents. Hideyoshi, frightened by these terrible signs of the dragon's presence, fled from the monastery and took shelter in a small house at the foot of the mountain. When about two hours had elapsed, the tempest abated, but Hideyoshi's unbelief in Kōbō's wisdom was cured for ever.

§ 7 The "Heavenly Dragon's Well" at the Suwa shrine.

According to the *Honchō zokugenshi* [1], one of the seven wonders of the famous Shintō shrine of *Suwa-Myōjin*, at the Suwa lake (諏訪湖, Suwa-ko), where the Tenryū-gawa (天龍川, "Heavenly Dragon River") takes its rise, is the *Tenryū no ido*, or "Heavenly Dragon's Well" (天龍ノ井). There was always water dripping from the overhanging roof of the temple into this well, which phenomenon was apparently ascribed to a dragon. When Kublai Khan's Armada attacked Japan, the God of Suwa flew in the shape of a long, five-coloured cloud, having the resemblance of a serpent, from the lake to the West, in order to assist the Japanese against the foreign invaders [2].

In the neighbourhood of the same "Heavenly Dragon River",

---

1 本朝俗諺志, written in 1746 by KIKUOKA SENRYŌ, 菊岡沾涼 (also called BEIZAN, 米山), Ch I, p 19, quoted in the *Shiojiri*, 鹽尻, written in 1749 by ZANSETSUSHA SOKYŪ, 斬雪舍素及, Ch II

2 *Taiheiki*, Ch XXXIX, p 12

in Tōtōmi province, a big dragon's head was preserved in a Buddhist temple called Zuda-dera (頭 陀 寺). It was taken to Yedo and there shown to the people. The river's name was said to have originated from the presence of this dragon [1].

§ 8 Kurikara Myō-ō, the dragon-shaped mountain-god.

Another Shintō shrine, the temple of *Kurikara Myō-ō*, 俱 梨 迦 羅 明 王, is dedicated to a dragon-shaped mountain-god, who is said to live in a waterfall on Mount Ōyama in Sagami province. As the *Nihon shūkyō fūzoku shi* [2] (1902) tells us, in olden times the Buddhist priest Ryōben was preaching there one day, when a violent thunderstorm suddenly arose and the water in the hollow, excavated by the cataract, was heavily disturbed. A huge dragon came forth from it and said to the priest: "I am the guardian-god of this mountain. After having heard your sermon, I wish to serve Buddha". Then Ryōben worshipped the dragon, and afterwards as little Shintō shrine was built on the spot and dedicated to the dragon, which was called by the Buddhist name "Kurikara Myō-ō", "Kurikara, the Light-King" (i. e *Vidyā-rāja*, the word Light being used in the sense of (mystic) Knowledge, *Vidyā*).

This was apparently an original Japanese dragon-shaped mountain-god, who was identified by the Buddhists with Fudō Myō-ō's dragon-shape, the *Shintō* shrine, however, remained his sanctuary. Kurikara is, as we read in MIURA's *Bukkyō iroha jiten* [3], Fudō Myō-ō's "*Samaya*" (三 摩 耶) shape, a black dragon coiled around a sword.

---

1 *Shiojiri*, Ch II, p 11   2 P 214
3 Vol III, p. 57, s v *Kurikara*, cf below, Ch VI, § 10

CHAPTER VI.

THE DRAGON-LANTERN.

Among the many *ignes fatui* of Japan the Dragon-lantern (*Ryūtō*, 龍燈) occupies an important place. It mostly rises from the sea and flies from there to the mountains, where it is seen hanging in some special old pine or cryptomeria tree before a (mostly Buddhist) temple. Old pine trees especially are famous in respect to these mysterious lights, which are evidently offerings sent by the dragons of the sea to the deities or Buddhas or Bodhisattvas worshipped in the shrines. There is an enormous number of legends telling of the Dragon-lanterns appearing along the mountainous coasts of Japan. In order to make clear the people's ideas on this point, however, it may be sufficient to refer to a few passages, because they closely resemble one another, and the same conceptions lie at the bottom of them all.

The old annals do not speak of the Dragon-lantern, nor do we find any mention made of it in other books before the fourteenth century.

§ 1. Dengyō Daishi's image of Yakushi Nyorai.

The *Kigegawa Yakushi engi* [1] says the following: "The image of Yakushi Nyorai in Jōkwōji (also called Shōryūzan, 青龍山, "Blue Dragon monastery"), in Katsushika district, Shimōsa province, is made by Dengyō Daishi [2] When Jikaku Daishi [3] stayed in Asakusa-dera (the famous Kwannon temple in Asakusa, the well-known district of Yedo), an old man with grey hair appeared to him and said. 'In the North-east there is a holy

---

[1] 木下川藥師縁起, written in 1327 by the Buddhist priest GIJUN 義純, Gunsho ruijū, Vol XV, nr 442, p 637.

[2] 傳教大師 (767—822), the founder of the Tendai sect in Japan

[3] 慈覺大師 (794—864), in 854 appointed head (zasu) of the Tendai sect

place, where I have dedicated a miraculous image made by Dengyō Daishi'. Thereupon the man disappeared, and Jikaku went outside and looked towards the North-east Suddenly a lucky cloud (瑞雲, zui-un, a cloud of a lucky colour) arose, and in it a blue dragon was visible. Then the Daishi secretly left the temple and went in search of this blue dragon, till he arrived at the cottage (where the above-mentioned old man had lived as a hermit and had obtained the image). There he worshipped the image and saw the blue dragon, which was still there. Jikaku turned himself to the lucky cloud and addressed the dragon as follows: 'I wish to say a few words to you, you sacred dragon, listen to me. I want to built a temple here, which you must guard and protect from calamity. From this moment I appoint you guardian-god of the shrine'. When the Daishi had finished speaking, the dragon, which had listened motionless, with his head bent down in reverence, disappeared. The priest considered this to be a good sign, and called the sanctuary 'Blue Dragon temple'. Up till this day from time to time a *dragon-lantern* appears there as a wonderful, lucky omen, probably in consequence of the above facts (i. e. because the blue dragon is the temple's guardian-god)".

The *Edo meisho ki* [1] tells us that from olden times many pilgrims went up to this temple, which is also called Jōkwōji (淨光寺, "Temple of the Pure Light"), to worship the dragon-lantern, which was sure to arise before the image of Yakushi Nyorai on the eighth day of every month, and on New-Year's morning.

§ 2. Kōbō Daishi's spirit.

In the *Tomioka Hachiman shaki*, "History of the Shintō temple of Hachiman of Tomioka" [2], we read that in 1628 Kōbō Daishi's ghost appeared in a dream to a Shingon priest and ordered all the priests of his sect in Kwantō, except the heads of Kōya and Sekigaku, to assemble in Eitaijima (in Yedo). They obeyed the saint's command and preached sermons for ninety days at a stretch. At the same time they erected a temple, dedicated to

---

1 江戸名所記, written by ASAI RYŌ-I, 淺井了意, who lived 1639—1709, and printed in 1662, Ch III, p. 19

2 富岡八幡社記, quoted by KURIHARA RYŪ-AN, 栗原柳菴 (1793—1870), in his *Ryū an zuihitsu*, 柳菴隨筆, written in 1819, Hyakka setsurin, Vol. 續下二, p 487

Kōbō Daishi's soul (Mikage-dō), and since that time a dragon-lantern arose before this shrine

§ 3. Jigen Daishi's spirit

The *Jigen Daishi den* [1], the biography of Jigen Daishi, i e. the Buddhist bishop Tenkai [2], who was greatly revered by Ieyasu, and who died in 1643, contains the following tale. — "In the evening of the second day of the eleventh month of the twentieth year of the Kwanei era (1643) a special service was held (for Jigen's soul) in the Sembakita temple (in Musashi), when a dragon-lantern rose from a well and hung on the top of a cryptomeria tree at the southern front of the kyakuden ("reception-hall" of the temple). Priests and laymen stared at the light with astonishment, and paid worship to it. Immediately a fast runner was despatched as a messenger to the Nikkō temple, in order to proclaim the news, and everybody was filled with admiration (for Jigen's holiness, for his soul was evidently believed to be connected with the light, like that of Kōbō Daishi in the preceding legend)" [3].

§ 4 "Dragon-lantern pine trees".

Very frequently mention is made of so-called "Dragon-lantern pine trees" (*Ryūtō no matsu*, 龍燈松), which stood before Buddhist temples, and in the branches of which a dragon-lantern was said to arise regularly. Now and then we read of such trees standing near *Shintō* shrines, but by far the greatest part of the passages concerning them, as well as those concerning the dragon-lantern in general, relate to *Buddhist* sanctuaries.

Before the chapel of Monju (Mañjuçrī), called Monjudō (文殊堂), at Ama no hashidate (one of the Nihon sankei, the three most beautiful places of Japan) in Yosa district, Tango province, situated near the so-called Kuze no to, or Kire-to, there stood a "dragon-lantern pine tree". At midnight of the sixteenth

---

1 慈眼大師傳.　　　　　2 天海.

3 Curiously rationalistic at the side of these passages sound the following words of the *Ensei meibutsu kōhōi* (遠西名物考補遺, Ch. VIII), quoted on the same page of the *Ryūan zuihitsu*. — "The 'Devil-lights' (*kirin*, 鬼燐) and Dragon-lanterns which appear above swamps, pools, broad plains, mountain temples, grave-yards etc are '*zwavelstofgas*' coming forth from rotten animals and plants". The word "zwavelstofgas", written in kana, is a Dutch word and must be "zwavelwaterstofgas", i e. hydrogen sulphide.

day of every month there appeared from the northeastern sea a dragon-lantern, which flew to this tree, and in the night of the sixteenth day of the first, fifth and ninth months another light, called the "Heavenly Lantern" (*Tentō*, 天燈) descended from the sky. Also a third light, the so-called "*Ise no go tō*", or "August Light of Ise", which is mentioned in the *Yūhō meisho ryaku*[1] (1697), where it is said to be named *Shintō* (神燈, the "Sacred Light") and to be made by the divinity of the Daijingū at Ise (Amaterasu), was visible on this spot. The image of the Bodhisattva Mañjuçrī (Monju Bosatsu), which was worshipped there, was said to be of Indian origin and to have come out of the sea.

The same temple is referred to in the *Ki zōdanshū*[2], where we read the following particulars concerning the light — "It comes from a deep spot in the sea, two chō from the "Broken Door" (Kire-to) of Hashidate, where the Gate of the Dragon-palace is said to be. When the weather is fine and wind and waves are calm, it goes from Kire-to to the Monju shrine. Unbelieving people cannot see it, or, if they see it, they think it to be the light of some fisherman. It stops on the top of a high pine tree which stands about 20 ken south of the Monjudō. After half an hour or shorter it is extinguished. From time to time a little boy is seen on the top of the tree, carrying the lamp which is called *Tendō*, 天灯, "Heavenly Lantern" (this word may also be written 天童, *Tendō*, "Heavenly boy") Formerly this boy (an angel) often appeared, but now rarely".

The *Nihon shūkyō fūzoku shi*[3] (1902) mentions an old "Dragon-lantern pine tree" which still stands near a Shintō temple called *Uhara jinja* (宇原神社), in Karida village, Kyōtō district, Buzen province. There Toyotama-bime, the Sea-god's daughter, in the shape of a dragon gave birth to a son[4], and at the same time a light (a dragon-lantern) came flying from the sea and hung in the same pinetree[5].

---

1 Ch XIII, p 18 About this work see above, p 170, note 4

2 奇異雑談集, "Collection of all kinds of strange tales", written by "the son of Nakamura, Lord of Buzen", in the Tembun era (1532—1554) (cf *Matsunoya hikki*, Ch III, p 4, and the work itself, Ch. II, p 15, where the author states that his father, Nakamura, Lord of Buzen, lived in the Bummei era (1469—1486).

3 P 436   4 Of above, Book II, Ch. I, § 5, p 139

5 Cf. the *Buzen kokushi*, 豊前國志, written in 1805 by TAKADA YOSHICHIKA, 高田吉近, who does not call the light a dragon-lantern, but states that it appeared even in his days.

We may mention here another Shintō shrine, the *Shirahige jinja* (白鬚神社) in Shiga district, Ōmi province, where a dragon-lantern was said to enter the worshipping hall (haiden) from time to time, instead of hanging in a pine tree [1], and the *Jōgū* (常宮), a Shintō temple in Tsuruga, Echizen province, where every New-year's night such a light arose in a "Dragon-lantern pine tree" which stood in the temple garden [2].

Before the Buddhist chapel of *Kasai Yakushi* (笠井藥師), situated on a mountain north of Okayama, in Bizen province, there stood a "Dragon-lantern pine tree". Every night, especially in summer time, will-o'-the-wisps were seen there [3].

§ 5. Tide-stones connected with dragon-lanterns

On the top of Kaneyama, a mountain very near the above-mentioned chapel of *Kasai Yakushi*, there was a big stone with a hole in it, about one shaku square. When tide was high, this hole was filled with water, and at low tide it was dry [4].

It seems that such stones were considered to be connected with the dragons who sent the dragon-lanterns, for also on the Sata promontory, in Hata district, Tosa province (30 ri west of Kōchi) there was at the same period (1746) the so-called *Ushio-ishi* (潮石) or "Tide-stone", a concave stone, filled with water at high tide and empty at ebb time, while on the same spot, near the Shintō temple of Ashizuri no Myōjin (蹉跎ノ明神), a dragon-lantern used to appear from the sea simultaneously with the descent from the sky of a Heavenly Light (*Tentō*, 天燈). The latter was one of the seven wonders of the place. Another of these wonders was a *dragon-horse*, which used to come at the hour of the ox (1—3 a.m.) and to eat the small bamboo, which for this reason gradually died out in the vicinity of the temple [5].

The connection between the tide-stones and the dragons at once reminds us of the legends concerning Toyotama-hiko, the Sea-god, who gave the tide-jewel to Hiko-hohodemi [6], and concerning the Empress Jingō, who was assisted by the gods of Kasuga and

1 *Yūhō meisho ryaku* (1697), Ch. VI, p 16
2 *Tōryūki kōhen* (see below, p 210, note 2), p 113
3 *Honchō zokugenshi* (1746, cf above, Book II, Ch V, § 7, p. 203, note 1), Ch IV, p 10   4 Ibidem
5 *Shokoku rijindan* (1746, see above, p 202, note 5), Ch III, Section VI, p 928
6 See above, Book II, Ch I, § 6, p. 140

Kawakamı by means of the jewels of low and high tide, taken from Sāgara, the Dragon-king [1].

§ 6. The Mountain-light and the Dragon-lantern of Gammokuzan in Etchū province

The *Tōyūki kōhen* [2] states the following about a temple of the Zen sect ın Niikawa district, Etchū province, called Gammokuzan (眼目山) or Sakkwazan. When this shrine was opened by ıts founder, the priest Daitetsu, a pupıl of Dōgen (道元, Shōyō Daıshi, 1200—1253), the Mountaın-god and a Dragon-god assisted and performed all kınds of miracles. Still in the author's tıme (second half of the eıghteenth century) ycarly on the 13th day of the 7th month (probably the date of the openıng of the shrıne) two lights appeared on the top of a pıne tree ın the temple garden. One of these lıghts (that of the Mouиtain-god) came flyıng from the summıt of Mount Tateyama, the other (that of the Dragon-god) rose up from the sea, and both stopped on the pıne tree. They were called the Mountaın-light and the Dragon-lantern (*Santō, Ryūtō*), and were seen every year by the people of the neighbourhood. "Although", says TACHIBANA NANKEI, "there are many cases of dragon-lanterns comıng out of the sea, they rarely appear sımultaneously and on the same pıne tree with a mountaın-lıght, as ıs the case at this temple".

§ 7 Kwannon's dragon-lantern at Ryūkōjı

On Itozakı yama, in Echizen province, Hannan (the present Sakaı) dıstrict, there ıs a Buddhist temple called *Ryūkōjı* (龍興寺, "Dragon's rıse-temple"), which was buılt by a Chınese prıest who came from Chına on the back of an enormous tortoıse, carrying a precious Kwannon ımage. When approachıng the coast the tortoıse emıtted a strong lıght, and the fishermen, seeıng this, went out to meet ıt and carrıed the image ashore. A temple was dedicated to thıs Kwannon, and every night a blue dragon appeared there ın a so-called "Dragon-lantern pine tree", carrying a lıght ın honour of the deity. When he appeared, there was always a large number of holy priests, clad ın magnificent robes,

---

1 See above, Book II, Ch I, § 7, p 142

2 東遊記後編, wrıtten ın 1797 by TACHIBANA NANKEI, 橘 南 谿 (1752—1805), Zoku Teıkoku bunko, Vol XX (*Kıkō bunshū*, 紀行文集), p 113

making heavenly music in the air. The priests could see them, but the ordinary people could only hear their music [1].

§ 8. Tōmyō-dake, Kumano Gongen at Nogami, Kwōmyōji at Kamakura and Zenkwōji at Nagano

Sometimes a mountain peak is called after a dragon-lantern, as e. g. the *Tōmyō-dake* (燈 明 嶽), or "Light-Peak", in Kawachi province, Ishikawa district (the present Minami Kawachi district), where such a light appeared at Kōkidera, a Buddhist temple, the guardian-god of which was the Shintō mountain-deity Iwabune Myōjin [2].

In the last night of the year, at the hour of the ox (1—3 a. m.), a dragon-lantern used to be seen near the shrine of Kumano Gongen at Nogami village, Suwo province, while at the same time another "sacred light" (*shinkwa*, 神 火) came flying, swift like an arrow, from the neighbouring "Dragon-mouth Mountain". While worshipping these lights the villagers entered upon the New year [3].

Another dragon-lantern was said to arise yearly from the sea to the clouds in the vicinity of Kwōmyōji (光 明 寺), the "Shrine of Brilliant Light" in Kamakura in two nights during the temple festival which lasted ten days [4]. And from the 14th to the 16th of the 7th month a similar light flew up from the Saikawa, a river in Shinano province, and, jumping from tree top to tree top it alighted on the south-western gable of the main building of Zenkwōji, the famous Buddhist sanctuary at Nagano [5].

§ 9 The light of Yotsukura.

A celebrated dragon-lantern was that of Yotsukura, a village on the coast of Hitachi province. It is described as a glittering fire ball, fully one shaku in diameter, and spreading a very clear light. Fishermen explained this (as well as all other so-called dragon-lanterns) to be a mass of flying insects born upon the water, which dispersed and disappeared as soon as they heard people approaching. Therefore they never appeared in storm and rain (because they were afraid of noise). "Sometimes", they said, "these insects cluster into one mass, which is seen hanging on

---

1 *Yūhō meisho ryaku*, Ch V, p 16.
2 Ibidem, Ch IV, p 59.
3 *Shokoku ryūdan*, Ch III, Section VI, pp 928 seq.
4 Ibidem   5 *Honchō zokugenshi*, Ch III, p 8

the top of a high tree or on the eaves of a temple, and which looks like a ball of fire. The so-called *shiranu-bi* (不知火, "unknown fire") is the same [1].

More details about the Yotsukura light are to be found in the *Tō-ō kikō* [2], which says that it moves, floating on the water, from the sea along the Kamado river up to the valley brooks. At the foot of Mount Akai-dake it flies up and is soon seen hanging between the branches of big cryptomerias, till it disappears into the depths of the wood, continually followed by other lights, in an endless row, from evening till daybreak In bright moonshine the lights are small, but in dark nights they are big like fire-flies or torches. A strange thing is that they are only visible from the so-called Enseki (Swallow-stone) on a projecting part of the mountain. The author calls it *inkwa* (陰火, *Yin*-fire), an expression borrowed from Chinese books, and compares it with the "Sacred Lights" (神燈) and the "Cold Flames" (寒炎), mentioned by Chinese authors

§ 10 The lights of Ushijima, Ishidōzan and Kurikara

In the last night of the year — a time when many dragon-lanterns were said to appear, as the above legends have taught us — three strange lights used to arise from differents spots near the island Ushijima and to join into one mass which flew to the "Dragon-lantern pine tree" of Asahizan Jōnichiji, a Buddhist temple at Himi, a little place in Etchū province, Himi district, and seen hanging between its branches [3].

It was also a dragon-lantern which the Buddhist priest Nansan saw on an old pine tree, when he crossed Mount Ishidōzan in the year 806, Amida Nyorai appeared there, seated on a wonderful cloud Nansan built a Buddhist temple on the spot and placed Amida Nyorai's image in it Four centuries later, when the Emperor Juntoku (1211—1221) went to Sado province and his ship was tossed on the waves by a severe storm, all of a sudden a dragon-lantern arose in the South on the same spot and served

---

1 *Ōshū-banashi*, 奥州波奈志, Onchi shōsho (温知叢書), Vol XI, p 50, 52

2 東奥紀行, written in 1760 by NAGAKUBO GENSIU, 長久保玄珠, and quoted by KURIHARA RYŪ-AN, 栗原柳菴 (1793—1870) in his *Ryū-an zuihitsu*, 柳菴隨筆, written in 1819, Hyakka setsurin, Vol 續下二, p 487

3 *Sanshū kidan kōhen* (1779) (cf above, p 174, note 1), Ch VII, p 990.

as a beacon to the Imperial ship, which safely reached the coast [1].

In the Kurikara [2] mountains, which form the boundary between Etchū and Kaga, there was a Shingon temple called Chōrakuji or Kurikara-san, with an image of Fudō Myō-ō. This sanctuary was miraculous beyond description, and famous for its wonderful "Mountain-lights" and "Dragon-lanterns" [3].

§ 11. Ignes fatui in general. The dragon-lantern is the only one which arises from the sea and flies to the mountains.

Not only in regard to the dragon-lantern, but also in other respects especially old pine trees were famous for their ignes fatui. So we read of the "gold-fire pine tree" on the road from Komatsu to Kanazawa, where phosphorescent light, the so-called "rinkwa" (燐火), or "kin-kwa" (金火, gold-fire) was seen to fly up and down. This fire, however, did not come from the sea, like the dragon-lantern, but was ascribed to the fact that formerly criminals used to be beheaded under this tree, whose blood, penetrating into the ground, had become so-called "ki-rin" (鬼燐) or "demon's fire"; or some one had in great anger committed suicide on this spot, and "the fire of his heart made the pine tree burn" [4].

The idea of blood causing these mysterious lights is borrowed from China; we read in De Groot's *Religious System of China* [5] that blood, identified with the *tsing k'i* (精氣), the breath or *yang* soul possessed by vital energy, especially the blood of men killed by weapons, and that of horses and cows, forms ignes fatui. They are soul-flames, especially to be seen on battle-fields. The identification of blood and soul is not only a Chinese conception [6], but is also found among some Indian tribes of North America, as we learn from Frazer's *Golden Bough* [7]. As to China, there the ignes fatui were believed to be produced especially by old trees and old blood [8]

Also demons were considered to cause will-o'-the-wisps, as the names "ki-rin" and "oni-bi" (鬼火), "demon-fire", clearly show. Moreover, old bewitching animals, like *tanuki* and *mujina*, were

---

1 *Sanshū kidan* (1764) (cf p 172, note 7), Ch IV, p 815
2 Cf above, Ch V, § 8, p 204 Kurikara Myō-ō, the dragon-shaped Fudō Myō-ō
3 *Sanshū kidan*, Ch V, p 835 (*santō, ryūtō*, 山燈龍燈).
4 Ibidem, Ch. II, p. 713, 'Hachiman's gold-fire"
5 Vol IV, p 80.   6 De Groot, l l, Vol I, pp 217, 268, note 2
7 Vol I (second edition), p 353.
8 De Groot, l l, Vol IV, p 80

notorious in this respect [1]. Besides *tanuki-bi*, *kitsune-bi* (badger and fox-fire) and *oni-bi*, the ignes fatui were called *inkwa* (陰火, or *Yin*-fire, Fire of Darkness), *kumo no hi* (蜘ノ火, spider-fire), *kaigetsu no hi* (海月ノ火, sea-moon-fire [2], *susuke andō* (煤行灯, sooty lantern) [3], or *bōzu-bi* (坊主火, monk's fire) [4].

Not always, however, are demons [5], or old animals, or dragons believed to cause the Jack-o'-lanterns, nor are these only considered to be angry souls of the dead [6], for also Buddhas and Shintō gods may be the producers of these wonderful "*burari-bi*", or "dangling lights". Amida Nyorai himself, as we have seen above [7], appeared with the dragon-lantern on Ishidōzan, and the name *Butsu-tō* (佛燈), or "Buddha's lights", is sufficient evidence of this belief. As to the Shintō gods, we may mention the ignes fatui near Gofuku village in Etchū, which were said to be caused by the jealous spirit of the goddess Fukura-hime no Mikoto, whose consort, the god Noto-hiko, during her absence took a second wife, whereupon she pelted his temple with stones [8]. And in the year 1770 the god Sannō made a sacred light (神燈, *shintō*) appear in the dead of night in the worshipping-hall of his temple in Sebamachi, at the western mouth of the Nami-kawa, after two nights he stopped it in consequence of offerings made to him and *kagura* dances performed in his honour [9].

So we see that there is a great variety of ignes fatui in Japan. The dragon-lantern, however, is the only one which arises from the sea and flies to the mountains; all the others start and remain in the woods, or fly from there to the sea coast, where they sometimes fall into the water [10]. The reason for this difference is clear: the dragon-lantern is believed to be an offering sent by the dragons of the sea to the deities, Buddhas or Bodhisattvas in the mountains, while the other lights, on the contrary, are ascribed to these divine beings themselves, or to demons, animals or spirits of the dead, all of which have their abodes in the mountains and woods or on the grassy plains of the battle-fields.

---

1 Cf my treatise on "*The Fox and the Badger in Japanese Folklore*, Transactions of the Asiatic Society of Japan, Vol XXXVI, Part III, pp 151 seq, 156
2 *Sanshū kidan kōhen*, Ch VI, pp 955 seq
3 Ibidem   4 *Sanshū kidan*, Ch III, p 752
5 *Mami*, 魔魅, cf. *Sanshū kidan*, Ch. III, p 770
6 *Sanshū kidan*, Ch I, p 664, Ch V, p 840   7 P 212
8 *Sanshū kidan*, Ch V, p 840   9 *Sanshū kidan kōhen*, Ch VIII, p 1001
10 Cf. *Sanshū kidan kōhen*, Ch. VI, p 956 a fisher catches them in his net, but the numberless small lights escape through the mazes, fly up, and join into one massive ball of fire which soars away through the air, perhaps, says the author, was it a transformation of old blood

CHAPTER VII.

THE CHINESE DRAGON'S EGGS IN JAPAN.

§ 1. The dragon-fetus remains in the egg for three thousand years

In the sixteenth century of our era a Japanese author [1] spoke of an old (certainly Chinese) tradition, according to which a dragon's fetus lives during a thousand years in the sea, for a thousand years in the mountains and, after having been among men ("in a village", says the text) for the same long period, it finally is born, becomes a dragon and ascends to the sky [2] During these three thousand years the fetus lives as a very small snake within a s t o n e, the dragon's egg, which is first lying at the bottom of the sea, then comes to the mountains (how it got there is not explained), where after a thousand years it is picked up by somebody who͵ carries it home and preserves it on account of its beautiful colours, or uses it as an ink-stone (*suzuri*, 硯) As it invariably has the remarkable peculiarity of constantly producing water (the dragon's element), it is a very convenient ink-stone indeed [3]. But woe him who possesses such a stone at the end of the millennial period which the fetus must pass among mankind, for then the stone splits, and a small snake creeps out of it, which in a few moments becomes larger and larger, and with a terrible noise forces its way to the sky, smashing the roof amid thunder and lightning, and ascending in a dark cloud. The little reptile has become an enormous four-legged dragon, which leaves the narrow abodes of men and frees himself in this terrific way.

---

1 *Ku zōdanshū* (1532—1554) (cf above, p 208, note 2), Ch III, p 16

2 Cf above, Book I, Ch III, § 16, pp 88 sqq

3 In the *Hyakka setsurin* (Vol 續下二, p 487) we find the following names of ink-stones. *Ryūringetsu-ken*, 龍鱗月硯, or "Dragon-scales-moon-inkstone", and *Ryūbi-ken*, 龍尾硯, "Dragon's tail-inkstone"

§ 2. Dragons born from beautiful stones picked up in the mountains

A remarkable ink-stone was preserved in olden times, says the *Kii zōdanshū* [1], in a Zen monastery at Kanagawa, Musashi province Drops of water were constantly dripping out of this stone, but nobody understood the reason of this strange pheno- menon Once upon a time, on a very hot summer day, when the monks were sitting together in a cool room, all of a sudden the ink-stone split of its own accord, and a small worm, about 2 bu (0.24 inches) long, crept out of it. The monks were about to kill the beast, but the head-priest forbade them to do so, and carefully carried it on a fan to the garden, where he put it into the lotus pond. All the monks followed him, and while they were looking at the worm, they saw with astonishment how the little creature. drawing together and stretching its body, grew larger and larger. In a great fright they ran back into the house, but even there they soon felt themselves no longer safe, for the sky, hitherto quite clear, at once was covered with clouds, thunder and lightning raged, and a pitch-black darkness filled the garden and enwrapped the building. Then they all fled away through the gate and saw from far how the dragon in an immense cloud ascended to the sky, first his head, then his four-legged body, and finally his enormous tail. When he had disappeared, the clouds dispersed and the sky became clear as before. The garden, the pond and the building, were all in a terrible con- dition. In the mean time people from the neighbouring villages came to the rescue, thinking that the monastery was on fire.

A writer of the eighteenth century, KIUCHI SEKITEI [2], relates the same accident as having happened in *Kanazawa* (instead of *Kanagawa*). Further, he mentions a round stone which was picked up by a boy in the mountains near Sammon, in Ōmi province. As water was constantly trickling out of this stone, the boy used it in later years to wet his ink-slab After fifty years, when he had attained the rank of Archbishop — the stone apparently had brought him prosperity — the curious object split and a dragon arose to the sky, after breaking through the ceiling and the roof. The stone existed still in SEKITEI's time, and in the middle of it there was a hole of the size of a bean.

---

1 Ch V, p 1

2 木内石亭, who lived 1722—1801, in the *Unkonshi kōhen*, 雲根志 後編, "Records on cloud-roots continued", written in 1779, Ch II, p 2 The first volume of this work (*zempen*) appeared in 1772, and the third (*sampen*) in 1801

A' similar dragon's egg was used by a Buddhist priest in Moriyama, Ōmi province, in 1774, for grinding his tea, till the dragon was born and ascended, leaving a round hole in the middle of the stone [1].

In another case such an egg was recognized before by a great scholar, thoroughly versed in Chinese literature, the famous ITŌ JINSAI [2], who warned a Court-noble, telling him that a magnificent stone, square and five-coloured, in the nobleman's possession was a dragon's egg, and that he had better throw it away in some lonely spot. The man followed the scholar's advice, and built a little Shintō shrine in the open field outside the capital, in which he placed the stone. A few years afterwards the shrine was smashed by the dragon which ascended to heaven. This stone was a so-called ryūshō-seki, 龍生石, or "Dragon producing stone" [3].

The name of "dragon-horse-stone" (ryū-me-seki, 龍馬石) was given to another remarkable stone, white as crystal and as big as the palm of the hand, which was lying on the desk of a samurai in Hizen province. In its centre a moving creature was visible, and the stone moved by itself from one side of the desk to the other. One day the man placed a tea cup filled with water on the desk, and when he came back the cup was empty. The next day he made the same experiment with a big bowl, and while he was talking with some friends in the next room, they heard a noise as of wind and waves. At once they went to look what the matter was, and discovered a lizard (tokage, 石龍子, litt. "little stone-dragon") running from the bowl to the stone, which it entered [4].

Two "snake-producing stones" (shō-ja-seki, 生蛇石) [5] were found in a hole at Kyōto in 1762, and in 1780 a "golden snake stone" (金蛇石) was picked up in the mountains by a child. Water was constantly flowing out of it, till it was cooked and the dragon inside was killed. Then it was split and the dead body of a little gold-coloured snake was found in it [6].

Although they were not dragon's eggs, we may mention here two stones which were believed to be connected with dragons. One of them was a big stone lying in a hollow excavated by a waterfall near Kayao village, Inukami district, Ōmi province,

1 Ibidem. 2 伊藤仁齋, a kangakusha who lived 1626—1705
3 Unkonshi kōhen, Ch II, p 8   4 Ibidem, Ch II, p 10
5 Ibidem, Ch. II, p 12   6 Ibidem, Ch. III, p. 7.

which was said to belong to the Dragon-god of the place and was called "Dragon-god-stone" (龍神石, *Ryūjin-seki*) by the villagers. In the Kyōhō era (1716—1735) five or six men came to the neighbouring villages and asked the inhabitants to sell them woman's hair in order to make a rope by means of which they might carry the stone as an offering to the Dragon-god of Seta. A short time afterwards the stone actually disappeared, but it was much too heavy to have been carried away by human hands (probably the men in question were transformed dragons)[1]. The second stone, which was black and about three shaku long, lay in a garden and was said to cause even a clear summer sky to become cloudy in a moment, when it was touched by somebody. In 1764 the stone was no longer outside, but within the castle, so that the experiment could not be made any more. "Perhaps", says HOTTA, the author of the *Sanshū kidan*, "it is a so-called 'cloud-root' (雲根, *un-kon*)"[2].

We find the following details in the *Shōsan chomon kishū* (1849)[3]. The abbot of a Shingon monastery had a so-called dragon-gem (龍ノ玉, *ryū no tama*), which was considered to be an uncommonly precious object. On cloudy days it became moist at once, and when it rained it was quite wet. In reality it was not a dragon-gem, but a dragon's egg (*ryū no tamago*, 龍ノ卵) Such eggs are hatched amid thunderstorm and rain; then they destroy even palaces and uproot big trees, and it is therefore advisable to throw them away before-hand on a lonely spot in the mountains. The abbot, however, deemed it not necessary to take this precaution with the dragon's egg in his possession, because it was dead. "Thirty years ago", he said, "the egg became moist as soon as the weather was a little cloudy, and its luster was magnificent, but as it afterwards did not show moistness any more even on rainy days, nor grew any longer, it is evidently dead". MIYOSHI SHŌSAN (the author) himself went to the monastery to see this wonderful egg, and gives a picture of it (p. 573), which shows the dragon-fetus inside. Its dimensions were · length, 4 sun, 8 bu; breadth, 4 sun, 6 bu, it was like a "diamond-natured thunder-axe-stone" (玉質雷斧石, *gyoku-shitsu rai-fu-seki*, called by the people *Tengu no ono*,

---

1 Ibidem, Ch II, p 13
2 *Sanshū kidan*, Ch IV, p 788
3 想山著聞奇集, written in 1849 by SHŌSAN SAI SHUJIN, 想山齋主人, Zoku Teikoku bunko, Vol XLVII, Kinsei kidan zenshū. Ch. IV, pp 572 seqq

天狗ノ鉄, or "Tengu-axe"), but it seemed to be still harder and sharper than these. Its colour was red, tinged with bluish grey, just like the thunder-axe-stones, but its lustre was more like that of glass than is the case with the latter. There were some spots on the egg, which SHŌSAN considered to be dirt left on it by the dragon which produced it.

§ 3 Thunder-stones.

In the same monastery there was a so-called "*thunder-jewel*" (雷ノ玉, rai no tama, or 雷玉, rai-gyoku), which in 1796 had fallen from the sky during a heavy thunderstorm, when the lightning struck a spot near Haseda. Its colour was white, tinged with a slight bluish grey, just like cornelian or marble Such thunderstones were called "*thunder-axes*" (raifu, 雷斧), "*thunder-knives*" (雷刀, raitō), "*thunder-hammers*" (rai tsui, 雷槌), "*thunder-blocks*" (雷碪, raitan), "*thunder-rings*" (雷環, raikwan), "*thunder-pearls*" (雷珠, raishu), "*thunder-pillars*" (雷楔, rai-ketsu), "*thunder-ink*" (raiboku, 雷墨), "*thunder-swords*" (raiken, 雷劍, "*thunder-pins*" (raisan, 雷鑽), and so on. They are found in spots struck by lightning. The black ones are thunder-axes, those which are white, tinged with blue, are thunder-rings, the purple ones, tinged with red, are thunder-pins If it is neither stone nor earth, but a lump as of lacquer, it is thunder-ink. The above-mentioned specimen was, in SHŌSAN's opinion, a kind of thunder-pearl [1].

We learn from this passage that the prehistoric stone weapons and utensils were considered by the Chinese (for all these names were borrowed from Chinese works), and in imitation thereof by the Japanese, as thunderbolts; this is the same conception which we find everywhere among primitive peoples Also meteors, of course, are believed to have been thrown by lightning upon the earth, or to be fallen stars. As to the dragon, his connection with rain and thunder is evidently supposed to begin long before his birth and to show itself in a terrible way as soon as he is born.

---

1 Cf DE GROOT, *Religious System of China*, Vol V, p 866, where the "thunderbolt stones" (霹靂碪), "thunder-nodules" (雷楔, cf the 楔 of the Japanese text) are said to be believed to remove the effects of *ku*-poison On the next page DE GROOT mentions thunder-hammers, thunder-awls, thunder-axes (supposed to have been used by the God of Thunder to split up things), thunder-rings (lost by that god) and thunder-pearls.

CHAPTER VIII.

THE TATSUMAKI (龍 卷), OR "DRAGON'S ROLL"

The works of the eighteenth and nineteenth centuries explain the heavy whirlwinds which cause the so-called water-spouts and in a moment destroy the products of human hands or whatever they may light upon, to be the work of dragons ascending to heaven. Accordingly the enormous columns of water, thrown up into the air by these whirlwinds, are called "*tatsumaki*" or "dragon's rolls".

§ 1 Dragons which ascended to heaven

Apart from the *tatsumaki* we may refer to two passages in the *Yūhō meisho ryaku* (1697) where dragons are said to have ascended to the sky The first passage [1] treats of the name of *Tatsuta*, the place where the Wind-god was worshipped from times immemorial [2], which name it ascribes to the fact that a dragon arose to heaven there. It was the Thunder-god himself, who in the shape of a boy had fallen down on Tatsuta yama (Higuri district, Yamato province), thirty or forty chō south-west from Nara. A peasant adopted the child and educated it, and from that time wind and rain were very favourable to that special village. Afterwards the child changed into a dragon and flew to the sky.

The second passage [3] explains the name of *Sennin-zuka* (仙 人塚, or "*sien's* grave") in Narumi village, Aichi district, Owari province, to be the spot where in remote ages a Chinese *sien* (*sennin*), who floating on a tree had arrived on this shore, lived for a long time till he finally became a dragon and rose to heaven. His soul was worshipped in the "Heavenly Dragon's shrine" (*Tenryū no miya*, 天龍宮), erected close to the spot where he had lived.

---

1 Ch III, p 15   2 Cf above, Book II Ch III, § 1, p 153.
3 Ch VIII, p 47

The *Wakan sansai zue* (1713)[1] describes how on lake Biwa a man saw a little snake, about one shaku long, which came swimming to the shore, climbed upon the water-rushes, danced about, came down again and swam about on the surface of the water, whereupon it several times repeated the same movements. Gradually the snake became longer and longer, till it reached the length of about one jō (10 shaku); then it ascended to the sky, which in the meantime was covered with black clouds. It became pitchdark, so that only the dragon's tail was visible, and a shower of rain fell down till the dragon had entered the sky, which then became as clear as before. "The climbing upon the rushes and dancing about", says the author, "was probably a preparatory exercise for ascending to heaven".

§ 2 Tatsumaki in Yedo [2]

The *Ichiwa ichigen* [3] makes mention of a *tatsumaki* which in 1735 arose in the vicinity of the Detached Palace in Shiba district, in the Yedo bay, and destroyed the roofs of many houses in Kyōbashi and Nihonbashi districts; at the same time a heavy rain came down and it became pitch-dark.

In the Kwansei era (1789—1800) there was in Yedo a Buddhist priest who went about and predicted that soon a dragon was to ascend to heaven in a heavy tempest, reason why he advised the people to stay indoors. When a samurai asked him how he knew this beforehand, the priest answered: "I know this from experience Always when the sky has been clear for a long time and it suddenly begins to rain, as is now the case, a dragon ascends". "Are you perhaps the dragon yourself?" asked the samurai, and when the priest answered in the affirmative, he requested him to rise to the sky at once. "I cannot do so", replied the bonze, "because I have no water". "No water?" exclaimed the other, "there is plenty of water in the river near by!" "That is of no use to me", remarked the priest, "for that is flowing water and what I want is heavenly water (rain)". "Well, then I will give you some rainwater", said the samurai,

---

1 Ch XLV (龍蛇部), p 673

2 I use the old way of transcribing this name instead of "*Edo*", because the name of *Yedo* has become familiar to all readers of the older works on Japan

3 一話一言, written by Ōta Nampo, 太田南畝 (1748—1823), Ch XL, p 41

and he gave him a bottle of ink-stone water (used for wetting
the *suzuri*). The priest took it and went away rejoiced, declaring
that he now would mount to the sky. Actually a few days later
a violent thunderstorm suddenly broke forth, accompanied by
heavy rains and wind. When it abated, the trees and the grass
had become quite black. The samurai alone knew the reason
thereof: it was the ink-water which he had given to the priest,
who had used this in rising to the clouds. The author of the
Miyakawasha mampitsu [1] heard this tale from the samurai's son,
to whom his father had told it.

In 1744 a tidal wave which destroyed a little Shintō shrine
near Yedo bay, as well as several houses and trees in Yedo,
killing a large number of people, was ascribed to a dragon [2].

Another *tatsumaki* happened in the Temmei era (1781—1788),
when a dragon arose from the famous Shinobazu pond in Ueno
(Yedo). A black cloud arose from the pond and destroyed the
houses in the vicinity. This is stated by Ogawa Kendō [3] in his
Jinchōdan [4], who adds that such a dragon often ascends on
summer days in the seas of Sado, Echigo and Etchū provinces.
"Then there descends", he says, "a black cloud from the sky,
and the water of the sea, as a reversed waterfall, rises whirling
about and joins the cloud. Tradition says that a dragon passes
from the water into the cloud ... On considering the fact that
a dragon rose from the Shinobazu pond we arrive at the conclusion that dragons lie at the bottom even of small ponds and
that the water, according to the weather, rises and a cloud
comes down, so that heaven and earth come into connection
and the dragon can ascend to the sky".

§ 3 Tatsumaki on the sea.

In 1796 four fisherboats sank and the crews all perished when
pursuing a whale in the sea near Kashima no ura in Hitachi
province. They were caught by a "dragon's roll" which all of a

---

1 宮川舎漫筆, written in 1858 by Miyakawa Seiun, 宮川政運;
Ch. V, p 13

2 *Mado no susami*, 窓ノ須佐美, written by Matsuzaki Gyōshin, 松
崎羮臣 (1681—1753), Onchi sōsho, Vol VII, p 130

3 小川顯道.

4 塵塚談, written in 1814, Onchi sōsho, Vol. IX, p 12

sudden covered the sky with dark clouds and made the surface
of the sea quite black [1].

In the *Shōsan chomon kishū* [2] a sea-otter which rose up from
the sea into a black cloud and ascended to the sky, is said to
have done so in the same way as the "dragon-snakes" use to
fly to heaven. The incident is described as follows. In a clear
sky suddenly a black cloud appeared which in a moment covered
the sea. A heavy storm stirred up the waves and raised the sand,
the rain fell down in torrents and the mountains shook. A hunter
saw a mysterious creature rise from the sea into the cloud and
fly to the sky. At once with a thundering noise the cloud came
straight in the hunter's direction, and he saw a dazzling light
in the middle of it. When he hit the cloud with a bullet, it
was dissolved, the rain stopped and the storm abated. A few
days later a big sea-otter was found dying on the shore, with
the bullet in its eye.

On the next page the author quotes the *Koji inenshū* [3], which
states that in the sea of Iwami fishes ascend to the sky and
become "fish-dragons" (魚龍), and in a note we find the remark
that "there are several thousands of dragons, messengers of the
divine *sennin* (神仙), and among these are 'fish-dragons' and
'otter-dragons' (獺龍, *datsu-ryū*), which can assume all kinds
of shapes" [4]

A curious way of driving away a *tatsumaki* is described in
the *Yūhisai sakki* [5]. A dark cloud came down upon a vessel sailing
from Yedo in a western direction, and the sailors were afraid

---

1 *Hitoyo-banashi*, "Tales of one night", written in 1810 by Maki Bokusen, 牧
墨僊; Ch II, p 9.
2 Ch II, p 460, concerning this work cf above p 218, note 3
3 故事因緣集, by an unknown author, probably a work of the Tokugawa
period
4 A "dog-dragon" (狗龍), a kind of mole, which, living under the ground,
haunted houses and devoured old women, is spoken of in the *Sanshū kidan* (Ch II,
pp 732 seqq, cf Transactions of the Asiatic Society of Japan, Vol XXXVII, Part I,
p 32), and "gold-dragons" (金龍) were, together with "spiritual foxes" (氣狐)
shown to the public by a sorcerer in Kyōto (*Sanshū kidan*, Ch IV, p 821) In Ch
III (p 517) of the *Shōsan chomon kishū* we read that big snakes (especially the so
called *senya*, 蜱蛇, or *uwabami*), and also small snakes, are a kind of dragons
which cause rain and wind and ascend to the sky Snakes all belong to the species dragon
5 有斐齋剳記, written by Minagawa Kien, 皆川淇園, who lived
1733—1807, quoted in the *Tōyūki*, 東遊記, written in 1795 by Tachibana Nankei
橘南蹊; *Kōhen*, 後編, Ch III, Zoku Teikoku Bunko, Vol. XX, p. 129.

that a dragon was about to lift up the ship and carry it to the sky. In order to scare the dragon away they all cut off their hair and burned it And behold, the terrible smell was apparently too much for the dragon, for the cloud at once dispersed.

Dragons are fond of money[1]. One day, when a *tatsumaki* was raging, an empty string of cash fell down, the coins had evidently been taken off by the dragon which had then thrown the string away. Another time a ship with much money on board was attacked by dragons in the form of a fearful storm. It foundered, and all efforts to raise the box of money from the bottom of the sea were frustrated by the greedy dragons which caused a storm to arise each time when human hands tried to deprive them of their prey[2].

§ 4 Snakes rise as dragons up to the clouds

A strange tale is found in the *Fude no susabi*[3] concerning a woman who had a severe headache on a day when a violent thunderstorm broke forth. During the tempest a little snake came out of her head, fled away through the door and ascended to the sky in a black cloud which suddenly came down

The *Mimi-bukuro*[4] relates a legend of a big snake, which lived under the verandah of a house and was daily fed by the inmates. If a girl who was waiting in vain for a husband gave food to this snake and prayed to it, her prayer was heard and she soon was married. One day, in the third month of the second year of the Temmei era (1782), the animal crept upon the verandah and lay there as if it were ill. While the man and his wife were carefully nursing it, clouds arose and it rained continuously. The snake raised its head and looked up to the sky, when a cloud descended upon the garden. Then the animal stretched its body and in a heavy rain ascended to the sky.

---

1 Cf above Book I, Ch III, § 3, p 69, with regard to the dragon's liking for the vital spirit of copper

2 *Saiyūki*, 西遊記, written in 1797 by the same author as the *Tōyūki* (cf. above, p 223, note 5), Ch II, p 259

3 筆ノ遊, "Pencil sports", written by KWAN CHASAN, 菅茶山, who lived 1747—1827, Hyakka setsurin, Vol 正上, p. 177

4 耳袋, written in 1815 by FUJIWARA MORINOBU, 藤原守信, Shidaikisho, 四大奇書, ni 4, p. 11, Ch, 1.

CHAPTER IX.

In the preceding chapters we often have mentioned mountains
and temples called after a dragon which was said to live there
or to have appeared at the time when the temple was built.
There are a large number of similar names to be found throughout
Japan, which are given in Yoshida Tōgo's *Dai Nihon chimei jisho*,
or *"Geographical Lexicon of Japan"* [1] The following details are
derived from this work

§ 1. The Japanese dragon (tatsu).

Tatsu no kuchi, or *"Dragon's mouth"* (龍口 or 辰口) is a
very frequent name. It is e.g. given to a hot spring in Nomi
district, Kaga province [2], to a little waterfall in Kōjimachi district,
Tōkyō [3], to a hill in Kamakura district, Sagami province [4], to a
dike in Kuji district, Hitachi province [5], and to two mountains
in Bizen and Rikuzen provinces [6]. On the hill of this name in
Kamakura district criminals were put to death during the Kamakura period, and it is famous on account of the legend concerning
Nichiren's miracle, whose life was saved because the sword refused
to cut off his holy head. Tradition said that a hill was formed
by the dead body of a dragon whose mouth was on this spot
and who in olden times had inhabited a large lake near by [7].
Even in the Anei era (1772—1780) a five-headed dragon was
worshipped there in a little Shintō shrine [8], and still nowadays
a "Shintō temple of the Dragon's Mouth" (*Tatsu no kuchi no sha,*

---

[1] 大日本地名辭書, by 古田東伍, published in 1907
[2] P 1912   [3] P 2884   [4] P 2715
[5] P. 3731   [6] Pp 921 and 4208

[7] *Enoshima engi*, 江島縁起 (time and author unknown), quoted by Yoshida,
l 1, p 2715.

[8] *Nichiren chūgwasan,* 日蓮註畫賛, quoted ibidem

龍口社) is to be found on this spot, while a Buddhist shrine
of the Nichiren sect, called *Ryūkō-dera* (龍口寺), proves how
the Buddhists adopted the old belief [1]. On the afore-said mountain
in Rikuzen a big rock in the shape of a dragon's head is worshipped
in a Shintō temple, called "*Tatsu no kuchi jinja*", or "Shrine of
the Dragon's mouth" [2]

Tatsu ga hana [3] ("Dragon's nose") is the name of a cliff in
Ōmi province, Sakata district, *Tatsu-kushi* [4] ("Dragon's skewer")
that of a rock in Tosa province, Hataya district. *Tatsu-yama* [5]
("Dragon-mountains") are found in Harima, Innan district, and
in Owari, Higashi Kasugai district; a *Tatsu-ko-yama* [6] ("Little
dragon-mountain") is mentioned in Hitachi, Taga district, and
Tatsu-zaki [7] ("Dragon's capes"), in Shimozuke, Sarushima district,
and in Iwashiro, Ishikawa district In Mutsu province, Higashi
Tsugaru district, we find a *Tatsu-bama-zaki* [8] ("Dragon-beach-cape"),
also called *Tatsubi-zaki* [9] ("Dragon's flight-cape"), and in Shinano,
Saku district, a *Tatsu-oka* [10] ("Dragon-mound") and called *Tatsu-
no* [11] ("Dragon-field"), also called *Tatsu no ichi* [12] ("Dragon-market")
is to be found in Shinano, Ina district, and another *Tatsu no ichi*
in Yamato, Soe no kami district, where a Shintō-god, Tatsu no
ichi Myōjin, is worshipped. In Harima, Iiho (or Iho) district,
there is a *Tatsu-no* [13] with an old castle of this name, built by
Nitta Yoshisada in 1334. Finally, we find villages called *Tatsuta* [14]
(Dragon-ricefield) in Higo province, Akutaku district, and in
Yamato, Ikoma district. Near the latter place is the well-known
ancient Shintō shrine called *Tatsuta jinja* [15], which is dedicated
to the Wind-god and where prayers are offered up for wind and
rain. Also a *Mount Tatsuta* [16], in the same vicinity, may be
mentioned, as well as a river, called *Tatsuta-gawa* [17]. On the
afore-said *Tatsu-yama* in Owari stood an old Buddhist temple of

1 Yoshida, p, 2715.　　　2 Yoshida, p. 4208
3 龍鼻, p 558　　　　　　4 龍串, p 1364.
5 龍山, pp 864 and 2272　　6 龍子山, p. 3743
7 龍崎, or 辰崎, pp 3445 and 3848
8 龍濱崎, p 4752　　　　　9 龍飛崎.
10 龍岡, p 2434.　　　　　11 辰野, p 2364
12 龍市.　　　　　　　　　13 龍野, p 894.
14 龍田, pp. 1671 and 229
15 Cf above, Book II, Ch III, § 1, p 153, and Book II, Ch VIII, § 1, p 220.
16 P 230　　　　　　　　17 P 228

the Tendai sect, called "*Ryūsenji*[1] ("Dragon-spring-temple"), which was said to have been built by a Dragon-king in one night; the original Japanese dragon-god of the mountain was probably identified with a Nāga by the Tendai priests On the "*Dragon's cape*" in Iwashiro there is a waterfall (the favourite abode of dragons), and a Bodhi-tree is evidence of Buddhist domination in later times.

By far the greater part of these names is found in Central Japan, and they are rare in the South and the North[2].

§ 2. The Chinese and Indian dragons (ryū or ryō)

A. *Names of mountains.*

The mountains are called *Ryū-zan* or *Ryō-zan*[3] (in Iwashiro and Uzen, near the latter is a place called "Sacred Tail"[4], which probably means a dragon's tail[5], *Ryū ga mine*[6] ("Dragon's peak", in Higo, resembling a lying dragon, and in Hida), *Ryū no* (or *ga*) *saki*[7] ("Dragon's cape", with a Buddhist "Blue Dragon temple", *Seiryūji*[8], in Tosa, and another, in the vicinity of which is a Buddhist shrine called *Kinryūji*[9], or "Gold-dragon-temple", in Hitachi), *Ryū* (or *Ryō*) *ga take*[10] ("Dragon's peak", in Ise and Uzen), *Ryūzu-zaki*[11] ("Dragon's head cape", in Tosa), *Ryūten-yama*[12] ("Dragon-Deva mountain", in Bizen); *Ryū-ō-zan*[13] ("Dragon-king's mountain, in Bichū, with a little Shintō shrine[14], dedicated to the Eight Great Dragon-kings, on the top, and two others in Kawachi and Sanuki. A *Ryū-ō-take*[15] ("Dragon-king's peak") is found in Chikuzen, and a *Ryū-zō-san*[16] ("Dragon's claw-

---

1 龍泉寺, p 2272

2 As to personal names, these are seldom connected with *tatsu*, except the three following Tatsu (龍), Tatsuki (龍木, Dragon's tree) and Tatsuzane (龍實, Dragon's seed)

3 龍山, pp 49 and 4393

4 神尾, Kan-o   5 Cf above, Book II, Ch III, § 12, p 177

6 龍峰, pp 1721 and 2234

7 龍崎, pp 1358, 3571

8 青龍寺.   9 金龍寺.

10 龍嶽, pp 606, 4414   11 龍頭崎, p. 1353.

12 龍天山, p 912   13 龍王山, pp 959, 311 and 1256

14 Cf above, Book II, Ch III, § 12, p 176

15 龍王嶽, p 1452   16 龍爪山, p 4455

mountain") in Suruga, with a temple of Ryū-zō Gongen [1], "Manifestation of Ryū-zō", "Dragon's receptacle (womb)", the Buddhist name given to the, probably dragon-shaped, mountain-god. Near Ryū-oka [2] ("Dragon's hill") village, in Igo province, there is a mountain where in olden times a Buddhist priest is said to have successfully prayed for rain. In Hitachi there is on *Ryūjinsan* [3] ("Dragon-god's mountain") an old Shintō shrine of a Dragon-god, and in Kii we find a *Ryūmon-zan* [4] ("Dragon-gate-mountain")

B. *Names of springs, waterfalls and rivers.*

A hot spring in Kii, famous for its curative powers, is called the "Spring of the Dragon-god" (*Ryūjin-sen*) [5]. In Ōsumi, Yamato and Higo we find "Dragon-gate waterfalls" (*Ryūmon-daki*) [6], and in Shimozuke a "Dragon's head waterfall" (*Ryūzu-daki*) [7]. The ancient Chinese considered the dragon to be so closely connected with waterfalls that they indicated these by means of the character "dragon", combined with the radical "water" (瀧). Rivers called after dragons are the *Ryūge-gawa* [8] ("Dragon-flower river", also pronounced *Tatsu-bana-gawa*) in Kawachi, the *Tenryū-gawa* [9] ("Heavenly Dragon's river") in Shinano and Tōtōmi, and the *Ryūkan-gawa* [10] ("Dragon's rest river") in Tōkyō.

C. *Names of islands, valleys and places.*

Two "Dragon's islands" (*Ryū ga shima*, or *Ryū-shima*) [11] may be mentioned, one in Echigo, the other in Awa; and a "Dragon-king's valley" (*Ryū-ō-dani*) [12], in Buzen. Also place names as

---

1 龍藏權現, deities of the same name are worshipped in two Shintō temples, in Uzen and Kii (pp 4455 and 754)

2 龍岡, p 1295

3 龍神山, p 3619

4 龍門山, p 701, cf above, Book II, Ch IV, § 12, p 194

5 龍神泉, p 739.

6 龍門瀧, pp 1781, 290, 1652, cf above, Book II, 11.

7 龍頭瀑, p 3517　　　8 龍華川, p 327

9 天龍川, pp. 2361, 2505, cf above, Book II, Ch V, § 7, p. 203

10 龍閑川, p 2886　　　11 龍島, pp. 2073, 3144.

12 龍王谷, p 1418

Ryū-mai[1] ("Dragon's dance"), in Kōzuke; *Ryū-ō*[2] ("Dragon-king"), in Buzen and Kai; *Ryū-toku*[3] ("Dragon's virtue"), in Chikuzen, *Ryū-ge*[4] ("Dragon's flower"), in Ōmi, and *Ryū-ge*[5] ("Dragon's hair") in Ugo, are evidence of the Chinese and Indian dragon's great popularity in Japan.

D. *Names of Buddhist temples.*

Among the names of Buddhist temples connected with the dragon *Ryūzōji*[6] ("Dragon's receptacle (womb) (or hiding) temple"), *Ryūsenji*[7] ("Dragon's spring temple"), *Ryūkōji*[8] ("Dragon's rise temple") and *Ryūmonji*[9] ("Dragon's gate temple") are the most frequent. Further, we find temples of the Dragon's horn (*Ryūkakuji*[10]), belly (*Ryūfukuji*[11]), mouth (*Ryūkōji*[12]) and head (*Ryōtōji*[13]). Moreover, mention is made of temples of the Dragon's cloud (*Ryūunji*[14]), pool (*Ryūenji*[15] and *Ryūtanji*[16]), sea (*Ryūkai-in*[17]), valley (*Ryūkeiji*[18]), spring (*Ryūgenji*[19]), river (*Ryūsenji*[20]), palace (*Ryūgūji*[21]), canopy (*Ryūgaiji*[22]), flower (*Ryūgeji*[23]), treasure (*Ryūhōji*[24]), felicity (*Ryūfukuji*[25]), rest (*Ryūanji*[26] and *Ryūonji*[27]),

---

1 龍舞, p 3370

2 龍王, pp 1418, 2443   3 龍德, p 1454

4 龍華, p 496   5 龍毛, p 4597

6 龍藏寺.   7 龍泉寺.   8 龍興寺.

9 龍門寺   10 龍角寺, in Shimōsa, p 3235

11 龍腹寺, in Shimōsa, p 3244, cf. above, Book II, Ch. III, p. 177

12 龍口寺, in Sagami, p 2715   13 龍頭寺, in Uzen, p 4509

14 龍雲寺, in Iwami and Shinano, pp 1072, 2431

15 龍淵寺, in Musashi, p 118.   16 龍潭寺, in Ōmi, p 2488

17 龍海院, in Mikawa and Shimozuke, pp 2316, 3350

18 龍溪寺, in Kazusa, p 3176   19 龍源寺, in Rikuzen, p 4205

20 龍川寺, in Yamato, p 305   21 龍宮寺, in Chikuzen, p 1505

22 龍蓋寺, in Yamato, p 262.

23 龍華寺, in Suruga, p 2555

24 龍寶寺, in Rikuzen and Tōkyō, pp 4098, 2962

25 龍福寺, in Suwō, p 1172

26 龍安寺, in Yamato, p 103.

27 龍穩寺(院), in Musashi and Iwashiro, pp 3034, 3870

prosperity (*Ryūtaiji* [1]), correctness (*Ryūshō-in* [2]), majesty (*Ryū-gonji* [3]), a. s. o.

E. *Names of Buddhist priests.*

Buddhist priests often have similar names, especially *Ryūzan* [4] ("Dragon's mountain") and *Ryūshū* [5] ("Dragon's islet") are frequent. Further, we find *Ryūsui* [6] ("Dragon's water"), *Ryūsen* [7] ("Dragon's river"), *Ryūtaki* [8] (Dragon's waterfall), *Ryūchi* [9] ("Dragon's pond"), *Ryū-en* [10] and *Ryūshū* [11] ("Dragon's pool"), *Ryūshin* [12] ("Dragon's depth"), *Ryūsho* [13] ("Dragon's islet"), *Ryūden* [14] ("Dragon's rice-field"), *Ryūtō* [15] ("Dragon's ascending"), *Ryūhō* [16] ("Dragon's peak"), *Ryūbi* [17] ("Dragon's tail"), *Ryūmin* [18] ("Dragon's sleep"), a. s o. The large number of the names referred to in this chapter is strong evidence of a fact which also the legends have taught us, i. e. of the great popularity of all three kinds of dragons, Japanese, Chinese and Indian, in old Japan.

---

1 龍泰寺, in Mino, p 2205.　　2 龍正院, in Shimōsa, p 3229.

3 龍嚴寺, in Uzen, p 4504　　4 龍山.　　5 龍洲

6 龍水　　7 龍川　　8 龍澤　　9 龍池

10 龍淵.　　11 龍湫.　　12 龍深.　　13 龍渚.

14 龍田　　15 龍登　　16 龍峯.

17 龍尾　　18 龍眠

CHAPTER X.

Conclusions.

The preceding chapters have shown once more how great China's influence was upon Japanese legend and superstition from the beginning of the spreading of Chinese civilisation in the Land of the Rising Sun until the present day. We have also seen how Buddha's powerful doctrine brought the Indian Nāgas to the Far-Eastern seas and rivers and ponds, as it peopled the Japanese mountains and woods with their deadly enemies, the Garudas. The idea of serpent-shaped semi-divine kings, living in great luxury in their magnificent palaces at the bottom of the water, was strange to the Chinese and Japanese minds, but the faculty of these beings of assuming human shapes and bestowing rain upon the thirsty earth, as well as their nature of water-gods, formed the links between the Nāgas of India and the dragons of China and Japan The Chinese Buddhists identified the Indian serpents with the four-legged dragons of China, and this blending of ideas was easily introduced into the minds of the Japanese people, which did not hesitate to associate their own, mostly serpent-shaped, gods of rivers and mountains with the Western deities of the same kind.

In the Introduction we have seen that the Nāgas were, as a rule, favourably disposed towards Buddhism, but that they were dangerous creatures on account of their quick temper, deadly poison and great magic power. They possessed numberless jewels and mighty charms, which they bestowed upon those to whom they were grateful and who often stayed for a while in the splendid Nāga palaces at the bottom of ponds, or rivers, or seas. The Mahayāna school speaks of eight Great Dragon-kings, mightier than the others, one of whom, Sāgara, was well-known as a bestower of rain. The rain-giving faculty of the Nāgas, which is not mentioned in the Jātakas, was apparently more emphasized in Northern than in Southern Buddhism. According to the original conceptions these semi-divine serpents, who had their abode in Pātāla land, *beneath the earth*, could raise clouds and thunder or appear as clouds themselves to terrify mankind. Northern Buddhism, however, made these frightful beings the rain-giving benefactors of men, to whom prayers for rain were sent up by means of special ceremonies. These rites were performed also in China and Japan. As to the division of the Nāgas into four castes "Heavenly, Divine, Earthly and Hidden Nāgas", this is probably also a Northern feature, for I did not find it mentioned anywhere in the Jātakas. Indian Buddhist art represents the Nāgas as serpents, or as men or women with snakes coming out of their necks and rising over their heads, or as snake-tailed beings with human upper bodies and snakes appearing above their heads Hot winds and hot sand, sudden violent storms and Garuda-kings are what the Nāgas fear most. When strictly observing Buddhist fasting, they may be reborn as men.

In Book I we have stated how the oldest Chinese books spoke of dragons in divination, as ornaments of clothes, and as river-gods who caused high floods by their fights. As they belonged to the four *ling* ("spiritual beings"), full of *Yang* (Light), they were omens of the birth of great men, especially of emperors, and of felicity in general, like the dragon-horses, but also of death and ruin, when they were seen fighting, or when their dead bodies were found, or when they appeared at wrong times or in wrong places. The Emperors were not only called dragons and compared to them, but were sometimes even considered to be their offspring, or to have them in their service. The dragons ascended to the sky, riding on winds and clouds, and were ridden by the *sien*, or they descended into the deepest wells Their transformations were limitless. They could become small like silkworms or so big that they covered the world [1]. Their wisdom excelled that of all other animals, and their blessing power was great. Next to these ideas, which made them the favourite subjects of poets and artists, a great many lower conceptions are found, prevalent among the people from olden times.

The principal water-god is the *kiao-lung*, the scaly dragon, other important dragons are the *ying-lung* (which has wings), the *k'iu-lung* (which has a horn) and the *ch'i-lung* (which is blue and has no horn). Then, there are several other kinds of dragons, but all of them are afraid of iron, the *wang* plant, centipedes, the leaves of the melia azederach, and five-coloured silk-thread, while their principal enemies are tigers and the demons of drought

---

1 This must be the meaning of KWAN TSZĔ 's words (quoted on p 68), instead of the obscure "lies hidden in the world"

who devour them. They are fond of beautiful gems, hollow stones with water inside (or the vital spirit of copper) and swallow-flesh Male and female dragons are different in shape As the dragon is very lewd, he copulates with all kinds of animals and in this way produces nine different classes of young, which according to their nature are represented as ornaments

Causing rain is the Chinese dragon's most important function, and he is compelled to do so by mankind by several magical means, especially by making clay images of dragons (and laying them in water), or by throwing poisonous plants or bones of the tiger (his deadly enemy) into his pools, or by annoying him by a terrible noise, or by using utensils adorned with dragons when praying for rain The dragons are called the "Rain-Masters", and rain is prayed for in front of their holes.

They transform themselves into old men, beautiful women, and fishes, or sometimes assume the shapes of trees and objects, as e. g. swords. They have a pearl under their throats or in their mouths. As to their eggs, these are beautiful stones to be found in the mountains or at the riverside; water is constantly dripping from these stones till they split and a small snake appears, which in a very short time grows larger and larger and in the form of a dragon ascends to the sky amid thunder, rain and darkness. Hurricanes and whirlwinds are all ascribed to ascending dragons. Their bones are considered to be a very efficient medicine and their spittle is the most precious of perfumes; their cast-off skins spread a brilliant light. Dragon-boats were pleasure-vessels of the Emperors, which had the shape of a dragon and the head of a *yih* bird, quite different, however, are the dragon-boats of the water festival of the fifth day of the fifth month, which are probably intended as sympathetic magic to obtain rain. As to Buddhism, this introduced into China legends concerning tranformation into dragons after death, Dragon-kings and palaces, a. s. o.

The first chapter of Book II, in which I treated of the original Japanese dragon, mentioned no later dates than the tenth century (*Engishiki*) Even the eighth century adorned her legends with Chinese and Indian features, as we saw in the tale of Toyotama-bime and Hiko-hohodemi. This was very easily done because the Japanese sea and river-gods, having the shape of a dragon or a serpent, resembled the Chinese *lung* or the Indian Nāgas. It is no wonder that the simple, rain-bestowing Japanese gods of rivers and seas, mountains and valleys, owing to their shapes were identified with and superseded by the similar but more fantastic Chinese and Indian gods of water and rain. The "water-fathers" (*mizuchi*), dragon-shaped river-gods who, just like the Chinese dragons, hindered men when constructing embankments but were pacified by human sacrifices instead of, as in China, being driven away by iron, soon had to give way to the Rain-masters and Dragon-kings of the West. Gradually foreign elements were added to the ancient legends, and their original form became hardly recognizable.

The second chapter shows how all the Chinese conceptions in regard to the appearance of dragons and dragon-horses as omens were embraced by the Japanese, and preserved by them from the ninth century down to the nineteenth.

In the third chapter the dragon's main function is treated of, i. e. the bestowing of rain upon mankind. Among the eighty five Shintō shrines to which in times of drought messengers were despatched by the Court, there were many dragon-shaped river-deities. As to the offerings made to the Shintō river-gods for obtaining rain or for causing them to stop a too abundant supply of heavenly water, these were hemp and fibre, black, white or red horses (the latter only for stopping rain) Yet, even the Emperors of as early an age as the eighth century did no longer sufficiently believe in the power of these gods, for at the same time Buddhist rites were performed in the three great temples of Nara. In the ninth century, especially, the Buddhist priests got more and more influence, also in this respect, and the famous "Sacred Spring Park" in Kyōtō became their special territory for praying for rain. Kōbō Daishi declared the pond in this park to be inhabited by an Indian dragon, and sūtras were recited on its banks by crowds of bonzes, sometimes to pray to the Dragon-king, sometimes to threaten him with persecution by his deadly enemy, the Garuda. If they had no success, however, the ancient river-gods enjoyed a temporary triumph and were elevated to higher ranks. But short was their glory, for soon the mighty foreign invaders prevailed once more. Either the Chinese dragon which had to be aroused by sounding bells and drums, by singing and dancing on a dragon-boat on the pond in the Sacred Spring Park (or by being deprived of his element, the water), or the Indian Nāga-king, were the gods from whom the blessing of rain was expected by the Court. The clever monk Kūkai (Kōbō Daishi) knew how to conquer his adversaries, not only the Shintōists, but also his rivals among the Buddhist priests. This was experienced by the mightiest of his colleagues, Shūbin, the abbot of the "Western Monastery" Besides prayers, incantations and the recital of sūtras a magical image of the dragon (which reminds us of the clay dragons of the Chinese) was used by Kūkai, who strived to spread his doctrine by the extraordinarily impressive art of making rain. And his success was marvellous.

Further, we have seen how during the thirteenth century in times of drought the Buddhist "Five Dragons Festival" was celebrated in the same Sacred Spring Park or somewhere else, or sūtras were recited before the Dragon-hole on Mount Murōbu in Yamato, in order to cause the Dragon-king who lived there, to give rain. The remarkable fact that a *Buddhist* priest was said to have erected on this spot a *Shintō* shrine for the Indian dragon seems to indicate that the Nāga had taken the place of a *Shintō* dragon, a mountain god believed to live in the hole from ancient times. In the same century horses were still offered by the Emperors to the famous rain-gods of Nibu (the "Rain-Master") and Kibune, white ones to obtain, and red ones to stop rain. And the Court officials themselves went to the Sacred Spring Park and prayed to the "Sea-dragon-king", at the same time performing "sympathetic magic" by sprinkling water on the stones near the pond. Numerous were the miracles wrought by Buddhist priests in forcing the dragons to obey their will. In later times, however, especially in the eighteenth century, we see the *Chinese* ways of making rain gain ground again. The Chinese conception of arousing the anger of these rain-gods by making noise or by throwing iron utensils or metal shaving or dirty things into their ponds and thus causing them to ascend and cause rain, was different from the Shintō idea of praying and offering to the river-gods, as well as from the Buddhistic way of persuading or forcing the dragons to benefit mankind by abundant rains. As I remarked above [1], the Chinese methods, which got the upper hand in later ages, are still prevalent among the Japanese country folks of the present day.

The fourth chapter gave the Japanese legends concerning Indian Nāgas (Dragon-kings). As the Indian tales reached Nippon via China and Korea, it is quite logical that their Japanese imitations showed many Chinese features. Among the eight Great Dragon-kings Sāgara, who was believed to reside in a splendid palace at the bottom of the sea, is the most frequently mentioned. Like other Dragon-kings he possesses the "Precious pearl which grants all desires" (cintāmani). During storms the sailors tried

[1] Book II, Ch III, § 13, p 178

to pacify the Dragon-kings by throwing all kinds of precious
objects into the sea, and succeeded if the object which these
water-gods wanted was offered in time. Ponds, especially mountain ponds, were very often believed to be the abodes of Dragon-
kings, who probably in many cases had taken the place of
ancient Japanese diagon-shaped gods. Sometimes one of the eight
kings incarnated himself as some famous Buddhist high-priest,
or the spirit of a man became a dragon-god. The temple bell
of Miidera is said to have been obtained by Tawara Tōda in a
Dragon-palace. Azure dragons (a Chinese feature) were often said
to have appeared on the occasion of the establishment of Buddhist temples and to have thenceforth been the guardian-gods
of these shrines [1]. Sometimes dragon-relics, as for example a few
scales or a tooth, were preserved among the treasures of a
Buddhist sanctuary. Finally, eight- and nine-headed dragons were
spoken of as the inhabitants of mountain lakes, being sometimes
reincarnations of Buddhist priests, and down till the Restoration
offerings of rice were made by Buddhist priests to the dragons
of some of those lakes.

The mighty influence of the Indian and Chinese ideas concerning
this subject upon the Japanese mind is also shown by the
way in which these conceptions were applied to ancient Shintō
gods In Chapter V some specimens of this have been given,
which were found in books of the thirteenth and eighteenth
centuries. In the former the eight-headed serpent, called Yamato
no orochi and killed by Susanowo, as well as the unhappy young
Emperor Antoku who was drowned in the battle of Dan-no-ura
(1185) and whose spirit is said to be the Shintō god Suitengū,
are identified with the goddess of Itsukushima, the daughter
of the Dragon-king Sāgara! And the precious Kusanagi sword,
found in the eight-headed serpent's tail, belonged to this king's
Dragon-palace, or, according to another legend, was carefully
guarded by a Dragon-king and brought back to the Atsuta
shrine, from where it had been stolen. The Thunder-god, according to an old legend caught by Sukaru, was called a "Dragon-
king" by the author of the *Gempei seisuiki* (thirteenth century),
which was all the more plausible because the version of the
Nihongi spoke of a huge serpent. Further, several old Shintō
shrines, where probably from olden times snake- or dragon-shaped
gods were worshipped, in later times, in the eighteenth century,
were considered to have connection with Chinese or Indian

1 Cf above, Book II, Ch VI, pp 205 sqq

dragons, and even old tree-spirits in snake-form were called dragons and said to cause thunderstorms.

The *Dragon-lantern*, treated of in the sixth chapter, was not mentioned in works dating before the fourteenth century It always rose from the sea, and was mostly a sign of a dragon-shaped sea-god's protection of, and reverence towards, a Buddhist temple or, in a few cases, of a Shintō sanctuary. The Chinese "azure dragon" was often mentioned in these tales, and sometimes was said to have been seen carrying the lantern, which nearly always descended upon some old pine-tree standing near the shrine, and hung between its branches These "dragon-lantern pine-trees" remind us of the Chinese ideas of old trees producing ignes fatui.

The *"Dragon's eggs"*, beautiful stones picked up in the mountains, out of which constantly water dripped and which for this reason were often used as ink-stones, were dangerous treasures indeed For sooner or later they split, and a little snake crept out of them, which in a few minutes increased in size and finally ascended to the sky as a dragon, breaking through the roof and causing a terrible thunderstorm Book I, Ch. III, § 16, in connection with Book II, Chapter VII, have shown that this is a Chinese conception, introduced into Japan, where it was prevalent from the sixteenth century down to the nineteenth.

Very popular was also the idea of whirlwinds and waterspouts being caused by ascending dragons, winding their way to heaven. We find this both in China and Japan, in the latter country especially from the seventeenth century until the present day. The Japanese name *"tatsu-maki"* perhaps indicates that it was not borrowed from China; but on the other hand the fact that we did not find it mentioned in works before the seventeenth century causes me to think that the general inclination of these later ages towards Chinese conceptions, which we observed also in the methods of making rain, may have caused the spreading of this idea too.

Finally, in the ninth chapter, the geographical names were evidence of the original Japanese dragon having been worshipped mostly in Central Japan, and of the popularity of the Chinese and Indian dragons throughout the Empire The large number of names of Buddhist temples and priests, connected with the Indian dragon, showed the important part played by the Nāga in Japanese Buddhism.

Herewith I conclude this treatise on the dragon in the Far East, in the hope that it may throw light upon his complicate nature of Indian, Chinese and Japanese god of water, thunder, rain and wind.

INDEX

of the Chinese translations of sūtras, vinayas and abhidharmas,
mentioned in the Introduction. The numbers placed
within brackets are those of NANJŌ's *Catalogue of
the Buddhist Tripitaka;* the other figures denote
the pages of this treatise.

INDEX

of the Chinese works quoted in this treatise, and the pages
where particulars about them, or their titles in
Chinese characters, are given

INDEX

of the Japanese works quoted in this treatise, and the pages
where particulars about them, or their titles in
Chinese characters, are given.

ERRATA.

P.   22, note 3: *Fah hai*, read *Fah lai*.

„   63, line 6 from beneath· he lies hidden in the world, read he hides (covers) the world.

„   91, note 4: *Pao chi lun*, read *P'ao chi lun*.

„   93, „ 4: 新唐, read 新唐書

„ 119, „ 3 Ch. V, read pp. 160 sq.

„ 136, line 1. Fudoki, read Fūdoki.

„ 143, note 5: 910, read 901.

„ 148, „ 7: 記, read 紀.

CPSIA information can be obtained
at www.ICGtesting.com
Printed in the USA
BVHW051920040320
574091BV00006B/399